'A revelation! As a wife and mother I w
years ago.'

A

'Take it from a professional cynic – this book shines a light on how individuals learn. With a willingness to be open-minded virtually everybody can benefit from the insights it provides. It endorses the view that great teachers focus on what and how they want their students to learn rather than what they want to teach. This book helps parents and teachers alike to identify how individual children learn and provides keys to unlocking true potential. It really does work.'

Adrienne Carmichael LLB, MEd,
Senior Inspector/Adviser 14–19 Education (UK)

'Having worked as an educator for many years, I can say that all students would benefit from the knowledge of different learning styles and most effective approaches to teaching presented in Connerr's book. It is an invaluable tool for educators, parents, and life-long learners who seek to understand and respect the varied ways that individual human beings learn and communicate.

This thoughtful book offers hope and real ways to help people gain insight and appreciate one another in times like these when many are becoming increasingly polarized, intransigent, and disrespectful. Heeding and implementing ideas and suggestions in this book would greatly reduce pain, frustration and feelings of failure in learning situations and interpersonal relationships.'

Diane N Taylor
Exeter (NH) Elementary Schools Library Media Specialist
and School Librarian
Camp Director, Camp Hawthorne, Raymond, ME (USA)

'If he were still around, Carl Jung would love this book's new archetypal categories. *Learning Without Tears* is a superb tool for taking a family from communication chaos to harmony.'

Rev. Bonney Rega, MEd, Educator, Artist, Actress,
Sufi Order International Senior Teacher (USA)

'An original and highly specific contribution to learning theory. Helyn Connerr's accessible information and guidance for parents, ensures all children will be enabled, empowered and encouraged towards a lifetime of successful learning.'

Kay Adamson Cert Ed, DASE, MA
Mother, Grandmother, Retired Teacher and
Senior Lecturer in Education (UK)

This book is a true celebration of diversity and individual difference. The skilled use of metaphor and charming employment of character-isation are effective ways of illustrating this model, helping to make it accessible to all and offering a potentially powerful tool for change. The reader will be unable to help but reflect on their own and their child's learning style with some fascinating revelations. It will be welcomed by any parent who wishes to encourage their child's learning and development and will be one you might return to during times of challenge within your relationship.

Sue Sanderson, BA, PGCE, MA,
Senior Educational Psychologist (UK)

'My son's learning profile is very interesting and helps me to understand why he is the way he is. Now I will be able to support him in his learning without wondering why he's different from other children. Thanks so much.'

Penny Bradshaw, Psychotherapist (UK)

Helyn Connerr has an MSc in physical and hot atom chemistry and was involved in leading-edge research in nuclear medicine in Massachusetts. She went on to study the subtle energies linking body, mind and spirit, mythic themes, archetypal patterns, traditional wisdom and the New Physics. She became managing director of Theater Workshop Boston, an experimental theatre and Sufi centre. Later she opened and operated Magus Light, a bookshop, art gallery, and holistic education centre providing alternative therapies, astrological consultations, classes and workshop programmes.

Helyn's UK-based businesses, Mercury Communications Ltd and Astro Innovation (which originated the Mercury Model) offer counselling, coaching and courses in communication to individuals, families and corporate teams.

She divides her time between the Lake District in the UK and the Lakes Region in New Hampshire, USA.

She can be contacted at Learning@mercurymodel.com.

to
NDP, TH

Learning Without Tears

Helyn Connerr

WATKINS PUBLISHING

LONDON

Distributed in the United States and Canada by
Sterling Publishing Co., Inc.
387 Park Avenue South, New York, NY 10016-8810

This edition first published in the UK 2008 by
Watkins Publishing, Sixth Floor, Castle House,
75–76 Wells Street, London W1T 3QH

1 3 5 7 9 10 8 6 4 2

Designed and typeset by Jerry Goldie

Printed and bound in Great Britain

Library of Congress Cataloging-in-Publication data available

ISBN-10: 1-905857-53-5
ISBN-13: 978-1-905857-53-1

For information about custom editions, special sales, premium and
corporate purchases, please contact Sterling Special Sales
Department at 800-805-5489 or specialsales@sterlingpub.com

www.watkinspublishing.co.uk

Table of Contents

Acknowledgements

Deepest gratitude to my teachers, Isabel Hickey, Francis Darke, Pir Vilayat Inayat Khan and Robert Berube, all of whom were keen observers of the subtle laws which underpin the evident and the obvious.

Sincere appreciation to Dr Charley Owens, my prime mentor in the art of scientific research.

Thanks to Cumbria Institute for The Arts and our Business/ Education Partnership – the diligent and exacting artistic contribution of Steve McCombe in creating visual characterizations of the 12 learning styles.

With joyful recognition of the many individuals who helped bring this book into being, I salute all the adults and children who objectified their own inner mental processes in order to offer valuable feedback on my verbal descriptions; Chris Ogilvie for urging me out into the public and for helping to shape the concepts which led to this work; Irene Gravenor, and her mental courage which fostered the Mercury Model's early trials within the business sector; Penny Quest and the Faction and Fiction Group who have provided encouragement and helpful input at every stage of the process; the Watkins team, especially Michael, Penny, Shelagh and Annie; my dear friends and relatives for their many contributions – from personal encouragement to technical advice: Meredith Szwed, Tom McCarron, Jo Bullock, Annie Hawson, Anne Clark, Maureen Jackson, Rachel Bell, Wendy Wilson and Paula Wilson; Alan Price, the self-proclaimed Goad, not only for believing I could do it, and reminding me of it every step of the way, but also for his ready assistance in all matters technical, grammatical and comestible.

And finally enormous heartfelt thanks and love to Nicholas, my husband, who has developed over the years the remarkable knack of stabilizing whichever limb I was out on.

Introduction

The instant someone discovers and truly acknowledges that we all think and learn differently, personal relationships magically transform. In that moment of acceptance there is forgiveness. The tight bands of criticism and judgement are released, old hurts are soothed, respect and empowerment can become mutual. Both people are off the hook. They are free to drop the negative, accentuate the positive and celebrate their minds' differences and similarities.

This book has been written with the spirit and intention to foster such moments.

Regrettably, particularly between parents and children, such moments have not been frequent. Historically, families have not been issued with guidebooks as to how each other's minds tick. That is about to change.

Parents scratch their heads, quite aware that they have no clue as to what is going on in their children's minds, or how to reach them. Children may not suffer the same confusion, but just assume that must be what adults are like.

Parents often decide that it's 'fair' to treat all their children the same – to avoid the favouritism and painful jealousies that can otherwise arise. But in striving for identical care, adults can miss encouraging the best and the special within each child.

After their children have grown up, parents frequently carry a level of guilt about their child-rearing. 'I never knew how to talk to him.' 'I didn't do a very good job of it.' 'Surely we could have a better relationship than this by now.' 'We did nothing but squabble as she was growing up.' 'I'll try harder with my grandchildren.'

New parents swear up and down that they will not inflict the same upbringing on their children as that inflicted on themselves. But then they discover they don't know anything else. A better alternative is not evident.

With absolutely the best of intentions, people who really love each other and strive for genuine close-knit family relationships still sometimes miss each other mentally like ships passing in the night.

Well, try this: our minds are geared differently, one from another, even if we are related. Each of us is born with our own set of unique learning requirements. It's natural! If people talk to us in a way that we understand, taking in their message is easy. Otherwise it's not. If we do not readily understand what is being said to us, it does not mean we are stupid, slow, incapable, insolent, resistant or closed down – though, it can feel or appear that way. It may just mean our learning requirements differ from the speaker's. Our needs may have gone unnoticed and were not taken into account. We missed each other.

But, can you imagine the harmony and peace at the dining table or on a family holiday when communication is clear and supportive, based on mutual understanding and respect for natural differences and similarities? Imagining one step further, what if the adults knew about the creative use of tension, which quite naturally develops where there is difference? What if they knew how to gently turn a brewing conflict into a positive experience with long-term benefits for everyone involved?

Can you imagine the invaluable advantage gained by children who are helped to recognize their natural mental skills and to develop them into effective tools to be enjoyed confidently and successfully for their whole lives – within your family, at school and in the larger community?

These are achievable goals. The book in your hands, inspired by traditional wisdom and the Mercury Model, provides what you need to make this a reality. Stir in your own intention and watch it happen.

Part I

Individual Learning Styles and How They Interact

Learning Styles

We All Think and Learn Differently

Let us peer into the domain of your child's mind, glimpse the territory, identify the lay of the land and detect what's happening there. Is a gala event under way, a serious business meeting or a dramatic presentation? Do you detect analysis in process; is an experiment in midstream? Are there bright flashes of enthusiasm or an overall calm? If there are other children, an entire scout troop, ball team or classroom full of them, let's repeat the process for each one. What emerges will be an impression of a vast diversity of mental experience. The differences can be staggering. You will never again hold the common misconception that a mind is a mind and, regardless of age, they all function in pretty much the same way. They do not.

All humans may possess a brain, a nervous system and several sensory organs, but these physical components link together and function under the guidance of uniquely distinct 'master programs'. Consequently, within those little grey cells between our ears we have entirely personal mental experiences – experiences of new information, of our existing thoughts and of our impulse to share those thoughts with others. Child or adult, we each handle information in our own way. We must – information is not the same thing to each of us. To some it's zigzags while to others it's round or parallel, or tangible versus insubstantial. Some of us are confronted or burdened by information, others are graced by it.

Whether we are aged 3 or 93 we each have our own natural reaction to new material. Some of us build strong barriers to keep it out while others open their arms widely to welcome any and all that is available. Whether we are learning to read, to tie our shoes, to master computer skills, or to understand the implications of genetically modified foods, each of us has a natural approach.

And, we all do best what comes naturally.

Along the complex path of dealing with new information, every step is personal. Our individual relationship with information guides each one of us through all the stages of learning:

- initially noticing or missing it
- embracing or defending against it
- deciding to learn or to reject it
- possibly taking it in
- considering it or excluding it
- recalling it over the long term or forgetting it instantly
- expressing it or containing it

The unique program that governs and interconnects all aspects of how we handle information is called our 'learning style'. Everyone has one, regardless of age, gender, intellectual capacity, health, personality or national origin. A learning style is part of a person's nature – it's personal and it's natural. A learning style is neither an option nor a preference. It is not a matter of upbringing or heredity. At birth our unique program is already whole. *For us to succeed, these individual differences need to be recognized and taken into account by our families and those attempting to teach or communicate with us .*

This book provides everything you'll need to understand all the learning styles in your family and to take into account the natural differences and similarities. The rewards will be worth the effort. You will come to know your children better, be able to get your messages across to each one of them, provide each child with an astounding educational advantage (learning without tears) and transform communications within your family. You supply the resolve to use the tool.

A learning style has to do with the dynamics of thought and this book is about your child's mind and how it ticks, your mind and how it ticks, and how the minds connect with each other. A learning style is not about ego structure or personality. In some people the mind and how it works can be reflected in behaviour, but in many of us it is not. Therefore, we shall set aside all behavioural elements. We will not be looking at how your child acts out, plays, runs or sits, nor at what your child likes or dislikes. Learning styles are not related to values, social impulses or ambitions. Your child's learning style does not assess intelligence, 'IQ' or intellectual capability. Thinking and learning are hidden inner processes, not visible by observation. The mind is its own place.

Our individually configured minds handle information differently. It is just that simple. You may have noticed that some of us take hold of huge amounts of data and weave it like threads into something brand new, a fabric never seen before, and not resembling the component strands at all. Others are naturally skilled at initiating brand new thought, moving forward, always forward. Some minds share information very quickly, no sooner has it gone in than it comes out again, while others secrete it away, keeping it safely within, only to be shared when the time is right.

And in Your Family?

It may surprise you to know that even among siblings or within a closely knit family there can be, and usually are, astounding variations in learning style. The inner mental landscapes can differ enormously – from a lush green meadow for one to a deep underwater cave for another. Family members often go about dealing with information each in their own way – beyond genetic inheritance, despite similarity in family training. This is normal and natural.

So, if you have ever wondered what in the world makes your children's minds tick, believe me, you're not alone! Something that appears to genuinely excite one seems to bore the socks off another. And, with all we hear about family characteristics, how can a child's mind differ so enormously from that of either parent?

But, there they are, as mentally different from each other as night is from day, like chalk and cheese. You can look in on them doing their lessons, one quietly sitting at a desk working away, another on the telephone discussing the assignment with a school friend, a third jigging around the room, headphones on, book in hand. You might be convinced that at least two of them are not learning or studying anything at all.

Parents might ask what 'learning' is all about. Is the experience of learning the same for each of us? Does it feel the same? Is one mind doing the same thing as another? And what about teaching? Does anyone actually teach something to another, or does one person optimistically present information to another and hope it will be taken in? Who is in charge of learning, the speaker or the listener, the teacher or the student, the parent or the child? Learning is a mysterious process.

The very word 'learning' propels most adults back into school, the sheltered or confining domain of a formal educational setting, and many shudder at the memory. Although school years do provide a highly concentrated learning experience, learning in a broader sense neither begins nor ends in the classroom. It is part of everyday life.

Learning can happen at every age and in every setting. It is not restricted to groups of children in classrooms but can extend to solitary outdoor adventures for an older person. Learning even goes on at breakfast whether in the childhood home, at university or in a nursing home. Your learning style directs your selection of a card for a friend, shaping how you want to convey your message of 'Thanks', 'I miss you', 'I am sorry' or 'Happy Birthday'. Your learning style is right there with you when talking about personal experiences with a good friend, the mode and style, and perhaps even the content. Instructions of all sorts are filtered through your personal learning style – the procedures at your new job, the techniques of a new sport or reading the hands of a clock. Your learning style finds out about computers, instant messaging and mail merge software. It tries to comprehend what the mechanic said is wrong with your car. And it will soon discover how your children's minds work, how to provide them with easily understandable information, and how to foster harmony within your family, because it certainly sits with you while you're reading this book.

Every tiny bit of communication within your family (talking, shouting, singing, emailing, giving the 'hairy eyeball' or the cold shoulder, saying it with flowers, written notes, recorded and text messages, silence, any non-verbal expression, etc., etc.) engages the learning styles of both people – the presenter and the intended recipient. Communication, and therefore the possibility of learning, occurs constantly – in your attic, in the shower, while dressing, cooking, eating, preparing your tax return and riding your bike. Both people's learning styles come forward whenever you as the parent want to get your message across, no matter what the message is.

Our minds may function quite differently, but that is not to say any one learning style is better or worse than any other. It is not! All are valuable and each has its own special skills and contributions to make, both within the family and out in the world. Without awareness of individual learning styles, you might observe differences among your family members and arrive at any number of sorry conclusions about relative worth and value. But consider this. Society needs the analytical scientist as much as the reflective poet. Your family might contain these opposite kinds of minds. The mediator, the organizer and the networker carry important roles as well as the philosopher, the pioneer and the detective. It would be a less exciting world if we all thought alike – easier, perhaps, but less stimulating, less creative and far less interesting.

Effective and joyful learning comes from knowing and respecting our own learning styles.

One part of our individual master program identifies our learning 'needs' or 'requirements'. We all have some critical parameters which must be satisfied if learning is to be effortless. Information in harmony with our learning needs can be taken in smoothly, without glitches, hiccups, stress or tears.

For example, you (or your child) may be exceptionally sensitive to physical surroundings, literally unable to think in some locations. On the other hand, you may be surprisingly unaffected by the setting, able to read in a tree or negotiate on an airplane. Such things are neither talents nor defects; they are simply personal learning requirements. Your mind might easily take in information only if it is seen to be useful, or you might require a lively discussion of ideas before accepting them. Awareness of such needs is the first step towards meeting them. For example, you could decide to avoid engaging in mental work in a location that disadvantages your thinking, or to provide the same option to your child.

You might be very surprised to discover what aids or inhibits another person's learning process. Possibly, you might never have dreamed that a factor could be significant for someone else, if it is not important to you. Most of us never objectify our learning needs. Nonetheless, they can be grouped into the following three broad categories:

1 For easy learning, some minds require that a specific quality exist within the information itself. This is not an exhaustive list but just some examples. Information must be: practical or applied or pure, logical, intuitive, useful, valuable, traditional, innovative, true, conceptual, functional, powerful, significant,

legal, sacred, exciting, fun, poetic, moving, global, detailed, political, smutty or grammatically correct.

2 Mode of delivery is frequently an important learning requirement. You could be speaking to a child for whom any of the following features might either assist or hinder learning: interaction, involvement, repetition, activity, drama, discussion, colour, time to consider, excitement, a fast pace, a slow pace, fun, action, emotion, the big picture, the tiny details, show-and-tell demonstration, visuals, written instructions or experimentation.

3 Physical and emotional surroundings are critically important to some learners, who take in information most easily if the setting is: comfortable, familiar, physically and/or emotionally safe, colourful, fun, quiet, noisy, out in nature or in a room with the door closed. Some children have learning needs for solitary versus group activity, or where action and movement are not just possible but encouraged.

Children who are fully aware of their own learning requirements from an early age can easily accept a mind's individual nature. They can ask for their needs to be met, later on in life, with confidence rather than shame, and they easily understand and accommodate natural differences.

Effective communication takes place when we take into account the learning requirements of others.

When your message is presented in a way that matches your child's learning needs, there is a good fit and information uptake can occur smoothly, with neither person becoming snagged on rough edges.

For example, your child's mind might be one of the very fast ones, breathing in information in a flash, needing no processing time at all, restless to get on to the next idea. If your words are presented quickly, almost on the run, matching pace with the child's mind, then your message will probably hit the mark.

Unfortunately, the reverse is also true. Learning can be seriously dis-advantaged when a mind's unique needs are not recognized, or much worse, when they are perceived as weakness. Let's look again at the child with the very fast-paced mind. Consider this scenario: The parent's natural mental style responds well to a slow and steady approach, perhaps requiring a few repetitions to really get the message. Moreover, the parent, being unaware of individual mental differences, thinks all minds are fundamentally alike. Does not bode well, does it? Lacking the tools to understand the absolutely natural top-speed, flat-out pace of the child's mind, the parent could view it as dangerously ungrounded, and even seek medical intervention to rectify the problem. Unfortunately, this is not uncommon.

> **Young Eddie's parents** were enchanted with his astounding curiosity – when he was a baby. His attention was drawn by everything from a passing bumblebee to a new sound in his own tummy. It all interested him and he responded to it. His parents proudly labelled him as 'quick'.
>
> This was great until Eddie's school reports said he didn't concentrate well. Suddenly concerned by the very quality that had previously pleased them, his parents sought further advice, obtained a diagnosis of attention deficit disorder and faced the dilemma of drug therapy.

Children (and adults!) whose learning requirements are not met can come away feeling just terrible about themselves. What might have been a joyful exchange becomes drudgery for both parent and child. Tension results. Self-confidence and self-esteem can be so easily and unnecessarily damaged. The child's natural flame of enthusiasm may be extinguished. Mistrust could develop. Family harmony could be right out the window. Nobody wins.

Years after leaving school, many adults still experience the shame of having felt slow or stupid. Worse still, they might think it's true. All this because nobody recognized the individual's natural learning needs.

Each of us takes in information most easily (and joyfully) if it is presented to us in a way that's compatible with our own 'master program', otherwise we have to struggle to get the message. There are ways to say things that will make it easy to hear and ways that will make it virtually impossible to pick up.

If information were tailored to make it easy for me to learn, I would take it in and feel good about myself and the process of learning. On the other hand, information could be tailored to benefit someone else and

I would not easily take it in. I would struggle and feel dumb and the speaker might see me that way also. Or a message could be shaped and delivered to reach me rather than my brother, and I would learn it but he would not. He's not dense, but he needs a message formatted differently.

For the sake of getting an idea across, a parent who is aware of natural learning styles can always modify and tailor a presentation to suit a child's learning requirements, and this practice honours the child's individuality. If we have the knowledge to do so, adults willingly change languages while travelling in foreign countries in order to interact with others. How much more important to adjust the mode of delivery and actually communicate with those we care about rather than missing them totally and just talking to ourselves.

It is likely that a variety of unique learning styles is represented in your family. A uniform way of presenting information simply will not benefit them all. A child (or adult) whose mental landscape figuratively resembles that lush green meadow will most easily take in information that harmonizes with that landscape. A presentation of the same message would have to be tailored differently if intended for a child whose mental landscape is more like the deep ocean cave. These two children will not both receive your message easily, if it is presented in only one way. One of them might understand what you are saying, but chances are the other will not. Or, if one of your children is a real stickler for detail, and actually learns by dissecting and questioning everything you say, and another needs to get the 'big picture' by taking a wide view first, then their minds will respond to quite different approaches on your part.

> **Loraine likes facts**. She is a child who takes in information most easily if it seems to be useful. But, Richard, her elder brother, needs to get the gist of ideas before really accepting them. Their father has solved it – at least about the matter of bedtime. 'Time for bed, Loraine; it's nearly 7:30' works well for his little daughter. But he and Richard have to chat for a few minutes about concepts such as age, fatigue and tomorrow's activities.

All family members, but especially the little ones, need permission to grow along the lines of their most natural and therefore greatest mental strengths. Your son or daughter might have mental qualities and ways of handling information which are quite unlike your own. Both your family and the larger community stand to benefit from their unique development. We all do best what comes naturally. A fish would have difficulty learning to tango and I am just as glad my family didn't expect me to learn underwater breathing.

In all of our early lives, well-meaning parents, teachers and big sisters, knowing what helped them to learn, have tried to convince us, usually with great success, that their method of information transfer and uptake is better than ours. That's when it happens, right there. At that point we become detached from our own natural mental style and attempt to mimic or imitate a mental style that works quite well for someone else. We separate ourselves from our strengths. It might be years later, if ever, that someone leads us back to our own way of handling information and our unique mental style.

Here's an example: Let's say one of your early schoolteachers learned most easily through discussion. His mind had always been like that. Even as a small child he had discussed notions about shoe-tying and clock-reading with his dog. This method worked for him, despite the dog's lack of verbal response. He got what he needed – the opportunity to form his thoughts into concepts and ideas and to express them. (Some discussion-style learners use computers as the chosen recipient of their fledgling thoughts while some use other people.) At any rate, your teacher grew to adulthood certain that learning is best accomplished through discussion. He had teaching cracked; he knew how to do it. The teacher simply involves the pupil in a discussion. Right? No, not for all students. If you are a natural hands-on 'I have to try it out to get it' type of learner, then the discussion method does not play to your strength. It will take you ages to get the message into your head if you abandon your own need for active involvement with the material in favour of your teacher's need for discussion. He did not hijack your learning process deliberately, but you may have been disconnected from easy joyful learning ever since.

Now, let's fast-forward a few decades to you as an adult, facing a steep learning curve with today's rapidly advancing technologies. A trainer is there showing you pictures of the inner workings of a big electronic device, a trainer who really has teaching cracked because he knows that people learn most easily when they are shown diagrams and graphs. No, this does not play to your mental strength. Go for what you need and get your hands on that machine! Try it out. See what it does and what its capabilities are. If you are a 'hands-on' learner, claim what you need. Do it! Try it! Get your hands dirty. Sniff it, taste it. Reconnect with your own natural style of thinking and learning. But, whatever you do, don't make the assumption that everyone else is like you mentally. They may not need to ingest and digest the dictionary to learn linguistics. But you might.

We have all heard these things. Now, they should make us very suspicious.

- No, not like that! Do it my way, it works for me. It will work for you too.
- It's how the human mind works.
- It's traditional. It's the way it's done.
- If you do not learn this material the way I am teaching it, you will fail at school.
- We wrote this test to find out if you have learned the material. If you fail it, you are dumb, slow, stupid, retarded, have ADD, dyslexia, learning difficulties, are disruptive in the classroom, non-cooperative, daydreaming out the window, could concentrate better, are not academic material and moreover, will never amount to anything.

Whew, all this to avoid looking at individual mental differences.

Profiles

The 12 Primary Learning Styles

This information is presented as 'Profiles' of 12 distinct 'Characters', each with its own well-defined essence, pace, style, interests and ways of doing things. Each one has a name and a child-tested illustration which represents its fundamental mode of gathering and handling new information.

Each Profile includes a clear description of how a particular mind ticks, how it learns, how it remembers (or does not), its openness to new information, its natural strengths and potential blind spots. Many of the Profiles mention how the mind may appear to other people. If relevant, a Profile identifies specific environmental features which are conducive to learning. Each one includes hints, tips and strategies for parents to encourage effective learning and improved family interactions. All include quotations from people with the learning style, as another way to access an individual point of view.

Mental traits and dynamics are neither masculine nor feminine. All people, without reference to gender, can elect to use their natural mental skills in any way they please, including the apparently opposite pursuits of reflective poetry or research science. Either a boy or a girl can have any of the 12 learning styles presented here. As a way of dealing with the language of gender without simply defaulting to the masculine or constantly using cumbersome structures such as 'his or hers', 'him/her' or 's/he', the Profiles are grouped as three written for a boy and then three written for a girl and so forth. This is simply for convenience. It is hoped that the parent will be able to juggle the gender words if their son's Profile happens to be one that is written for a girl, or vice versa.

As learning styles are not about behaviour or personality, they are not discernable by observing your children in action. Your children's mental styles may bear no relationship to their other component qualities – feelings, egos, values, social impulses, ambitions, etc. A learning style does not comment on mental or emotional intelligence or capacity. It is a style, a mode, a manner.

However, the Profiles which follow use some behavioural terms in describing the activities of the 12 Characters. They are ways in which the Characters themselves might behave and are not intended to correspond to your child's performance. You may or may not observe the Characters shining forth in your children's activities, as they represent purely inner mental styles.

Before reading on, this is the perfect time to quickly and easily identify learning styles for your children and yourself. Just turn to Part III page 163 and follow the instructions for using the Tables. A worksheet is included on page 162 to help you keep track of all the learning styles in the family and how they naturally interact.

Scout – The Trailblazer

Quick on the uptake, this mind is active, direct, energetic,
positive, lively and bright. It can be unflaggingly forceful and
competitive. And to a parent it can be both stimulating
and exhausting.

Unless you were born with this style of learning also, you could be surprised, excited or perhaps just plain puzzled by some facets of your child's mind. You might anticipate that he will outgrow the qualities you are now observing, his flippant youthful enthusiasms or mega mental confidence. Well, you'd better get used to it because 20, 30, 60 years from now, your child will still be a mental Trailblazer.

Whether young or mature, Scout is first off the starting line when it comes to new information. He literally runs at it, like a gladiator, charging with his sword drawn. He likes the idea of knowing something before anyone else does. Scout is first to get his hand in the air, first to speak – first to put his foot in his mouth. However, he likes having the last word. This mind is dynamic, eager, assertive, robust and tireless. A Mental Warrior, Scout persistently moves forward, thriving on challenges as he goes. He rarely, if ever, looks over his shoulder.

Your child's mind is naturally creative, originating new ideas and initiating new lines of thought. Don't be surprised if you have not heard them before from anyone else. Scout likes to veer suddenly along uncharted mental pathways, inventing as he goes. He is good at this – starting is one of Scout's mental strengths. So when a fresh new approach is needed, ask your young Brainstormer. You probably won't even have to ask – he'll be right there.

Your little Warrior is fearless about the unknown. He's brave, bold and courageous about mental exploration. Some may find it a reckless mind, exciting, enterprising, but reckless. He's wired to respond to red.

The Trailblazer may not ask for your permission or for your help in making a decision. His mind is tremendously independent. Without reference to other minds, he just 'goes for it'. Scout is at the centre of his own universe. He is identified with his own thoughts – they are closely related to his ego, his sense of self. Your child takes his own ideas very seriously and is attached to his own point of view. To question one of his ideas is to question his essence, and this can be experienced as a personal challenge. Other learning styles do not respond like this, it's very specific to this one.

Your child learns by reference to himself – it's natural – and as another expression of the link between his mind and his ego, he may tend to begin most sentences with 'I'. Although the rest of your family might spot this as a serious 'me first' attitude (and perhaps it is), it will not be helpful for the child to be criticized or told he is egocentric or self-centred. It may be more helpful for Scout to recognize and respect the value of other family minds and to realize how his constant 'I' statements make others feel.

> **Game Idea:** For some period of time, all family members engage in 'I' sentences and talk about themselves. Little Scout has the opportunity to be on the receiving end of all those 'I's, while the rest of the family has a chance to try it out for themselves. This is not intended to ridicule or to be a Scout bashing session, but as a loving experience of similarity and difference in family thinking and learning styles.

Scout's natural mental impulse is to start things, to take initiative, to speak out, to introduce himself, his topic and his thoughts. He may have learned to curb that impulse or he may bravely take responsibility for his own ideas and fearlessly tell others about them. If someone disagrees, that's often OK as he quite likes an argument and doesn't mind being controversial. In fact sometimes he quite likes to stir things up. It is exciting! Thriving on challenge and risk, he may leap in impulsively where angels fear to tread. His mind is naturally competitive. But the tendency to defend his own point of view and to regard every question as a personal challenge may interfere with both learning and getting along with people. It can be a steep learning curve for Scout to accept the possibility of holding back, of selecting the tone and the time to speak. Along that path he might explore the option of snapping shut like a clam. All of this may require a great deal of patience, understanding and guidance from you.

His natural impulse, to energetically (forcefully?) share his thoughts with everyone, may appear out of line to adults and those in authority – classroom teachers, the headmaster, grandparents. It can mature to engage courageously with powerful forces like the boss, the board of directors, the drill sergeant or the government. Some help from you during his childhood will go a long way toward his learning to avoid pitfalls later.

The trick is to convey, lovingly, supportively and without damaging the child's courageous but delicate spirit, that impulsive action on all his natural inclinations does not always bring his desired results. Inspire him to engage with the challenge of modifying his expressive behaviour while remaining connected to his natural mental strengths. This blend will allow his mind's creativity to flow constructively as a great gift to the rest of us as well as to himself. The art is conscious socialization – learning to live in community with others, family members and other children, while still retaining one's fine qualities and talents.

Although Scout can be challenging and confrontational, he is not stubborn. Unless the fight is just too interesting or too much fun, he is usually ready to move on. There are so many other conquests out there!

You'll find your child learns best if he applies his mind in short bursts separated by periods of activity. Thinking is stimulated by movement – his brain slows down with immobility. A marathon session with the schoolbooks accomplishes little in the way of learning but will certainly create a volcano of restlessness. Try encouraging a period of mental focus, then a run or walk, and then back to the topic at hand. Any activity that gets the blood moving seems to help mental concentration: swimming, skating, stretching, bike rides, chopping wood. (If you are lucky, household chores might be effective.) Scout likes to take in information on the move. 'Think while doing' is his motto.

Your little Trailblazer is very quick on the uptake. He seems to just breathe in information without needing to process, integrate or digest it at all. He can inhale fully developed ideas in the blink of an eye. But then, while he waits for everyone else to catch up, restlessness takes over and boredom sets in. So, off he dashes in hot pursuit of the next exciting new idea.

He is not very interested in follow-through, completing, reviewing, revising or repeating. He is not interested in practicality, punctuation, logic, or your opinion. This mind rushes forward inexhaustibly and rarely looks back. Scout's mental energy works in intense blasts, like fireworks that brilliantly illuminate a dark sky and then quickly fade. It's natural for an idea to captivate his enthusiasm for a while and then die away. Completing a project, sticking with it to the end, dotting all those i's and crossing all the t's, goes against the grain. Taking care of the details is not a favourite mental activity. It will not be easy for him to accept that life does not seem to allow us the luxury of using only our mental strengths all the time. Many projects do require completion, and many ideas need to be followed through. It will take extra energy and will power for your child to do this. The mind wants to move on to new and more exciting ideas, not stick with the old, boring ones. Striking out, speeding like a rally driver, his mind's forward momentum can often carry your child straight on past the point of success.

Try using tricks to help your child learn to stick with a project, topic or lesson until it's completed. A useful strategy is to find ways to make the old project seem new again and thus re-enlisting the mental enthusiasm that naturally occurs at the beginning.

> **Game Idea:** How many new titles can he discover for the same (old) project? How many different directions of approach arrive at the same (old) point? How many different facets of the same (old) project can be explored as if it were a new activity? Can doing the same (old) project in a different study space make it seem totally new?

Your little Trailblazer might notice and wonder about others taking longer to catch on to new information. Even most adults do not realize that we all think and learn differently and that no particular learning style is better or worse than another. It would be helpful in the long term if your child avoids the widely held misconception that quicker translates into smarter, that those who catch on faster are better students than those who require more time. For example, the 14-year-old Trailblazer son of a friend adopted the policy of telling his very busy mother something once, and only once. He would not repeat it. But, he would judge and condemn his mother's quite different learning style if she just happened to forget something weeks and sometimes months later. 'Mum, I told you my sports schedule at the beginning of term. Why should I have to tell you again? I have a game today! Are you stupid or what?'

Help him to see that other people are not inferior because their minds work more slowly, but that a different kind of mental processing is going on. Unlike others who pause to reflect and check out all the angles, or to digest or feel the information, Scout leaps impulsively upon a new idea with enthusiasm and boldness. To some this may look heedless but, to him, almost everyone else seems painfully slow.

What helps your child to learn?

- Recognize that he will have the most mental energy at the beginning of a project and that finishing is likely to take more effort. Help him to find creative new ways of 'restarting' in order to actually finish.
- Activity aids his learning. He is mentally restless and likes to physically move while thinking. This may be difficult in a group situation as his moving around may disturb those who need stability and calm. Look for creative solutions.
- Work with him in short sessions with activity in between.
- Try recording information onto an audiotape or an MP3 player for him so he can listen during a variety of activities.
- Field trips, dramatizations, modelling, visits or role-play can positively stimulate his mind.
- Energizing music may help to dispel restlessness and boredom.
- Present ideas with enthusiasm, emphasizing their newness.
- Learning by rote is a sure route to impatience and boredom, so avoid this strategy.
- Present information in a way that makes it personal to him.
- Make learning fun and let him take the lead as frequently as possible; it allows his mind, which likes to be first with new ideas, to have a free rein.

- Ask him questions about things that he has done. Encourage him to tell you about what excites him.
- Introduce him to flashcards or other fast methods of learning, making connections or testing his knowledge.
- Shock him, surprise him – use jokes or punch lines.
- Keep it short.

Quotes from people with this learning style

'I think that the quickest way to gather information is the best.'

'I had a great new idea ten minutes ago and I've given it a great deal of thought.'

'Look I've told you once. I'm not telling you again.'

'I think while I'm driving.'

'I have great enthusiasm, especially at the beginning.'

'I find I can move on with new initiatives at work. Others find it hard.'

'I do like to poke people a couple of times to get them to say what they really mean.'

Steady – The Vault

Have you heard the one about leading a Highland calf to water
only to find the decision to drink it is totally his own?
That statement was first written about a boy with this learning
style. Sometimes you can't even get him within half a mile
of the trough.

Raising a youngster with this learning style will be easier if you recognize that he decides what to learn and what not to learn. Perhaps this may not be within the realm of choice for most of us, but it is for him, and it's totally natural. Any new information coming his way will be subjected to tests. If it does not pass muster, he will not learn it – no matter how much you might want him to, no matter how much you cajole, threaten, plead, or yell. Sometimes he can fool you into thinking he has taken in certain information, when in fact he has not. He may be just using it for a while. Time will tell. If it looks as if he has forgotten something, then he never actually learned it; he pretended. Young 'Vault' does not forget.

Affectionately known as Steady, his mind approaches new information slowly and with reserve. As you know, he will not be rushed. This type of mind does not jump to conclusions or to anything else. It ponders and deliberates.

Regardless of his age, he quite naturally compares all new ideas against his own emerging mental values, and in this way thoroughly tests the new information before he even considers learning it. His mind is very concerned with the appeal and charm of new information. Does it have worth? Does it delight him? Is it beautiful? Does it please all his senses? Does it taste good, smell good, look good, feel good, sound good? Will knowing this information increase his attractiveness, security or stability? Later on he will ponder the financial or artistic benefit. Will it enhance his beloved earth? Is it practical, worthwhile and valuable? Will it endure over the long term? Only when criteria of this sort have been met will Steady elect to chew on, take in, actually learn, the information.

As part of this scrutiny, he even reaches behind and beneath the new information to evaluate where it came from, weighing the appeal, the reliability and the solidity of its source. The information's origin has to pass the value tests as well. Books have to be in clean and good condition. A top-quality hardcover or first edition might be best. Believe it or not, your child finds it almost impossible to learn from anyone, even an adult, who lacks beauty or style or who does not dress according to the child's sense of quality. Sorry, but he is not fabricating this. It's real for him. You might as well forget about making helpful suggestions first thing in the morning, if you're still wearing your old dressing gown.

For example, a friend's teenage son was doing well with most of his schoolwork, but was struggling with his guitar and piano lessons, pursuits which he especially loved. His parents were stunned by the strength of his reply to my question about the music tutor. 'No, of course I can't learn anything from him, he doesn't even dress properly.' The lad thought his reaction to the man would be evident, obvious and shared by everyone else.

In truth, it is a very good thing that your child carefully considers new information before taking it in. He learns by consuming new ideas just as the body ingests food. He chews things over – and swallows! Ideas become part of the fabric of his body, incorporated at the mental equivalent of physical cells. Steady will not be changing his mind soon. The decision to learn something is a mental commitment that can last his lifetime. That's why we call his mind The Vault. It contains all the thoughts, ideas, data and information he considers valuable. But, if your child had failed to stop, look, and listen before accepting every new concept that came down the road he could have found himself with a vault full of useless and unappealing drivel.

This is the key to Steady's great mental tenacity and 'groundedness'. He tests the value of new information by his attraction to it. Any idea deemed valuable enough to be learned is deeply integrated and will be retained and preserved over time. Your child simply cannot change his way of thinking like his clothing as many other people can. You probably thought he was just being stubborn and wilful; well it does appear that way.

And just a word about appearances. Little Steady lives, and has always lived, with this learning style. He was born with it and it comes totally naturally to him. He may not realize for many years to come that others interact with information quite differently. He just does what he does without self-conscious awareness of difference. Not for an instant does he wonder how his natural mental style might appear through the eyes of someone else. None of us does! Unless you too have this learning style, you might occasionally view his steadfast commitment to ideas as obstinate, inflexible, intractable or even 'bull-headed'. You may know how disturbing it can be to patiently wait for his decision on something simple, like what he wants to wear today, and then to observe him slowing down even further when he feels pushed. May I point out that any criticism will fall on totally deaf ears? He will not understand that he has done something 'wrong', or what it could be. We are on the thin ice of damaged self-esteem here. Please be as patient as possible, working toward 'right relationship', which stems from the mutual respect for difference.

When a piece of information or an idea has met Steady's tests of quality, attractiveness, etc., and he has decided to learn it, he does so most naturally and most easily through a 'hands-on' approach. He learns by getting involved with the material. He would be delighted by wooden objects, driftwood, pebbles or beach stones, mineral samples like geodes and crystals of all colours, playing with and learning from all the natural, beautiful things that earth has produced. He might not need any encouragement to pick them up and examine them. It's natural for him to involve his senses in the learning process – taste it, practise it, look at it, sniff it, try it on, act it out. He is a practical thinker who takes easily to common sense.

Because of his mental persistence and reliability, it might seem that your young one has a very old head. You might think his mind is 6 going on 60 and isn't having enough fun. Relax. This is normal for

Steady. To him an idea has merit if it can be applied to real life in a useful and down-to-earth way. Actually, it surprises him to discover that other people can value ideas just because they feel right, or are interesting, or are new, while totally disregarding the importance of practicality. But, we do!

Sometimes, you might admire the relatively more freethinking, more upbeat, fun-loving mental styles of other people's children. You might wonder why yours has to be a 'stick-in-the-mud' sort of child who rejects nearly all new ideas out of hand. It's probably fairly predictable by now that he will. You certainly notice other children's easy acceptance of exciting new suggestions from parents and teachers, and their enjoyment at trying out new thoughts and ideas.

Because we each have a unique and individual style of learning, thinking and communicating, it's desirable that we interact differently with information. It makes the world go around. Society needs all kinds of thinkers, with each expressing different mental strengths. This is as true of your child as of the others. Just think about it – children who easily embrace new ideas by the bucketful discard them just as quickly, changing their minds with every passing breeze. By necessity, we all grow up to make quite different contributions to the larger group. If we all thought alike, the world would be a far less interesting home.

So let's look at some of the special qualities of your child's mental makeup. His mind is very stable with great powers of concentration enabling him to ignore outside disturbances and stick to the matter at hand. It's steady! Most children are much more easily distracted. Your child's mind considers things carefully. He is unhurried and refrains from leaping to conclusions or onto bandwagons. Whether telling you about his day or preparing a school assignment, he will tend to cover the groundwork thoroughly. Steady speaks his mind deliberately and with intention. He doesn't leave big gaps in his stories.

Steady's natural appreciation of beauty and design may express itself as mental gracefulness and artistry. Learning is physical – his senses are instruments of learning, with touch possibly better developed than hearing. But if you ask him to describe how something feels or tastes or smells, you will discover a growing ability to capture these sensory experiences in words. He can recall how things taste. Ask him for menu ideas; he will know which flavours blend well together. Encourage his natural sense of colour and line, of how furniture can be rearranged for a pleasing effect, of which flowers or fabrics add the perfect touch.

Of course, The Vault does not forget easily. The proverbial elephant would be challenged by the reach of your child's memory. His mind holds ideas over the long term, carrying them, preserving them and sustaining them – no matter what. Adults with this mental commitment provide cultural stability in thought, ensuring that what's beautiful and valuable is not lost. Wherever would we be without them? Who else would have the patience, interest or capacity to shape the living earth, to design and sustain elegant gardens which please the senses with their harmonious colours and fragrant perfumes? Who would see to the continuity of financial investments or countryside and agricultural policies and practices? Who would be interested over the long run in preserving the arts, architecture, and the well-being of the earth?

As an adult your child might find particular appeal in projects with long-term growth and with sustainability. He will be favourably challenged in areas that touch his sense of beauty and value.

What helps your child to learn?

- To relax and take his time. He is bringing new ideas all the way down to earth and into his body when he learns, not just into his head.
- Learning is best when his mind is allowed to proceed at an unpressured pace. He may have to ask for the space to learn according to his own time frame.
- To become aware of testing the appeal of new information.
- To realize that he decides what he will or will not learn. The 'teacher' has not 'failed' if he himself chooses not to take in something that has been offered.
- To see the practical benefits of any information. Relate ideas to usefulness, comfort, durability and beauty. Abstractions unrelated to everyday life are often rejected.
- To dig into topics as if he were digging the garden, even if he gets his hands dirty. Provide a variety of 'hands-on' activities so that learning can be through experience and direct involvement.
- To see how he might apply new ideas or thoughts to a real-life situation.

- Link new information to what is already known.
- Give demonstrations, and then let him try it himself.
- Allow him time for careful consideration of ideas and delay before asking him questions. The length of 'wait time' will depend upon the child and the topic.
- Present information concretely with tactile sensory aids – blocks, beads, Lego, measuring tapes, etc.

Quotes from people with this learning style

'I can learn anything as long as I'm interested in it.'

'I sometimes persevere with something long after I know I should leave it alone.'

'I like this school – the teachers have style.'

'I don't forget things.' (Joshua aged 5 years)

'I can never face a new idea cleanly, without the filter of the baggage of what I already know.'

'I only read fact books. I can't see the point of reading fiction.'

'Others may call me stubborn, but I am proud of the fact that I am consistent and hold onto what I believe.'

'I do not like short-term things. I like things that are solid.'

Buzz – The Curious

*Here is a child who is inquisitive about absolutely everything,
from bison to butterflies. One WHY question will follow another,
and another, and another.*

You might as well get accustomed to being asked 'Why?' as this will not go away with the terrible twos, or threes or even fours. This is a lifelong pattern. Your child really is interested in both the questions and the answers, but for just about as long as it takes to get the ideas into words. Then he is off on another tangent, to another set of fascinating inquiries.

We affectionately call this mind Buzz. It's full of interests, full of ideas, and loves to dart and flit among them. To him, an idea is complete in and of itself. Buzz does not need to do anything with it. He does not need to actualize it, analyse it or retain it in memory. Having the idea and maybe sharing it with someone else is enough. To Buzz, ideas are tangible and can be batted around like ping-pong balls. The more balls in the air at a time the better, and the absolute minimum is two. Your child's mind rates highly on levity and agility!

Buzz is a generalist. Just as a garden butterfly naturally touches lightly on every flower, stalk and stem, this Curious mind dashes across the surface of a wide spectrum of information. Its job is not to plumb the depth of a topic, any more than the butterfly's job is to reach down into the roots of your garden plants. It gathers what it wants from the exterior and moves on. Buzz likes to know a little about a lot.

To learn, he only has to fit a new idea into a concept, grasp the sense or logic of it. In the overall scheme of things, this mind is a little slower than one which just breathes in information without requiring conceptualization. However, it's considerably faster than those which need to filter new information through the feelings or take it into the physical cells. So Buzz seems very fast on the uptake to some people and slower to others. This quality links with relationship dynamics, not intelligence. Speed does not reflect intellectual capacity. It is just a natural feature of some learning styles.

Because Buzz is a conceptual type of mind, your child can take in new information from either the written or the spoken word. He can come away from a teacher's classroom presentation with the message intact. He can read a book once and have it. Other children may need to go over lessons a few times, but not our Buzz! Others might need time to ponder or feel their way through new information, or try it out for themselves. Not Buzz. He reads it, he hears it, he has it. This does not mean that he will remember it.

The Curious child (or adult) thrives on new information. He evaluates its merit by its newness and its interest factor – not usefulness, intuitive truth or human component. If he has not heard it before, he wants to – now.

Let's talk about memory. Do you think the butterfly remembers the lily it lingered on yesterday or even the tulip it touched upon earlier today? Not very likely. As soon as Buzz moves on to the next task at hand, the whole mind moves along too. When a project is finished (reading a book, viewing a DVD, having a conversation) his mind is apt to jettison information associated with that activity (the author's name, the starring actor, what the plan was). Data which is not being used on an ongoing basis is forgotten as quickly as this morning's news. His mind is then ready to approach the new, which is much more fun than holding on to old stuff.

Fortunately, information which is in active use is retained, and in adult life his mind will be very well suited to what is called project work. For example, let's look at a journalist assigned to a story. First he gathers a mountain of new information and then he moves it around into a logical and cohesive pattern. The article is composed, written and submitted, with luck by the copy deadline. Our reporter instantly forgets all about that assignment, becoming mentally uncluttered and ready to move on to his next activity. Sometimes projects last for years and years, with the necessary information staying right there at the mind's fingertips. But as soon as it ends, out goes the then unnecessary mental clutter.

Buzz's memory is something of a mixed blessing, and it is met with a variety of different responses from others.

On the positive side – and if you are Buzz's parent you might really need to know there is a positive side – the mind doesn't become encumbered with old baggage, ideas that were bright and lively ages ago, but are now dry and dusty. It just does not happen to him. Remember, the archetype here is The Curious, and this fits Buzz at any age. Your child does not become mentally obsessive, that's for sure. He does not even want to think about the same things today as he did yesterday. The mind is fresh and clear and ready for whatever new thoughts are coming his way. He has such mental agility, such levity, such buoyancy. He gives a natural lift to any conversation. He is clever and funny, and fun to talk to. He always has interesting new ideas.

It's best if people with other kinds of learning styles view Buzz's 'short-term memory' as a positive quality. It's not always easy, as his mind can infuriate other people, especially those blessed with very good long-term memory. Punctuality does not seem to be in his vocabulary. Plans and promises are forgotten, resulting in cold or burned meals, missed deadlines and unused tickets to musical or athletic events. Please do remember that Buzz is not being disrespectful if he forgets what you say. He is not doing something to you; he is simply being himself and doing what comes naturally. He just buzzed off when a new idea caught his fancy. You have the choice of accepting this and letting it be, recognizing the positive/creative/charming side of his mind, different as it may be from your own, or of rejecting it and suffering. You will simply not change The Curious into The Rock.

Hint: You can introduce strategies to make both your life and his run more smoothly. To be effective and last a lifetime, they will have to be fun, not drudgery. Try Post-it notes in his lunch box, surprise messages tucked into his schoolbooks or drawers, an annual/weekly/daily diary system created just for him, novel and amusing 'penalties' for forgetting simple practical things, even the time-tested string around the finger. Get creative with this, make it a game. It may help you as much as him.

One of Buzz's mental strengths is his ability to take in an enormous volume of information, stir it around and synthesize something brand new from the component parts. His particular specialty is synthesis on the conceptual level and he's good at it. He will look at a body of data through his own unique lens and will reshape it. He will paraphrase. He will enlist his natural mental flexibility and adaptability to put ideas, lyrics, jokes, concepts, views and suppositions into his own words, with his own twist, giving it a totally unique imprint.

This mind has fun and likes fun. He learns best if the learning process is fun. Other children may need repetition to learn. Some require silence, nature, movement or a beautiful environment. Some children even require a sense of emotional safety and security in order to learn. But your child needs fun, levity and logic.

And while on the topic of fun, this mind is very funny. It has its own take and twist on humour. It loves to laugh and to make others laugh. Is this not a gift? Sometimes other minds don't get the joke. Not everyone can follow Buzz through his conceptual maze and realize that the last sentence was in fact the punch line. But it was.

Buzz loves words and games that involve words and letters: crosswords, puns, Scrabble, blocks. His mind enjoys and is stimulated by notice boards, books (better to be reading two at once!), libraries, comics, newspapers, telephones and all the newest gadgets of communication technology. It loves paper, pencils and pens. Watch the wallpaper!

To others Buzz can appear to be forgetful, flighty, insubstantial, airheaded, motor-mouthed, indecisive, frivolous, superficial, ambivalent, wishy-washy, unstable and changeable, to list just a few appropriate words. But, without minds like Buzz, life would become so totally serious, heavy, sombre, sober, grim and grave that, well, it just wouldn't be as much fun.

You may have read about the increasingly widespread diagnosis of a condition called ADD, attention deficit disorder. You may have been concerned that your child suffers with this condition and you might even have been considering medicating him to make him more 'normal'. His mental restlessness is entirely normal for him. It is part of his nature. He loves variety, diversity and anything new. He thrives on leaping from one topic to another. Please think carefully about this before medicating Buzz.

What helps your child to learn?

- Recognize his short-term memory as a strength, not a failing. He does not need to apologize for it!
- He has a much more flexible and adaptable mind than most people with good long-term memory. Encourage him to enjoy it.
- Writing things down or saying them aloud helps him to learn.
- Encourage him to tell others about things he has learned.
- Give opportunities for discussion and debate.
- Indulge his curiosity.
- Ask questions, especially those that arouse his curiosity.
- Help him to find answers to his own questions
- Learning for its own sake can be a joy. Make learning fun for him.
- Provide lots of books, audio books, taped lectures, journals, TV and radio programmes, magazines, newspapers, podcasts, DVDs and videos
- Tell stories, jokes and anecdotes.
- Encourage him to find common themes and connections among different ideas.
- Suggest he apply his mind to a task in short bursts. It's a curious mind, and may chafe against concentrating on a single topic for a long time. He wants to learn a little about everything.
- Teach him about lists, diaries and notes to himself, as strategies to help him keep track of things and live in harmony with others.
- Suggest he prepare for a test or report shortly before the event, not a long way in advance.

Quotes from people with this learning style

'The funnier something is the easier it is to remember.'

'There has to be a reason for this.'

'I wonder why…?'

'Tell me that again.'

'Did you know that…?'

'Have you heard the one about…?'

'Why is a banana called a banana?'

'You wonder if I related to the Profile for my learning style? Well, yesterday when I read it, I read it seriously and considered it. It easily slipped right in, and now it seems to have slipped right out again.'

'I've just watched two films on TV at the same time. Why? Because neither of them was interesting enough on its own. I just watched one until I saw where it was going and then flipped over to the other for a while.'

'Oh, sorry, would you repeat that. My focus went elsewhere.'

Sponge – The Sensitive

Regardless of this child's outward behaviour, despite how robust
she may appear to be, she has a supersensitive mind. By the
time she's a teenager she will be sick and tired of hearing people
say 'Oh, why do you have to be so sensitive?'
Well, here's the simple truth: she just is.

It would be really helpful and supportive for her family to understand and work with her sensitivity, as it is a natural part of her learning process.

Sponge does not have the option of taking a giant step backward from new information or pausing to decide whether or not to take it on board. No, she soaks it up like a kitchen sponge in the vicinity of a puddle. Nor is she able to distance herself from information by keeping it in her head, in the safe realms of intellectual concepts and flashes of insight. No, afraid not. This mind drinks in messages from the environment and filters them through her personal feelings. So there is always emotion associated with learning, with hearing new ideas, with seeing pictures (TV, videos, photos, etc.). This is her natural learning dynamic and will not be outgrown in time. Even great big adults with this learning style can flood with tears just watching a TV commercial.

Information coming from the outside gives rise to feelings on the inside.

Furthermore, this reaction is deeply personal. As she learns, Sponge relates the new material to herself and to those close to her. She may position herself in the plot of whatever she's learning about and feel the impact of being in the midst of that situation. Or, she might mentally reframe a news story to include you or other family members, and then experience an emotional response to having people she loves actually involved in the episode. Reading stories and watching TV programmes can become emotional events, full of joy or sadness, enthusiasm or despondency. This just happens. It is a natural mode of learning and is unrelated to either choice or control.

While on the topic of family, many of your child's ideas and attitudes come from you – home and family are very important to her thinking. The images she absorbs there are foundational. Throughout her life, she is apt to reference her family members in conversation, their exploits and life experiences.

Sponge evaluates the merit of an idea by how it feels. She knows good ones from bad, interesting ones from boring, right from wrong, exciting from dangerous, by the personal emotional reaction generated within her. A good idea is one that feels right. This interwoven blend of mind and feelings is totally natural to your child. Like the rest of us, she will be surprised to find that all minds are not like hers. She might be stunned to realize that others judge an idea's value on grounds of logic or practicality. She may consider others too cold and detached because they separate feeling from thought. But others might observe that Sponge can be swayed by an appeal to her emotions, sometimes against the dictates of 'common sense'.

Have you noticed that you can ask her what she thinks but she responds with how she feels? Has it puzzled you that she comes forward with so much emotion when you ask for just factual information? This combination of head and heart is natural for her but perhaps not for you.

We say a picture is worth a thousand words. This is especially true for your child! Her mind very definitely links ideas with pictures. If you show her a picture, she will get the sense of it instantly. But if you offer her the thousand words, she first creates in her mind's eye a picture version of what you said and then she takes in the picture. Her mind requires the extra step, the translation from language to visuals, in order to learn. And she will remember ideas in visual form – she may have a 'photographic' memory. Words simply do not produce the necessary direct emotional resonance but pictures do.

For this reason, Sponge does not take in either the written or spoken word as easily as other types of minds do. The stock-in-trade of traditional education does not benefit children with this learning style. Although their particular requirements for testing/evaluating as well as for learning often sadly go unrecognized, these children learn easily from visuals of all sorts. Pictures directly engage their feelings.

> **Helpful Hint:** To enhance her learning, provide your child with a wide assortment of graphics, photos, videos, charts, illustrations, abstract and realistic diagrams and drawings.

A quiet and safe learning environment is essential for your child. This becomes obvious if you just think about what she is coping with while absorbing new material. Her mind works by linking ideas with the feelings they call forth. Strong emotion, loud noises, raised voices and even very bright colours can totally overpower the gentle work of her learning process. If the home or classroom feels 'unsafe' to her, a predominant feeling of fear or worry can be ever so much more powerful than the delicate inner emotional message generated by an ordinary session about history, science or music. The lesson will not have a chance – the material will just not be learned.

As an example, here's a story about a school inspector with this Sponge-type mind. She is a strong, powerful woman whose behaviour conveys supreme confidence, totally masking her mental sensitivity. She reports that when her family moved from a small town to a sizeable city during her childhood, she was so frightened in school that she didn't learn anything at all for a year and a half. Nobody understood.

> **Her Hint:** Although it may be very difficult to arrange, try to have someone personally greet your child at the door of a new classroom, sports centre or meeting place, introduce her to the other children and allow a little time for her to settle in before beginning the activities.

It does not take much to overwhelm the delicate sensitivity of this learning style. But if you provide or insist upon safety and emotional security in her learning environment, your child will flourish. Otherwise, she might much prefer to stay at home with you, where protection and well-being are assured.

You must be wondering by now if there are any compensating benefits to all this sensitivity. Resoundingly, yes!

Sponge's unique mental strengths stem from, actually grow out of, the activity of translating between words and pictures. Your child may develop considerable skill at interpreting verbal or written language into visuals, a skill with enormous possible applications in her future. For example, this natural mental talent could be focused toward logo design, concise graphical representations, leaflet and brochure design, packaging and other examples of high-impact advertising where a specific message is conveyed at a glance. If you need a simple picture that can speak volumes, here's your girl.

Enjoying design activities of all sorts, Sponge's highly imaginative mind can fashion powerful emotional messages from both musical and visual imagery. Her skits, songs, videos, photos and even plays can pack an emotional wallop. Her cards, invitations, posters, announcements and letters convey meaning with strong emotion.

Perhaps you have noticed that your child picks up the feelings or 'vibrations' around her. Many things do not need to be spelled out – she doesn't need to be told when you are unhappy or when something is wrong. She may often come away from a conversation with considerably more information than anyone intended to provide. Over time she may develop an ability to absorb an entire picture from just a few sketchy words, an advantage in both personal and professional situations. She just feels it – and usually is correct. However, when she speaks, she might not realize that the rest of us need a more complete explanation, with more words, to get her drift. Most people present information in the mode that best satisfies their own learning requirements, thinking it will be just right for others. Little Sponge may need to learn to fill out her stories and presentations.

Sponge is very talented at initiating ideas which are concerned with emotional issues or have an emotional impact. For example, she may be the first to suggest a project aimed at providing assistance to children needing a helping hand in one way or another. She can originate ideas which have a very positive effect on your family or other families. Her thoughts quite naturally tend to nurture, to look after – plants and animals as well as people. She thinks about and responds to others' feelings, and, adopting the role of a young counsellor, she can easily talk to others about themselves.

At the same time, nobody can stir things up like Sponge. She can really get your entire family going with just a few words, especially if she's bored or there isn't 'enough going on' around the house. Sponge can experience an emotional threat when someone questions one of her ideas, another feature of the strong bond between her mind and feelings. But, if she reacts to the perceived threat, it can thoroughly confuse communication, agitate the other person and ultimately generate a whirlwind.

At the deep place within her where thinking links with feeling, she quite naturally dreams up new ideas – one after the other. She thrives on beginnings; she is very good at starting new things, but she is not skilled at completing. When an idea loses its emotional appeal, goes cold and no longer interests her, her first inclination is to flow toward something more stimulating. Although this comes naturally to your child, she might benefit from knowing a few tricks to help her finish projects.

Helpful Hint: If her big project has gone cold, show her how to isolate a component part and establish a renewed emotional connection to that section. Help her to drum up a bit of appreciation or perhaps exalt in its beauty! Do this a few times and presto, project completed.

Sponge is sensitive to other people's feeling responses and consequently can make a significant contribution to any activities in which the human factor is important. Further down the road your child's natural mental skills could be creatively applied to taking care of others, making people feel happy, safe and comfortable, either at home or away, by engineering the ambience, colour schemes and interior-design features of clubs, hotels, hospitals, airplanes, trains and restaurants, in addition to private homes. Her mental sensitivity could lead her toward the human resource field, counselling, or nurturing and looking after others in any of a variety of situations.

Of course this selfsame awareness may drive her in the opposite direction. Who would know better how to scare a moviegoer to death? Someone has to advise on or write modern drama and films – someone's child grew up to conceive, write, and stage *The Rocky Horror Picture Show*!

What helps your child to learn?

- Appreciate that she needs to feel comfortable and safe in the learning environment in order to do her best mental work.
- Assist her to create a positive, supportive learning space at home, perhaps with an eye to colour, music and pictures.
- Encourage her to embrace the emotional dimension of her learning process and make a friend of it. She might as well recognize this as a strength; it is not going away.
- Seek out illustrations or videos about whatever topic is at hand.
- Present information to her in picture form using visuals of all sorts, gestures, word pictures or dramatization.
- Suggest she take notes in graphical forms, charts, diagrams, mind maps and use them to help commit information to memory.
- Recommend that she take time and space to reflect upon activities and lessons.
- Engage your own emotions when presenting information to her and ask her to do so in return.
- Use colour to present and record information.
- Explain, demonstrate and use visualization techniques.
- Encourage the use of symbols, metaphors and stories.
- Present information in a way that is relevant to human needs and feelings. Talk about it; ask for her feedback and opinions.

Quotes from people with this learning style

'My job is getting the feel for a client's business and then designing a logo or visual which captures the idea of what they are trying to do. After I have visited a business I always know a lot more than they have told me. I just absorb it.'

'How does it feel to be an eyeball?'

'I think the British people need someone in public life to
give affection, to make them feel important, to support
them…'

(Princess Diana)

'When I was sent away to boarding school it broke my
heart, but I then just got on with it and had no hard
feelings toward anyone.'

'I hear the words and I see the pictures.'

'My mind seems to flow over the surface of life, consuming
by absorbing. I take it all in.'

'Information is the fuel that feeds my emotion.'

Rex – The Dignified

Your child might try out new ideas, have a good sniff around
them, but she absolutely will not invite them into the kingdom of
her mind, unless she knows they will be worthy subjects.

Certainly not! Her mind is a special place. Plain old ordinary thoughts are simply not welcome there. Ideas have to be of the highest quality to gain entry, and the perimeter wall is carefully guarded and diligently defended. Each and every new piece of information presented at the gates is examined for worth and value. Each one is considered and tested individually. Oh, jubilation, if a thought satisfactorily passes the test – it's in! And there it will remain, indefinitely, a respected resident of the kingdom with all the associated high-level rights and privileges.

So, what is the test all about? What criteria must be met? Which ideas will be accepted and which will be forever banished? And does Rex really have individual choice and total authority about what to learn, what to take in? Well, yes, she does and her selection is related to the role which ideas and thoughts play within the kingdom of her mind.

The crux of the matter is this: her thoughts are closely related to her identity. Information held in her mind contributes to her sense of selfhood. She is what she thinks. Any idea that she takes in, goes right to her heart, to her core. So, she will single out only those ideas on which she is willing to stake her identity. They must confirm who she already senses herself to be. She has to be proud of them. When Rex speaks, she speaks from the heart. When she proclaims her ideas, she proclaims herself.

Information that has gained entry is well and truly ensconced within the walls. But you might wonder how Rex handles simple daily information which not even she would bother to remember, let alone use as building blocks of identity. Well, it depends on the particular child. Some are surprisingly rigorous about this but your child can develop the skill of just 'using' material without learning it. Essentially, it camps out for a while on the grassy area outside the perimeter wall and performs some temporary service for the kingdom. Rather like a travelling minstrel, it entertains without belonging, and soon departs. If young Rex forgets something, it's because she never actually learned it to begin with. The material never truly became 'her own'. Otherwise, it should go without saying, her memory is phenomenal!

Selecting ideas need not be either a lengthy or a conscious process. Your child doesn't ponder: to learn or not to learn. She doesn't concern herself with the future benefit or liability attached to taking in particular ideas nor with the ensuing consequences to her identity. These things are not reasoned out. It's not a logical process. She is unlikely to be objectively aware of it. Her mental process is intuitive. She just knows if something is for her or not. If it rates a thumbs down, she will reject it, stop it right at the gates – outcast!

Possibly you will have observed her doing this. For example, you may have made a pronouncement of your own and she failed to respond – perhaps about bedtime, bath time, or wash your hands, it's lunchtime. It may have seemed that she didn't hear what you said or that she was not listening. But, just as likely, your words were repelled at the outer ring of her mental defences. They didn't harmonize with her self-image.

However, if she recognizes and welcomes incoming information, she simply inhales it, she breathes it in – quick as a firefly flash. Your child does this without any additional mental processing. In order to learn something, her mind does not need to try it out with a hands-on application. She does not need to discover its logic by conceptualizing it. She does not need visuals as many other minds might. None of this! Rex is fast, direct and positive, once she opts to grant access to her mental domain.

After reading about her granddaughter, Rex The Dignified, Cheryl reports: It was as if you'd watched her grow for the last six years. As you said, she has her own way of learning and although extremely bright, she can sometimes make you think she needs a hearing test.

Did I mention that the perimeter wall, including the gate, serves as a defence in both directions? Worthy ideas, having walked the red carpet, are expected to become loyal subjects and stay inside. No little trips abroad or wandering off. Of course not, what would become of Rex's identity? Your child is not whimsical about her ideas. She commits herself to them. She is passionate about the subjects residing in her custody. She will neither toss them out nor allow them to leave. They are in for the long term. This is not a take-it-or-leave-it situation.

Her mind is persistent, determined, tenacious, resolute and obstinate. She can apply herself to a mental task and keep on keeping on, through thick and thin, like a dog with a bone, against powerful opposition. On occasions when her will is pitted against yours, you might use alternative words like stubborn or headstrong. But now you know what's beneath it. To change her mind is to change her identity. It will not happen easily or willingly. It will certainly not be precipitated by force. Her mental convictions are the subjects of her kingdom, whom she will protect and defend against assault from the outside world. They comprise her strength, her stamina and her constancy.

The mental courage of some adults with this learning style is legendary. Often they are unaware of it, neither objectifying their bravery nor seeing it as anything special. Their committed minds do not falter in the face of adversity, especially in the form of unfairness or injustice anywhere. Fearlessly standing alone with an unpopular opinion, they can hold fast to their principles, refusing to compromise mental integrity. They can be well suited to serve in the challenging role as spokesperson for causes which strike their hearts – from groups which lobby for environmental protection and human rights to those dedicated to defending a nation's interests. These individuals can advocate vigorously – for homeopathy as an alternative approach to health, for the highest quality TV programming especially when the children are watching, or for equal rights of access for the disabled. Their mental dedication sees things through and provides society with stability and continuity. It can be a mixed blessing in a political leader who, on the one hand, sticks to his guns no matter what and, on the other, has a hard time even hearing suggested alternative views. There have been some notable Rex-type minds on the world stage, both currently and historically.

This Profile is not intended to comment on your child's behaviour, but to focus on her natural style of handling information. Performance is evident and observable and it can be modified to suit an individual's intentions. Actions can mask the strong, unseen mental dynamics being described here. For example, some Rex-minded children quite naturally present themselves with a soft, gentle or even retreating behavioural style, while others outwardly express the power and conviction of the learning style. Communication moves information from within the person outward into the world. It is the component of 'handling information' that could be viewed as the out-breath, while learning is the in-breath. But it also has a component of performance, and that part can be altered under the direction of the will. Being such a dramatic mind, Rex will have a natural way of expressing ideas, but your child will filter the presentation through her own particular behavioural style or personality.

Rex's natural mode of communicating has pizzazz, colour, spirit and often high volume. Because conviction comes from the heart, Rex speaks with authority, whether delivered with a velvet glove or a sledgehammer. She can even be bossy. The addition of a little costuming and acting can make her presentation even bigger than life itself. Rex can be very entertaining; she can put on a great show. But, she can also carry it a bit over the top and adopt centre stage in the drama of life, failing to note the rest of the cast (us). But, she's young – she's practising. Here is a gentle warning: If you occasionally feel the need to 'take her down a peg or two', please remember that your child is sensitive, in the extreme, to humiliation. It would be so easy to overshoot the mark, thinking her apparently robust mind could withstand it. A shamed Rex can be a long time recovering composure.

What helps your child to learn?

- Help her to see that she makes choices about taking in the information that is offered to her. She may not know this.
- Reduce the burden on yourself and her teachers. The fact that she decides what to learn and what to leave is not always a

direct reflection on the methods or quality of the teaching.

- Help her recognize the link between doing well in a subject and opting to learn the material. If she does poorly in a subject, it may be from lack of interest, not lack of ability.
- Once something is learned it is never forgotten. If it seems that she has forgotten something, it is simply that she did not choose to learn it. It's helpful for her to be aware of the difference.
- Accept that she learns and tests more easily when no one is pressuring her.
- Experiment with dramatization, modelling, role-play and storytelling. Encourage her to participate and contribute.
- She learns best when allowed and prompted to make a creative, personal contribution to an idea or project.
- Let her take centre stage once in a while to express what's on her mind.
- Make the information personal but be careful to respect her dignity.
- Present ideas with enthusiasm and passion. Dramatize your points with gestures.
- Allow her to move around while learning. Physical and mental activity are linked for her.
- Organize field trips, either to places of specific interest or just to get out and about.
- Realize that what she says is important to her. She expects it to be received with respect and attention.

Quotes from people with this learning style

'I always thought that if I spoke from the heart then people would understand me.'

'I remember people who are interesting, who talk with energy about what excites them.'

'You know, one of my colleagues actually disagreed with part of my report! I took it as a matter of personal disloyalty.'

'I can remember being bottom of the class in maths, because I hated it, and top in English. This really confused my teachers. Is she dumb or smart? They were very black and white.'

'Everything I teach has to come from my heart and experiences. I have to believe in something to teach it. If I don't understand or believe in an idea, I will not try and preach it to others.'

Details – The Analyst

As a person who was a child with this style of learning, I have the greatest sympathy for both you, the parent of this long-questioning youngster, and for the child herself.

As an adult, I have learned to apologize to those I interrogate, explaining that it's me, not them; that it's just the way my mind works to ask so many very detailed questions. It may appear that I am not quite convinced that they know what they are doing, when in fact I really am. Some believe me, some don't.

Your child, the little Analyst, experiences an ongoing mental critique of everything which comes her way. Oh, look at that! Mother missed a spot on the window she's washing. I wonder why little brother just sank below the surface of the bath water. I better find out how my doll's arm attaches to her shoulder. Wouldn't it look pretty to outline the pale-coloured flowers on the wallpaper with my new red pen! If I do it really carefully, the whole family will love it.

This is far more than just idle curiosity, it's definitely active. Her mind learns by separating large pieces of information into tiny bite-sized bits. It dissects. It analyses. It can tear an idea apart limb from limb in the blink of an eye. It has to do this in order to learn. Understanding comes with the process of breaking down and breaking apart. Her mind thrives on discovering the details, and this is what generates all those questions. Your child is not being intentionally difficult with the never-ending WHYs, she is digging for more detail in order to learn. Annoying isn't it, to be interrogated on a daily basis?

Additionally, your little Scientist is a hands-on learner who wants (needs) to become involved with all incoming information. Talking about it is simply not enough. She has to get her hands dirty with it, try it out and see if it works. An idea which does not work is not worth taking in. If it cannot be applied to real life, in a practical and tangible way, it is not worth its salt. She is not a theorist. Abstraction does not cut the mustard – unless ultimately it will have a practical application further down the road.

When your child wants to know something, try to think of a practical demonstration or activity which will provide the direct involvement she requires. Otherwise, your answer to her apparently urgent question will pass straight through her head and out the other side. You will know this because she will ask the same question again at a later time. If information remains just a spark of an idea, or stops its descent to reality at the level of the intellect, or even comes down to the emotional sites but fails to be integrated at a cellular level, then it's not learned. For example a child with some other learning style might take in information about fractions as a beautiful idea, on the conceptual level. But to learn the same lesson, your child needs application rather than theory. She would benefit from using a measuring cup, calibrated in both fluid ounces and millilitres, please, and a recipe which needs to be cut by a third for a smaller group event (which will be held in the school lunchroom, the day after tomorrow at 2:15 PM, with six people attending).

The eldest of Annette's four sons is a Details, The Analyst – she absolutely is not. As a young mother, very interested in her child's early education, she thought learning should be fun. After all, he was a little boy. She tried teaching him through a wide variety of games, and was particularly drawn to using flashcards. She can laugh about it now, knowing not only how his mind ticks, but that it does. It was not funny at the time. His responses to her best, but totally misguided, efforts put her off trying to 'educate' any of the other boys.

Buzz, The Curious might need learning to be fun, but it's

the last thing on Details' mind. Learning is something you knuckle down to. Flashcards, or other devices designed to speed up Details' pace of analysis, serve to befuddle his neural connections not encourage them. His need to digest new ideas in his own time was overpowered. His mother had tried, but it would have been hard to miss the mark of his learning needs by a broader margin.

Here are some of the annoying but real facets of Ms Details, The Analyst:

1   That which has been dissected is not made whole again. Putting the pieces back together is not the interesting part. The act of breaking down into the little components is important. For example, if your vacuum cleaner has been subjected to 'analysis' you may need to take it to a specialist for reassembly.

2   If the answer to the urgent question is not going to be used in a real and tangible way, it will not be retained. In fact any information which is not part of an ongoing 'project' is likely to be cast aside – rules of good behaviour, what time you said she should be home, Dad's birthday.

3   This mind can become a wee bit picky or critical. It's only trying to make things perfect. Hey, someone has to do it. Please make it a point to remember that she is far more critical of herself than she ever is of others.

That's it. Everything else is perfect.

Young Miss Scientist widely opens her little arms to any and all infor- mation. She loves it and can take on mountains of it. Then she tends to break it down to tiny bits, move the pieces around, reshape, recolour and make something brand new from the component parts. This is called mental synthesis and your child is very good at it. Let me offer an example: if one activity involves being blindfolded while performing certain tasks, while another involves preparing breakfast for Dad, and yet another calls for collecting bait for a fishing trip, your child might suggest some fascinating examples of synthetic genius by blending these, as if they were component parts, thus inventing a most disgusting new game.

A child with this learning style can create a dilemma for herself. Firstly, she is very fond of new information and gathers considerable amounts of it. However, her mode of processing it, separating and analysing, takes dedicated time. Consequently, young Details seems to always be surrounded with piles of information, which she honestly wants to read, she intends to learn and digest, but she has not finished it yet. These things take time. There may be little stacks of papers, books, information in any form at all, birthday cards, magazine pages, comic books (a collection of insects, vacuum cleaner bits or dolls' arms) covering all available surfaces – especially the kitchen table. Those piles are at varying stages of mental processing. Please ask her to tidy them away herself before supper. If you do it for her, you will contribute to befuddling her mind. This is true; I will personally vouch for it.

What helps your child to learn?

- Help her to recognize her short-term memory as a strength rather than a weakness. However, do guide her toward coping strategies (lists, notes, diaries) that work on a practical level to keep really important information at the forefront of her mind.
- Suggest she recopy untidy class notes into her own format with her own sense of organization. It will help with revision further down the road.
- Point out her mental flexibility and adaptability so she can observe and appreciate it.
- Be sure to allow her time and space to digest and assimilate new information and to carefully consider new ideas. For your child, processing information is much like digesting food. Neither activity can be pushed or hurried. Forget about flashcards!
- Give her time to process information before asking her a question about it. She wants to give a quality response and will do so, but only after new information has been adequately integrated. She responds poorly to pressure. If she learns this about herself as a child, she will more easily ask others for this most necessary space later on.
- Help her to recognize the onset of information overload and to

avoid it. You could suggest, kindly and without an edge of criticism, that she go outside for a walk, clear her head in nature and then resume her mental activity.

- She responds well to practical demonstrations, but then needs to try it for herself. Provide 'hands-on' activities so that she can learn through experience.
- Supply practical applications for new ideas.
- Help her to break down large topics into smaller chunks, like dismantling a jigsaw puzzle.

Quotes from people with this learning style

'Anyone who reads through this information quickly will not appreciate it for what it is and what it has to offer.'

'Of course I didn't read the instructions, I just tried it out.'

'Well, you could have an instant, off-the-cuff reply now; but, if you wait until tomorrow, you can have a quality response.'

'My mind is in total disarray. Someone tidied my office and moved all the piles of paper around.'

'This stretch of road has a somewhat shinier surface than the last one. I wonder if it is new or has a different chemical composition.'

ProCon – The Diplomat

Always ready for an exchange of ideas, your child thoroughly enjoys conversation, dialogue and debate. His mind establishes relationships with all kinds of information – with the spoken or written word, with other people's ideas and with the variety of points of view within himself.

Your child's mind likes the idea of harmony and will go to considerable lengths to achieve or preserve it. He dislikes any expression of unpleasantness, finding no need for a raised voice or a harsh word. To him, a message is certainly not clarified by shouting – communication is never improved by crudeness or coarseness. He prefers to be polite and, as he grows up, will really enjoy learning the rules of good behaviour. The very last thing he would intend is to hurt someone else. On the contrary, he would go out of his way to put others at ease, to introduce them and include them in conversations. He is a natural Diplomat. Etiquette makes his world go around.

ProCon learns by approaching new information along at least two tracks and at least a few times. His mind sees the validity of opposite points of view and understands a central idea by looking at it from both sides. His mind swings like a gate – it's back and forth, back and forth, relating to a concept from alternating vantage points. He looks at one side and then the other. He is apt to consult other people, asking for their opinion about a topic, as it provides a new and possibly different outlook. And then ProCon will go back and forth again from his view to the other's view and back around again, always looking for the balance between them. Yes, and no and, well, maybe – what do you think? This is all part of his natural learning dynamics. Be assured there is nothing 'wrong' here.

To really learn a new idea, your child needs only to frame the information into a concept – to take a vague whiff of an idea and firm it up with some good rational structure. He has to grasp the logical sense of it. He responds to clear-headed reasoning, a sound principle, a detached presentation of fact. Don't bother showing him pictures, just talk to him. Unlike some children, he does not need to filter ideas through his emotions to see if they feel right. He does not need to test for practicality or for long-term validity. Information just has to be interesting, sensible and coherent – his mind evaluates intellectually. He can easily learn from books, magazines, letters and any other print media. He can learn from lectures, radio programmes, conversations and any other form of oral presentation. His mind is well suited to chalk-and-talk teaching methods of the traditional classroom setting. (Many teachers have this learning style! Having both enjoyed and succeeded with their school's methods, they pursued education as a career. This learning style self-perpetuates in the field.)

Learning Strategy: When teaching ProCon to read an ordinary old-fashioned clock, try presenting the logical structure of 60 minutes comprising 1 hour and 24 hours comprising 1 day. It will make sense to him and will carry more impact than either the visuals of looking at the clock, or the practical approach of physically moving the hands by himself.

Your child learns most easily through discussion, but not just because it provides a forum for experiencing multiple viewpoints. He actually can discover what he knows or thinks while telling it to someone else. The learning event can happen during a chat. Here's how it works. To speak he must identify the correct words and link them together in an appropriately composed sentence. But first he needs to have something to say. Until an idea is verbalized, it may not have been conceptualized either, and therefore has not been recognized, acknowledged or understood. All these subtle mental dynamics can happen in an instant, prompted by his impulse to exchange points of view. How important conversation is to his learning! We have all heard people say: 'To really learn something you have to teach it to someone else.' Any bets as to their learning style?

If your child prefers to study lessons with a friend, either in person or by telephone, it's because the verbal exchange benefits his learning. In the absence of a study-mate, ProCon can hold a conversation between components within his own mind, going back and forth on the topic at hand. Many adults with this learning style have used a computer in the role of 'the other', as it can hold one point of view while the mind generates a comeback. Although other learning styles might not, The Diplomat seems to favour computer-assisted learning.

ProCon likes words. He likes their sound and their appearance on the page. There is a good chance he would dislike tatty textbooks as they do not properly respect the ideas they contain. He might be unwilling to relate to a book previously read by someone else. He likes pristine new volumes, comics and even newspapers. His mind establishes relationships with both the information itself and with its sources – the words, the book, even its critics and publisher. When he is old enough, you might notice him reading the author's biography on the jacket before buying a book. It actually enhances your child's ability to relate to the content if he knows something about the author. Proper introductions are important. He will want and need personal relationships with his teachers.

His mind treats concepts as if they were tangible objects, batting them around like tennis balls, weaving them into intricate patterns. To the Diplomat, any idea is worth considering. There is no reason to establish mental limits along lines of truth, practicality, feasibility or permanence. An opinion he states emphatically today may change in the future. You may hear: 'It was true at the time. I meant it when I said it.' Good ideas are those which are sensible, reasonable, rational and wise. He takes a balanced and impartial approach. He may even argue both sides of an issue, developing excellent skills for debating, politics or law later on. Ideas of fairness and justice are fundamental to his thinking, starting in childhood.

Even as a child he will enjoy the equality of an adult-style exchange of ideas, the back and forth of speaking and listening. It's a beneficial way to interact with him. But, be fully prepared to justify your ideas in terms of fairness. The old strategy of: 'I am the parent. You are the child. You will do it because I say so' is unlikely to achieve the desired effect. It simply does not seem reasonable to this child. Mental harmony, or at least the impression of harmony, is pivotally important. Have a chat about the house rules. Keep up the appearances.

ProCon is mentally original. He likes starting new things – ideas, concepts, essays, conversations, petitions. And he is good at it. His natural mental strength is beginning; finishing is not as easy. It may appear that your child goes from one interest or project to another without completing anything. Yes, it's probably true. But, as we well know, life does not allow any of us to do only what we do well, and you can help your child develop an ability to bring a project to completion. It will not be easy as it's not his natural strength. But here's an idea:

> **Learning Strategy:** When the initial buzz of enthusiasm for a new mental activity is fading, suggest alternative ways to view the project – ways that actually make it seem brand new. Or, isolate a facet of the project and show him how to apply himself to just that small component piece as if it were an exciting new task. Carry on with that method and, without tears, the job is finished!

Sometimes ProCon does seem to consider and reconsider endlessly. He may hesitate before committing himself to almost anything – what to wear today, which book to read next, if he wants a second helping. You may hear phrases like: 'but, then...' or 'and on the other hand...' as he sits on the fence looking back and forth. You may find such indecisiveness frustrating. So does ProCon, but there is little he can do about it and still be true to himself. If he really does see an issue through equal and opposite lenses, then landing firmly with a decision on one side rather than the other is like joining the opposition. It seems like a judgement against half of himself. At those moments he cannot win. Even in small ways like: 'Do you want the green one or the yellow one?' you might glimpse the terrible struggle. And he will turn to you and ask what you think. (Do notice, however, that he is not asking for advice, just for your opinion, and he is very apt to ignore it down the road when/if a decision is ultimately reached.)

Or he may defer to you and say, 'Oh, I don't care – whichever one you want.' You may discover years later that he did want the yellow one but wanted to please you by selecting the one he thought you wanted him to have. Back and forth, his point of view, your point of view, what he thinks is your point of view, and the even more subtle lens, what your point of view would be if he were you. Which decision or reply will benefit the relationship by leading to conceptual harmony or its impression? Which is logical? Where is the balance? These are all great dynamics for a Diplomat.

What helps your child to learn?

- Offer him opportunities for discussion and debate, especially one to one.
- Ask questions. Receive answers.
- Encourage him to talk, for example, about a book he has read, a current lesson or what his day was like. Share yours.
- Suggest he ask himself questions and find the answers by holding conversations in his head.
- Provide balanced feedback on his work and encourage him to request it from others.
- Assist him in making his study environment harmonious and pleasing.
- Let him explore the many ways in which a computer can help him learn. For example, a computer may provide the one-to-one interaction he needs. He will probably appreciate how beautiful his work can look when word-processed and with the addition of colour.
- Recognize that he will have most energy at the beginning of a project and that finishing is likely to take more effort. You can help him find ways of 'restarting' in order to finish.
- Suggest he work with schoolmates on assignments or projects.
- Encourage him to say aloud things he has to remember.
- Provide attractive-looking books, audio books, taped lectures, radio programmes, journals, magazines and newspapers.
- Tell stories and anecdotes.

Quotes from people with this learning style

'Can I just roll this past you so you can tell me what you think?'

'That's not fair!'

'I think that it might rain today. On the other hand, there aren't many clouds and they're very high up.'

'What do you think about…?'

'I like to get a sense of the person behind the book, so I go along to 'Meet the Author' evenings.'

'As a teacher I have trouble with grading and evaluating. I can see why the student said or wrote what they did and cannot call it wrong.'

'When I don't know how to do something I phone someone and ask.'

'I just couldn't concentrate. The scraping noise of all those chairs on the wooden floor was awful.'

Sherlock – The Detective

The Detective attempts to conceal his extreme sensitivity.
And you will tend to observe the defensiveness more than you
will see what's going on inside him.

Here's how it works. When little 'Sleuth' encounters new information he peers into it with X-ray vision that allows him to see right to the core of the issue, the person, the lyrics, the news story, the painting, the game plan or whatever it is. He may not understand the full adult meaning of what he perceives. He always realizes quite a lot more than you tell him or intend to tell him. With a mind like a laser, he evaluates 'truth' through his intuition and, over time, his gut feelings will prove to be accurate. Your little Detective learns on the level of instinct, which is a deeply interior part of a person. Now this has some important consequences.

Little Sleuth naturally perceives more than he actually learns, senses more than he takes right in. He absorbs information from all around, at every level from the obvious to the subtle. He may even experience extreme sensitivity to loud noise or bright light. He can be aware of the energy of other people's emotional states. Consequently, his mind is so sensitive that he can feel vulnerable and need to protect himself. One common defence is to try to frighten an 'opponent' away by any of a number of tactics. Another is to retreat into the depth, into the comfort zone, and as a result of practising the art of concealing his sensitivity, young Sherlock will create a rich inner life.

Once Sleuth is securely nestled into his inner mental spaces, he is reluctant to venture out again. This is what gives the appearance of secrecy. Believe me, your child does not even know he comes across as withholding information, let alone intending to do so. He is just settled down into a place so deep within that most of the rest of us don't even know that place exists. But to him it's home. Any attempt to draw him out, like a question about what he would like for lunch, can be experienced as interrogation and can produce a snippy snarl. Sometimes it will seem to be too much trouble for him to come all the way up to the surface to say 'Good morning'. This is natural. While bringing up a Sleuth child, or relating to an adult with this type of mind, we need to honour his natural protectiveness toward his own sensitivity while still encouraging him to recognize our relationship needs as well.

From the vast sea of all possible information to which he is exposed, your young Sherlock will carefully select only those ideas which he is willing to live with for a very long time. But before he makes a commitment and actually learns new ideas, he subjects them to rigorous (intuitive) testing. For example, the new information must in some way increase his personal power, the power of his mind or of his personal database. The source must be authentic, truthful and sincere. The definitions and decisions are his, not yours or anyone else's. When the time is right for him, he will commit himself to new ideas, containing and preserving them, possibly forever.

Once an idea has been absorbed and also accepted, it is lodged way down in the deep recesses of instinct. The idea has been 'captured' – it and the mind have merged and become one. Your child's mind wraps around an idea like heavy cream around a strawberry. It will not change easily. The idea would not have gained entry without passing the test of power. Asking little Sherlock to change his mind is like asking him to destroy part of himself. You might view this as simple stubbornness and maybe it is. But it's a natural feature of this learning style. They know what they know because their instinct told them it was true and valid, and if they change their mind they are going against themselves. These minds know how to hold on. A tantrum in the grocery shop will probably not be soothed quickly or easily, especially with a threat or a bribe you have tried before.

Your child may have seemed skilled from birth in wrapping his parents around his little finger. He may appear to know a great deal about the power of words at an incredibly young age. You may hear him at the age of three telling your adult friends about who is having a special relationship with whom. He will just know these things.

Your child may need some assistance in the correct use of his insights. Because of the laser-like perception he knows the depth of things. Others may often be shocked when he casually discusses their own deeply held secrets. They can feel exposed and violated, or uplifted and healed, depending on how Sherlock phrases and delivers the words. He cannot disallow the perceptions, but, with your gentle guidance, he can learn delicacy and sensitivity in the way he speaks to people about them.

Your child will not take to ordinary lateral thinking. There are unusual twists and turns to his thinking as it flows around in the sea of intuition. You may see this as a quirky sense of humour, sometimes veering toward either the bathroom or the barnyard, which links totally unexpected elements. This same trait can express itself in extraordinary diagnostic or problem-solving abilities. He will tend to see a unique solution reflected upon the screen of his inner eye.

All this talent and still the young Sherlocks of the world may experience difficulty with traditional educational practices. Their minds, which absorb information so easily through visuals, are not benefited by the usual lecture style used by many schoolteachers. At a deep level these children are students of the power of thought, the power of words, and even the power of silence. They can be (unknow-ingly?) intimidating and can so easily see straight through ploys of manipulation, deception or incompetence. They can make themselves unpopular with teachers.

Once interested in something, the young or the mature Sherlock can become fascinated (perhaps obsessive) and dig ceaselessly until an answer is revealed. The Detective is an excellent researcher in any area on which he chooses to focus, from art and architecture to science and technology, to humanities, law, psychology, cosmology, forensic or spiritual studies.

The Sleuth child, like all children and many adults, will believe that everyone else's mind is much like his own – in this case, deeply insightful and excruciatingly sensitive to subtlety. These children may have difficulty understanding how or why people can be cruel to each other or that others can be so totally oblivious to what is crystal clear.

Don't waste your energy trying to trick or cajole this child. He will not be deceived. You will only lose his respect and drive him more deeply into the caverns of his inner life. Even if you are as scrupulously honest as you can be, with time this child, who so enjoys puzzles and mysteries, will reveal and possibly expose character strengths or defects that lurk within your own depths.

What helps your child to learn?

- Relaxation. He may appear to be mentally tough, but unless he feels safe and secure, he cannot learn anything.
- Work together to create a suitable learning environment, one which feels positive and supportive to him, one which excludes subtle distractions and discord and includes colours, music and visuals.
- Gently let him know about his resistance to taking in some ideas and his compulsive capturing of others. It will be helpful for him to sense himself doing these things in order to realize that he can decide to learn anything he wants to learn. Such is his will.
- Help him to sense how he might benefit by learning particular information.
- His solutions to problems will be original and different, as his mind is unusually good at non-traditional, sideways thinking. Help him to value this.
- Point out the funny side.
- Rational logic is not your child's strength. Instead he tends to take in information by osmosis. Encourage him to get the feeling sense of what he is trying to learn, get a picture of it and absorb the picture.
- Realize that proof of having learned something is in his gut, not in his head.
- Allow him time and space to reflect.
- Engage your own emotions when presenting information.
- Present information in picture form, either with visuals, gestures, videos or picture words.
- Use colour to present and record information. Have visual displays around the room.

- Try visualization techniques.
- Present information as mysteries, puzzles and problems to be solved.
- Most of all, practise not taking it personally if your child will not learn what you want him to learn. He decides what he will or will not take in according to personal parameters. This is natural, not obstructive.

Quotes from people with this learning style

'I don't understand why you have to communicate all the time.'

'I cannot imagine why you think I'm secretive. I'm an open book.'

'Oh didn't I mention that?'

'I don't seem to remember well, only what's deeply important.'

'I like getting to a deep level very quickly.'

'Horrible things, mobile phones. When I see one on the road, I take aim and try to run over it with my car.'

'For a person like me, it's easy to hide the fact that I am hiding things from people.'

'As a child I needed a vivid internal world – perhaps as a buffer against the outside. I was a vulnerable child and remained so into my teens when I created appropriate defences which have continued even into adulthood.'

Flash – The Pioneer

If you are raising a child with this learning style, you'd better have your mental roller skates on just to keep up. His mind might seem like a little ball of flame rampaging through the house, a pint-sized conflagration on the loose.

This is one of the fastest minds of the 12 types – fast on the approach, fast on the uptake, fast to pass around any new ideas, fast to forget, fast to get onto the next new topic.

He is so curious about absolutely everything, that there is just no stopping him. As soon as he breathes in a new idea – and that's really all he has to do to learn, just breathe it in – he is ready to move on to something else, something new, or expand upon the idea, adapt it, contort it, twist it or forge it into something new. Then he's ready for a mental move. Anyplace! Just not here!

His mind wonders what's over there, what's around the corner, what's down the street? What's it like on the far side of that hill? Oh, gosh, look, there's another hill. I wonder… There is so much to learn! It must be infinite! And, he wants it all – right now!

Flash is a positive, forward-driving mind. It's optimistic and enthusiastic. It's bright and lively and spunky and adventurous. It likes to boldly go where no mind has gone before, to explore every far-flung horizon of thinking (at least!), to dare, to challenge, and to goad. It thinks big thoughts. It wants to expand on what's currently available. If one is pretty good, five is ever so much better. It doesn't matter if we are talking about building blocks, horses, or DVDs. *More* is better, *bigger* is better, *louder* is better.

EXPAND! INCREASE! INFLATE!

How exhausting for everyone else. Sometimes being with Torpedo-mind is like having a forest fire bearing down on you. For sure, it is exciting.

This is one of the most restless minds of all. Full-on all the time, it wants constant stimulation. Otherwise it gets bored. Your little Pioneer does not have to filter new information through concepts to learn it. He does not have to compare it to his existing ideas to see how it fits or if it stacks up. He does not have to pass it by his emotions to determine if it feels right. And he certainly does not need to integrate it physically. No, none of this! All your child has to do to take in new information is sidle up to it and just breathe it in. Then he has it! He gets the whole idea instantly. But then, while the rest of us do whatever it is we each need to do in order to learn, Flash gets fidgety. He starts to twitch. He gets fed up. His mind becomes a truant element, and races off in search of more life, more mental excitement and more immediate action.

If you ask your child to sit down, fold his hands and look tidy, his mind will close down instantly. Your little Adventurer needs motion, both mental and physical, in order to learn. Learning is linked with action and can be promoted by alternating periods of mental focus with periods of physical activity. It is simply not productive for your child to sit at a desk for a long time. Adult Pioneers can benefit from this tip as well. Try it out.

> **Tip:** Encourage bending and stretching exercises between intervals of focused mental attention. Suggest frequent short bike rides or walks – any physical activity will do.

It is not easy to implement an alternating rhythm of focused mental work and physical activity in a group setting where children with different learning needs are in close proximity. But it is possible. For example, a classroom teacher cleverly asks a young Flash to run quick errands for her while she recaps lessons for other types of learners. She keeps him moving with occasional chores like distributing materials to the group. Furthermore, the teacher uses the opportunity to help all the children recognize and respect their own and each other's quite different learning requirements.

We need to discuss little Torpedo's way of communicating. This is one place where he really needs a bit of your loving guidance. Some direction from you when he is still young could make a big difference to the potential success of all his future interactions and relationships.

You might find your child to be candid, frank and downright direct. Some would say he speaks his mind. Here is what's going on behind the mental scenes. Your young Philosopher loves Truth. He searches for it everywhere. He knows Truth on the experiential level as an enormous blast of intuitive perception. Truth is a gigantic, all-inclusive, holistic, multifaceted Aha! moment. And, in light of that sort of experience, his mind just KNOWS when something is right – beyond question. It happens in a flash. Who could possibly argue with it? Who could know better? An insight gained in this way is not analysed, questioned or refuted. It's Truth! And when this truth is spoken, which of course it will be, and quickly, it is often experienced by the rest of us as BLUNT. For example, Gosh, Mrs Smith, you look fat! Hey, look over there, that person has scaly (green, bumpy, black, purple-spotted, pink) skin. Why does it smell so bad at your house? My Mother said we do not have two sticks to rub together. Guess what my Dad said about your Dad!

> **Tip:** To help your child smooth out some big potential potholes along his path of life, try working with dramatization and role-play concerning which kinds of Truth are seriously hurtful to others. Although we cannot control how we take in information, we can surely do something about how we express it. We can all learn to regulate our behaviour.

Now let's address Flash's memory. Obviously your child's mind quickly inhales all information in its general vicinity, without restraint or discrimination. What happens next? Does his mind carry on inhaling and inhaling until it blows up like a balloon? Does it just as rapidly exhale and actually forget everything it learned in its mad dash for the next exciting topic? What, if anything, is retained? Well, interestingly enough, ideas will be retained, *if* they are going to be used as part of an ongoing process or project – but only for the duration of the project. Then they will be blown out, jettisoned, dismissed, forgotten. Tomorrow's spelling test or language quiz will hopefully be included in 'ongoing projects' and the correct information will be retained overnight. By the day after tomorrow, it might all be gone. This is a natural process; it is not a defect.

> **Tip:** Prepare for tests, reports and presentations just before them. Long-term advanced studying or revising is not useful for your child.

Please do not worry unnecessarily about your child's future prospects. Some 'ongoing projects' last a very long time, for the duration of a person's career, for example. An adult may easily retain a grasp on both the fundamental and subtle principles of financial planning, accident and emergency nursing or particle physics right up to the point of retirement or a job change. However, during those successful careers, the Mental Traveller might just as easily forget important family events like birthdays and anniversaries. He could forget to return a borrowed book, pay a bill on time or arrive at an agreed eatery to meet you for lunch.

> **Tip:** Write lists, keep a diary, employ a reminder service.

Your young Pioneer could be among the best brainstormers going. Fresh new insights and ways of looking at things may abound in that little head. He may demonstrate a totally original way of putting ideas together. Nobody else may have noticed that innovative twist on an old theme before. Give it space, new ideas have to come from somewhere. Risk-taking on the mental level enlivens academics, philosophy, politics, science, business, etc. and propels society forward.

His creative spark is fragile and can easily be damaged. Do be careful not to extinguish his glow of enthusiasm with a wet blanket of disapproval or a bucket full of the sand of practical assessment. A flame blown out by premature criticism might not easily be rekindled.

> **Tip:** Look for his occasional brilliant core idea, albeit in the rough. Encourage the inspiration. A good idea can always be refined at a later time.

What helps your child to learn?

- Present ideas with enthusiasm and make learning fun.
- Accept his short-term memory as a strength. He does not need to apologize for it! He has a much more flexible and adaptable mind than most people with good long-term memory.
- He may need to use notes, diaries and appointment books more than others, to keep track of things.
- Activity aids learning. He is mentally restless and likes to physically move while thinking.
- Short lessons or periods of mental activity with movement in between are beneficial.
- Learning by rote is a sure route to impatience and boredom.
- Record material onto an audio cassette or MP3 player for him to listen to while out walking or bike riding.
- Activities are always helpful: field trips, dramatizations, modelling, visits, role-play, even energizing music.
- Suggest he teaches what he has just learned to another person.
- Put new information into a story format for easier remembering.
- Present the expanded picture when introducing a topic.
- Remember that he grasps things very quickly so don't labour the point.
- Use symbols and metaphors – these will appeal to his mind.
- Match the pace of this mind. Ask sudden questions; use flashcards; shock or surprise him with a joke.
- Keep it short and snappy.
- Allow for spontaneity.
- Introduce a few foreign words.

Quotes from people with this learning style

'I sometimes listen to people and just wish they'd get on with it! I've got the message in the first few sentences and they insist on going over and over.'

'I've got this great new business idea which connects some of the ideas I've been having for a while and will catch the latest trend in Internet shopping. It'll be mega!'

'At the beginning of the course I quickly read through all the handouts. Then I was bored for the rest of the day.'

'Are you taking steroids? Your face is much fatter than before.'

'When I was a very young girl I used to spend ages playing with dolls and telling them stories about things that I wanted to do.'

Exec – The Achiever

This group thinks along more responsible, more adult lines than much older children. Don't worry, it's natural. They are still being themselves and enjoying childhood.

But, you might ask, how can such a young person have such an old head?

Your child's mind tends to be disciplined and very well organized. There is a place for every idea and every idea should be in its correct place. It's like a mental filing cabinet. Thoughts and ideas with something in common will be filed together. New information is subjected to the filing system in existence at that time. These are the rules.

Let us track the very interesting adventure of a piece of information offered to your child.

1 **The Presentation:** Right from the beginning, a piece of information will be viewed in a more positive light if it is attired correctly. For convenience let's name it 'Data'. Data needs to look right or it will be out of the door, with a rejection slip in hand, without even an interview to show for its trouble. Your little Exec prefers Data to arrive outfitted in clean, pressed, traditional lines. It should not be rumpled, crumpled or misspelled. It should have proper form in shape and sentence

structure. Ideally, Data should not be too avant-garde. It might still be accepted sporting spiky pink and purple hair, but only after very careful scrutiny.

2   **The Rationale**: OK, Data gets an interview. But Exec will be looking for assurance. To be considered for acceptance, Data will have to serve a useful and practical function. It must work well in real time. It must possess and offer qualities that are applicable to real-life situations. It needs durability, profitability and originality. It must have both feet planted firmly on the ground, or prove beyond question that it can get its feet on the ground in the near future. Exec is simply not interested in any fly-by-night Data. Theory is fine if it can be made real. Abstraction is highly questionable. And if it is smart, Data will not even consider an emotional appeal.

3   **Acceptance:** Now here is where our little analogy becomes tricky. You see, your young Achiever is a hands-on learner. She will not learn by looking, reading, talking, intuiting or feeling. To really learn any new information, she has to get involved with it. She has to try it out, test it, apply it in different circumstances. She has to touch it, smell it, use it, measure it. On their way to the mental filing cabinet, ideas are being integrated at a physical level.

4   **Learning**: (Working with mental organization/structure) If young Exec is going to take in Data, she needs somewhere appropriate to put it – like behind an office desk or out in the corridor or in the storage room. This keeps the mind organized. As with any well-planned system, similar items will be filed together. Ease of managing this creation improves with age. Let me explain.

Initially your little 'Organizer' has a challenging task. She was not born with a ready-made conceptual framework into which incoming Data could readily be slotted. At first there were no partition walls, doors, or even floors. She has had to build all the little cubbyholes from scratch. Her primary tool has been the old tried and tested technique called repetition. She has forged new mental pathways, like grooves in the grey cells, by going over new material, maybe just once or twice, maybe several times. Repetition – from the old school – does not work for everyone, but it suits this learning style down to the ground. Her other useful tool has been introducing new incoming Data to information already properly filed. Slowly, she has linked ideas together. It takes time to do this, sometimes quite a lot of it. Eventually it will be completed, and your young Achiever will have laboriously built a fully personal and very reliable, well-organized mental structure.

5 **Considering additional new Data:** Let us fast-forward to a point in time when your Exec is not quite so little and her personal conceptual framework is coming along nicely, one step at a time. By then, both you and she recognize, appreciate and embrace her good friend Repetition, having long since let go of the limiting belief that quick is best for everyone. Here comes more New Data, and it seems to be very new indeed and quite different from that which is already on file. Your child will have to choose among a few options.

- If she had previously decided to cling to the traditional, and this New Data is not just new but too unconventional, innovative or weird for her, she will simply reject it, untested.
- If she can find a similarity between today's New Data and some file folder already in position, she can opt to subdivide the current storage area. For example, she might be able to integrate 'email' into an existing file labelled 'tools for communication', a file which also contains information about her grandfather's antique fountain pen.
- Or, if she does want to embrace New Data but cannot subdivide an existing storage folder, she can enlist the help of Repetition and construct a new cubbyhole, from bottom to top. This method will always work for Achievers of any age.

Mental Strengths and Talents

There are some among us who are traditional thinkers, whose ideas help bind the fabric of society over time, keeping things on an even keel. These are The Achievers of the world and we simply could not get along without them.

When other minds might be oriented toward forward motion, progressive thought and innovation, the Achievers hold to the traditional ways, providing stability and continuity to group life – to the family, the tribe, the community, the nation.

Their talents include identifying, developing and upholding the rules and codes. This single mental trait can be widely applied to many facets of group life. Football games, for example, would be even less disciplined events without the formal game rules. Driving cars without our consensus and imposed traffic regulations would be chaos. Can I turn right on a red light after stopping in this country? On which side of the road do people drive in Bermuda? And think about holiday recipes and customs. If minds like your little Exec's were not looking after the traditional ideas, we might lose our rich cultural experiences like a Firemen's Field Day, Pace Egging, July 4th fireworks and November 5th bonfires.

You may notice your child's natural interest in the proper use of the language. She has to do this. She is part of the group charged with preserving the rules of correct grammar, sentence structure and word usage. She disapproves of personal creativity in spelling. Individuals should not take liberties with rules. Languages of all kinds – music, maps, mathematical formulae – belong to the group, after all. Your child may really enjoy combing through the dictionary and poring over maps. You might consider this when thinking about a birthday gift.

As your little Historian tends to know where she is by looking back at where she has come from, she may have a particular interest in, and therefore ability with, anything old – antique furniture, cars, equipment or buildings, archives, museums, genealogy, ancient civilizations and their calendars, artefacts and lifestyles. You may notice she has a strong affinity with older people.

History could be a favourite subject, especially if it can somehow be made current – the history of science, of artistic movements, of religion or spirituality, the history of people. She will find her own niche. Do not be too surprised if she becomes the youngest member of your local historical society. All of this relates to her tendency to focus on the traditional and to retain traditional values.

If you need someone who would be exceptionally well suited to looking after and preserving the customs and traditions of the royal household, vernacular architecture, the morris dancers, the veteran and vintage car club, she's your girl. Or if you want someone to collect and archive all the world's ethnic and folk music, here she is.

Young or mature, Exec naturally puts things into a framework; she perceives the inherent order in things and organizes them accordingly.

Her mind will express itself comfortably in business, government, boards of education and any system that has organizational structure and runs according to established regulations. She also has the mental style which could bring a company out of chaos, to restructure a failing business and turn it around.

Your young Exec has remarkable originality at developing new ideas with definite practical application. (This quality allows adult Execs to generate profitable new business ideas.) Given the opportunity and a bit of encouragement she could enjoy creating new games, complete with formal structures, procedures, a rule book, etc.

> **For example**, one Exec child, at about the age of 12, fabri-
> cated an athletic organization, with strong similarities to the
> football pools. All the teams had proper names. They were
> formed into divisions and regional groupings and played each
> other according to very formal rules. There were play-offs and
> awards ceremonies. He and his friends kept themselves enter-
> tained for months, thoroughly enjoying this very clever frame-
> work.

If I were writing a grant proposal to fund a project, I would want an Achiever-style mind on my team. If my business records were in good order and if I were looking for an accountant to ensure my annual return utilized every possible tax advantage, I would be looking for Exec. This mind can organize anything from a family gathering to a state visit. And it would be done correctly.

To Achiever, time does not matter. This mind quite naturally sets goals and determinedly puts one foot in front of the other until an objective is achieved, whether it involves pulling weeds, completing an assignment, tidying away one's toys or brushing one's teeth.

Pitfalls and Strategies

Your child tends to be a perfectionist about all things related to her mind. (Please, remember that we are commenting on dynamics of the mind, not behaviour.) Although it's great to strive toward excellence in all things – spelling, grammar, formatting, and so on – it is something else to become inhibited, or even temporarily paralysed, by one's Inner Critic. This can happen to both adults and children with this learning style, from time to time. It is similar to 'writer's block' when one sits looking at a blank piece of paper or computer screen, unable to start. Your child can be blocked from writing the first draft because she is concerned that it will not be perfect. From her point of view it should be. She might be blocked from sharing her real and true ideas, at school or at home, for the same reason, a reluctance to present her thoughts in a form less than perfectly arranged and developed. Better to remain silent than appear stupid. Better to play it safe and present ideas that will meet with approval, surface-level ideas, not serious ones.

> **Strategy:** Your child might benefit from being reassured that other people (you) do not expect adult perfection along these lines. Stepwise progress toward a mental ambition is just fine.

Exec likes to make sure all the bases are covered when telling a story or writing a report. Because she requires New Data to be presented to her with thoroughness, she works hard to provide the same to others. Sometimes she can come across as pedantic, wordy, bookish and rule-bound to those with different learning requirements.

> **Strategy:** Make a game (with clear rules, please) out of systematically reducing the number of words required to get a point across, whether in writing or speaking. If she has written five pages, ask her to distil it to three, and then to two pages. Perhaps she could summarize the central idea in a single paragraph. She would still be working with form, rules and pattern, but with the added goal of identifying the essence of a story.

The educational paradigm of fast is best, that the child with a quick answer and her hand in the air instantly is the 'smartest' child in the class, really disadvantages those with many learning styles, and certainly those with this one. The young Achievers of the world simply do not function that way. They require hands-on learning experiences and repetition to physically integrate the material. This takes real time!

Regrettably, these children can sometimes experience exclusion, being labelled as 'slow' learners and unfortunately can leave school with scars as a result. What a shame. These are children for whom learning takes time – they may be careful, but they are not 'slow learners'.

Strategy: Make sure both you and your child recognize and respect this important difference.

What helps your child to learn?

- She learns through experience, by doing. Don't worry if a hands-on approach results in dirty hands. It's natural.
- Show how new information links with existing ideas or prior learning.
- Repetition is her ally, even if it is not yours. Going over things a few times is essential to her learning, and some ideas will be integrated more quickly and easily than others.
- Present information in a structured form.
- She will have more energy at the beginning of a new project, while finishing is likely to take more effort. You may need to help her find new ways of 'restarting' an ongoing project in order to complete it.
- Allow time for her to carefully consider ideas, time to really integrate a new thought, before asking her questions about that information.
- Relate all new ideas to practical application. Emphasize the usefulness and concrete nature of new information. Suggest examples and analogies.
- Her mind likes to initiate new ideas that have practical applications to daily life. Encourage her to design some facets of her own learning process – schedule, content, timing, testing, field trips and other activities.
- Give demonstrations. But then she needs to try things out for herself.

Quotes from people with this learning style

'Let's get all these ideas organized into some sort of framework. I'd like to have some idea of where we're going with this.'

'My son doesn't know anything about the proper structure of poetry. I don't see how a person could really appreciate poetry without understanding the rules.'

'As I read a book, whether fiction or non-fiction, I write notes in the margin.'

'One thing I really hate is attending badly run meetings where there is no control and everything dissolves into general chit-chat. Inevitably I stage a takeover bid when this happens.'

'I have never played any of the games on my computer. I just can't see the point.'

'I think the reason I work so hard is because I'm the type who has to understand everything, from the foundation upwards, before they feel they can do or say anything worthwhile.'

Boffin – The Innovator

There are some among us who are traditional thinkers,
whose ideas help bind the fabric of society over time,
keeping things on an even keel.
There are others who seem to be charged with the task of
cracking the mould of the Traditional, the Customary and the
Expected in current-day thinking, allowing an opening for the
New, the Unusual and the Innovative.
Would you like to guess which group your child belongs to?

You may have noticed that your young Innovator can become completely captivated by an idea. Like a dog with a bone she will fixate on it, no matter what! Phrases like 'wilful child' might spring to mind, but many years from now only the 'child' part will have changed. At a very young age, in fact from birth, your toddler knew all about mental commitment. Sticking to it comes naturally.

So, how does she select ideas, take them in, remember them, and communicate them to us? Does she ever change her mind? How does this mind appear to us, how do our minds appear to her?

Selection

To Consider Learning It or To Dismiss It Out of Hand?

Since this mind is like a steel trap, serious preselection of what material to take in and what to ignore is a most important part of the mental equation. Without it the little mind would quickly get too full to function. So, we ask, are there certain types of ideas that will potentially captivate your child's thinking? Will the ideas that have appeal share any common ground? Well, yes and no.

The most favoured category contains the set of all those ideas which nobody else has – the completely original ones which spring into/from her own mind, ideas which can become statements of her own individuality.

But, if your child takes to an idea which someone else has had first, chances are it will have to do with friends getting together, belonging to a group with shared ideas, caring about friends and how friends are treated, cliques, how people link together into groups. Adults would use terms like 'humanitarian', 'political', and 'community'.

Your little Nonconformist does not like to find herself thinking just like everyone else. She is more of a mental trendsetter than a follower. If a trend she sets happens to catch on and become popular, she will stop thinking that way, freely moving off in a different direction.

Many with this learning style like modern technology, many do not. The real draw is not necessarily to the technological gadgetry itself but more to the thought process behind the idea that originated it. Boffin can become captivated by an original seed idea, back when it was just a concept, not yet actualized into a clever invention, a video game or a political ideology.

Frequently, the fascinating idea itself, to which your child commits, may be out of step with mainstream thinking in some way or another. It may be either too new or too old for current times. Other people simply do not think like that right now. Perhaps they did during the hey-day of Atlantis or will do during the 22nd century, but certainly not now.

Here is where it all becomes very personal. Any new information will have to pass a particular test if it is going to be learned. This test is absolutely unique to your child – other Boffin children will have their own quite different criteria. Your child has already constructed a conceptual framework that is both wide and deep. It is incredibly important to her and will not be infiltrated easily. Her mind will compare any new information to the body of what she already thinks.

If it fits, on a conceptual level, it's OK to come in. Otherwise, she does not even hear it. You may know very well the times when your little Rebel is not listening to you, but she does not see it that way. She thinks she is totally open-minded to all sorts of ideas, concepts, thoughts, principles, or suggestions. Ha!

Do not be too surprised if your Boffin has very mixed school reports. She will tend to do very well in areas that stimulate her mentally and quite poorly in those that don't. This is not a matter of ability but of interest, another issue of Selection. For example, one child became captivated by world music and diligently studied languages as a route into the ideas expressed in the lyrics. Meanwhile she shunned ordinary class work. Another child applied her mind, for several years, to studying aboriginal tribal cultures following a brief school project.

Uptake
How To Learn It?

Your child's mind needs only to make intellectual sense of an idea in order to learn it. After engaging in all the preliminary screening stages, her mind only has to fit the information into a concept and it's in – for the duration. That's it! There is no need for repetition, application, contemplation, reflection, discussion or anything else. The bottleneck comes at Selection not at Uptake.

Memory
Here is the Steel Trap

Once information is taken in, it is not forgotten. It is completely natural for your child's mind to remember it all. The elephant is downright forgetful by comparison. If it looks as if she has forgotten something, it's more than likely that she never learned it in the first place. That piece of information probably didn't pass the qualifying test. She may have looked as if she were listening, nodding her head, smiling angelically, but she was not. The blinkers had already come down.

Changing Her Mind
Like a Bolt of Lightning or Not At All

Little Boffin's mind has an extraordinary method of shifting mental gears. It is not so much a change of mind or a change of opinions, but rather a full-scale mental revolution.

The basis for your child's absolute commitment to a particular idea is that she became captivated by it at some point in the past. There are two ways that she can become 'uncaptivated', and this is essential if she is going to change her mind. As long as the captivation lasts, so does the commitment. One route is for her to suddenly see a flaw in the closely held concept. If it appears wrong or incorrect in some way, she will drop it instantly, like a hot potato, and will *never* pick it up again. So, don't bother trying to convince or cajole the little Inventor to review and reconsider an idea she has cast aside. It won't happen. And don't bother to seek an explanation as to why she no longer belongs to the youth group, scouts, or dance club. You may be left wondering why she traded in her calculator in favour of a slide rule, or abandoned her devotion to the French horn. The simple fact may be that she saw a flaw in her earlier perception and just went off it.

There is a second way this mind can become 'uncaptivated' by a previously closely held set of ideas. If new information comes her way and it's just too exciting and too right for words BUT it does not fit with a portion of the conceptual framework already in place, then the stage is set for a revolution. She is apt to excise and discard an entire section of the framework to which she has been committed for ages – her own personal criteria against which she has measured all other new ideas. Then, released from previous mental commitments, she is able to make a most unexpected leap and adopt a way of thinking which is very, very different from what it replaced. A mental revolution like this does not happen often, maybe a few times in a person's life, but when it strikes it strikes like lightning. This is a completely natural process for Boffin. Of course, it can be worrying for a parent (or later a partner, a child, a boss) but there is nothing 'wrong' – she just changed her mind in her very own unique way.

In Other People's Eyes
Different Viewpoints

People who do not have this learning style tend to describe those who do as: stubborn, closed-minded, not listening to other people's suggestions, weird or unusually creative. But the Boffins themselves tend to flatly reject all of that. No sir, not me.

Your little Inventor does not feel closed-minded and will certainly not admit to being fixed or stubborn. She absolutely thinks she is listening to what you suggest. She sees nothing either weird or particularly creative about herself – she'll tell you she is just normal, like everyone else.

Let me say again that your child is charged with the task of breaking the mental mould of the Normal and the Conventional in order to allow space for the New. Have you ever seen a revolutionary (inventor, innovator or scientist) without serious commitment to a cause?

What helps your child to learn?

- Mapping new ideas on paper may help her fit them into the existing conceptual framework in her head. It can help her find common themes and connections among ideas.
- Accept that your child may not choose to take in all the information that is offered to her, and do not take personally her decision to reject some topics. It's based on her choice, not your presentation.
- She likes to learn in her own way and at her own pace, when no one is either pressuring or holding her back.
- Saying things aloud helps your child to learn. Provide opportunities for discussion and debate. Encourage her to summarize her ideas after a discussion as this helps put information into a framework.
- Ask her questions to draw out her responses.
- Allow her opportunities to be inventive and experimental.
- Computer-aided learning may appeal.
- Metaphorical stories and drama may help her to explore ideas.
- Tell stories and anecdotes.
- Encourage her to think about the idea behind an invention.
- Provide plenty of books, audio books, taped lectures, radio programmes, magazines, newspapers, podcasts and DVDs.

Quotes from people with this learning style

'I flatly refuse to believe that I am stubborn.'

'I have clear ideas on how I think things should work and see people who don't embrace equality as quite backward.'

'Unless I'm really interested in something I only half listen.'

'Some of my best work has come from being given the opportunity to be inventive.'

'Going into technology deflects away from the ideas behind the technology, which is what's really interesting.'

'I will not stand for injustice if I can do anything about it.'

'I have a dream that one day this nation will rise up and live out the true meaning of its creed – we hold these truths to be self-evident that all men are created equal.'

(Dr Martin Luther King, Jr)

Sonar – The Intuitive

You will know at a deep intuitive level, if you and your child share this learning style. And, you might watch DVDs together, listen to music or perhaps just sit happily – sharing the subtleties of silence. Otherwise, you may be bewildered by her mind.

Her mind is highly visual and extraordinarily sensitive to what feels like a swirl of information around her. Sonar receives, absorbs and can become skilled in interpreting subtle signals that the rest of us easily miss. Ebbing and flowing, it never stays in one place very long.

While a different kind of mind might separate, dissect and analyse information as a way to understand it, Sonar does just the opposite. Her mind links pieces of information together – it unifies, it includes. It naturally sees the big picture in which everything is connected and integrated. Your child takes a global view – even of tiny things. She understands a new idea by sensing how it fits into the context of the larger whole. Other minds may examine details in order to build a composite; your child's mind starts from the overview. Sonar blurs the edges which otherwise separate one thing from another. She sees the forest as a whole rather than looking at individual trees, and she very much likes it that way. Frequently preferring abstraction, she could, but often would rather not, work her way toward the details.

Your child actually perceives quite a different reality from most other people. It's natural! And, accepting this fundamental fact will help you to understand her better. Studies confirm that people who have been present at an event often describe it quite differently; they report widely contrasting versions of the incident. The courts are full of them! Where, we might ask, are the actual facts in such a situation? And can they be separated from individual perception? Good questions, perhaps, but how do they relate to your child's thinking? Well, her mind chafes against the constraints of pure logic and refuses to be pinned down by hard facts. That which is purely rational seems cold, angular and only partially complete. It does not supply her with enough information. She could never make this a guiding principle of her life. On the contrary, Sonar's mind naturally connects to a different perception of reality, through the softer facts of instinct and intuition. In this way she gets the whole picture – the cause as well as the effect. Her mental state of 'un-focus' can reveal the all-important but subtle energetic underpinnings upon which hard facts appear to float. Don't doubt that this is real to your child.

A little Sonar boy called David would share his own observations about the neighbours as his contribution to the family's lively dinner time exchanges. Without fail his sister would aggressively demand proof. The fact that he 'just knew' was not good enough! With his intuitive feelings discredited, he gave up both talking during dinner and valuing his ability to read people's situations accurately. Having learned before the age of 10 that only facts were important, David detached from his best and strongest mental qualities for about 25 years in pursuit of a career that valued rational proof. But, you should see him now! As one of his grateful clients, I personally attest to his extraordinary abilities in a highly specialized area of alternative medicine.

Your child absorbs information from all around her, as if by osmosis. She just soaks it in, without discrimination, without the opportunity of selecting what to take in and what to reject. Her mind does not submit available information to qualifying tests, as do many other minds. She looks, she sees, she drinks it in. And then she filters the impressions through her personal feelings. Learning is an emotional matter, carrying an emotional impact. The mind and the feelings are intertwined for all Sonar people. Ask what they think, they tell you what they feel. A good idea is one that feels right. It need not be practical, timely or conceptually logical.

Sonar's mind is curious, it loves new information! It's also wide open, taking in all that's available like an open-shelled clam takes in sea water. The analogy does not stop there. Neither the clam nor your child's mind captures and retains everything that enters. Neither one can absorb endlessly without damaging their capacity to be receptive. In both cases it appears that most of what flows in flows right out again. Sonar's mind seems to forget much of what it learns. The analogy continues. From the stream of sea water flowing through it, the clam filters out and incorporates exactly the nutrients it needs for its survival and growth. Similarly, Sonar's mind selects the little pieces, the details, the facts that it wants from within the big mix. It can focus on some ideas and use them for as long as it decides to. But when those little bits of information are no longer in active use, they are discharged and returned to the sea. Sonar's facts sink below the surface of specificity into a great pool of unfocused awareness. Or stated simply, they are forgotten.

Some minds have a natural capacity to remember facts or ideas over the long term. Part of their contribution to the larger group is to preserve and sustain thought. These people tend to be very proud of their fine memories. Your child is not one of them! On the contrary, being blessed with a 'short-term memory', she makes quite a different contribution. For her, information is easy come, easy go. Because she can jettison unused information, she is always mentally free to approach the new. She does not run the risk of becoming clogged with rusty old obsolete ideas. Part of her mental mission is to be constantly open to new influences, to absorb them, to stir them around, adding in a pinch of this or a measure of that, and then to synthesize from the concoction something wholly original. Her mind is adaptable and flexible, giving a new slant to old ideas. Her particular kind of memory should not be viewed as a shortcoming or a defect. It's natural to her and you can choose to view it as a strength too.

Tip: You can help your child learn coping strategies to remember what's really important – lists, hard copy or electronic diaries, personal phone directories, string around the finger, etc. Note: adult Sonar types warn that your child must not only store important pieces of information, like event times and locations, but also she must remember to update and to consult her lists.

Sonar's mind is highly visual. She will naturally speak in visually descriptive terms. She thinks in pictures and she learns from pictures, photographs, DVDs, films, illustrations, diagrams and charts. If you provide your child with a picture, or just part of a picture, she will take it in easily, even filling in the missing sections. However, if you speak to her in words and concepts, she has to translate them in her mind's eye into a picture of what she thinks you have said, and then take that in. The same thing happens as she reads a book – a picture develops within her mind and she absorbs the picture, not the words.

Tip: Ask her to draw or describe what she sees when reading a book or listening to music – how characters are dressed, how they talk, the action, the local scenery, etc. You may be amazed and delighted.

Sonar-style minds often encounter some difficulty with the older, more traditional teaching procedures. Classroom teachers, regarding these children as diffused, drifty, vacant, unfocused or lacking in concentration, have sent home school reports that proclaim 'could try harder'. In fact the actual mental strengths of the Sonar group frequently go unnoticed, their natural learning requirements neither recognized nor understood. But who would ever realize, without being told, that these minds experience links between simultaneous events – that the cloud formation in the sky outside the schoolroom window carries the same message as the teacher's words? Needless to say, many do not tend to test very well by ordinary methods. Their unusually creative imaginations are often undervalued.

Because your child's mind is enormously curious as well as immensely absorptive and vastly receptive, she is easily 'distracted'.

Here is a story from the memory of an adult Sonar: As a young child, he was sidetracked by the intricacies of the hedgerows along his way to school. One delight led him on to another – the creatures, flowers, seeds, webs and their mutual interactions. He became enthralled, touching the beauty of creation, experiencing it, being part of it. Eventually some inner impulse guided him toward his destination, without guilt or awareness of tardiness, only to discover that his teacher and classmates had been observing his meandering from the upper window and were all waiting there for him.

This was one of those pivotal moments which could have separated the child from his own genuine mental strengths, leaving him humiliated and with a commitment of 'never going to do that again', as if his natural mental function were all wrong.

Another Sonar adult says the hardest thing for people to understand about her is that her mind never stays in one place very long – it simply flows off in another direction. If you will appreciate the mental fluidity which naturally draws your child from idea to idea and if you can celebrate this mental quality together, then she will feel supported, no matter what message comes from the outside world. You will be able to defuse potentially damaging episodes which your child might otherwise carry into adulthood. Perhaps you could help her learn to work creatively with her unique brand of flow, distraction or diffusion, to bring it into harmony with some pleasing musical, artistic, verbal or conceptual structure. Is this not how poetry is born – by containing inspiration in an accepted linguistic form, or a cloud in a bottle?

Because learning is so closely linked to her feeling nature, your child does her best mental work when she feels emotionally secure. The tranquillity of her classroom or home learning environment is considerably more important to her than to many other learners. Remember our clam analogy and consider the potential effects of a raised voice or other loud noises, powerful emotions like anger or fear, or a messy, unattractive or uncomfortable space. A clam snaps its shell firmly closed when it's frightened. So will your child. And it might take a long time to rebuild the confidence or security necessary to reopen it.

Tip: You could work together to establish a suitably peaceful yet visually stimulating study/play area for your child. Knowing she has that safe spot will mean a great deal to her. She benefits from time away from others to recharge herself and rebalance her sensitive nervous system.

The juncture between reality and fantasy is comfortable territory for your child, although many other people would rather avoid that terrain. She has a unique ability to detach from facts in order to imagine or dream. The original ideas she plucks from that place would never come from pure logic or rationality alone. Her mind enters other realms where she is able to connect with whimsical thoughts that can delight the rest of us. Her fertile and creative imagination has wide scope of expression in any of the traditional pursuits that reward a love of fantasy, for example music, film, acting, writing, entertaining. But also, the Sonar mind can be extremely successful in entrepreneurial activities from business to furniture design to computer programming. She has a most sympathetic ear and a compassionate understanding which allows her to identify with others' problems, from the personal to the corporate and the emotional to the professional. She can uplift others with an ability to soothe and heal with words.

While some Sonar children, in keeping with their learning dynamic, naturally present themselves in a tender, sympathetic or even a retreating way, others express themselves quite differently. Sometimes an active, robust confidence, an easy assertiveness completely masks Sonar's soft, intuitive quality. Behaviour can camouflage unseen mental dynamics. Don't be fooled. What's visible on the surface only sometimes reflects what's happening deeply within the mind. Child or adult, we filter communication through a particular personality or behavioural style.

Now, tuck this away for the future: The receptive nature of Sonar's mind involves a measure of permeability – she can be impressionable. Far more open to suggestion than most, she might change her views and opinions with her associates, unknowingly sacrificing her own thoughts. Her fluidity can mimic absent-mindedness, confusion or indecision. Sonar is sensitive to her own suffering and to the suffering of others. She can easily be hurt by people's words.

Your little Intuitive is apt to make reference to books, movies, articles and songs written by others whom she thinks did a good job expressing a point she would like to make. It's not easy for her to put into words the mass of what she feels, although there are many good options, like poetry, music and dance. And, like nobody else in the world, Sonar can say it with flowers.

Your child's diffusive nature allows her to blend with other people's mental modes and to unconsciously cater to their learning requirements in conversation. She has an uncanny way of asking the question which is at the forefront of other people's minds, such is the measure of her link into collective thinking. This mind has an innate refinement and gentleness. Creative imagination is high, the mind can be poetic, visionary and possibly psychic or even telepathic.

On the mental level, your child is a tender and gentle flower who needs your loving support to feel comfortable and get off to a good start in this rough and tumble world. Then there is no limit to what she may achieve.

What helps your child to learn?

- Present the big picture first. Details do not help her to learn.
- See her short-term memory as a strength rather than as a weakness. She tends to remember things she needs for the project at hand. Letting go of the rest leaves her free to embrace the new.
- Help her to recognize and value her mind's adaptability.
- Discuss how she gets the feeling sense of what she wants to learn.
- Test how well she is learning with suitable measuring sticks, designed specifically for your child. Tests designed for other kinds of minds do not always work well for her. Creative uses of the visual or the non-verbal, like collage, drawing, fabric/ texture, movement, sound or clay sculpture may allow her to express her understanding.
- Help her identify what choices she has about working consciously with the sea of information in which she is immersed and her sensitivity to it.
- Teach her how to sense the onset of mental overload and to develop a number of strategies to avoid it.
- Show her the value of relaxation and of spending time alone.
- Allow her time and space for reflection.
- Create a positive, supportive learning environment, perhaps with soft colours, music and pictures.
- Engage your own emotions when presenting information.
- Present information in picture form, with visuals, gestures, videos, images, charts, graphs, illustrations, drawings, etc.
- Use colour to present and record information.
- Teach her to use visualization techniques.
- Offer a wide range of ways for her to express her ideas.
- Encourage the use of symbols, metaphors, drama and stories.

Quotes from people with this learning style

'The feeling is too big for the words.'

'How can you talk about the scientific result or see its beauty unless you know what the engineer was feeling when she designed that bridge, and her vision for the whole community.'

'I do have a fertile imagination but it is not necessarily a dreamy type of thing.'

'I can pick up and hold a piece of wood and know how it will sound and its qualities of resonance, when I fabricate it into a guitar.'

'I do not remember things for very long. They merge into a "just below awareness" wholeness from which I cannot retrieve them easily.'

'I take in information, like an action, then another action comes up and I forget the first. Not necessarily because the first action was worse than the one I noted.'

'It's absolutely horrifying to realize what percentage of my life I spent trying to negate my own natural way of learning and be someone else. I tried to get as far as possible from the absorptive receptivity in the pursuit of the facts.'

'It's not that I don't like facts. I do, the more the merrier. I am a magpie for information, useful or otherwise.'

Style Groupings

Areas of Similarity and Difference

Groupings which share common characteristics can be called families. Think of the bird family. They all have wings, feet, bills, and eyes. Most of them can fly. Yet they have many differences as well. Some are very large like storks and ostriches. Others are tiny like wrens. Or consider the family group we call trees. Again they have much in common – roots, trunks, branches. Yet they also have many differences – some have leaves while others have needles. Some drop their leaves in winter, others hold them. There are enormous size differences among trees. Yet when we spot one, we know we are looking at a tree, not a bird. There's no doubt about it! And, of course, there is the human family. Although we come in all colours, sizes and shapes, we instantly recognize each other as human.

Similarly, people's natural mental qualities form groupings or clusters based upon shared features. Such common ground suggests a similarity of viewpoint and fosters ease of communication. For example, those with exactly the same learning style seem to be on the same wavelength. They communicate easily and effortlessly. One person's natural mode of speaking suits the other's natural mode of receiving information. The exchange is comfortable.

On the other extreme, we all know people whose minds are so different from ours that we just cannot figure out what makes them tick. They might as well be trees. Communication is neither easy nor satisfying. This can even occur within a close family, where individuals are naturally highly motivated to communicate with each other. Sometimes people who love each other very much, and even with the very best intentions, find it quite impossible to talk to each other. And generally, to each person the other appears to be at the root of the problem.

Most relationships fall into a middle range between these extremes of simple understanding and acute awkwardness. We can usually find at least some areas of familiarity, foundations on which to connect enjoyably with each other. This Section arranges different minds into clusters of compatibility, the potential cornerstones of harmony in the family. Section 4 applies these ideas by providing the parent with tools, wood, nails and a set of plans to build long-term mutual respect and open lines of communication.

Let's start by looking at broad areas of similarity and difference among the 12 learning styles.

Twelve is a special number. It pops up everywhere – in music, literature, mythology, religion and even in the physical sciences. Twelve is divisible by many smaller numbers and an interesting mosaic emerges when we divide our 12 learning styles into 2 clusters of 6 styles, 3 clusters of 4 styles, and 4 clusters of 3 styles. Each grouping refers to a different component of how we deal with information. The Divisions listed in the table below relate to single steps along the path to learning – A. *Reaction*, B. *Approach* and C. *Mode* of taking in new information. The clusters or Families within the Divisions relate to stylistic similarities and differences.

A **Reaction** to new information: to share it now or contain it until some later time? — 2 Families, each with 6 learning styles

B **Approach** to new information: the degree of openness vs reserve. Initiate, sustain or adapt? — 3 Families, each with 4 learning styles

C **Mode of uptake**: as easy as breathing in air or as deliberate as wading through molasses? — 4 Families, each with 3 learning styles

A: The 'How shall I REACT to this information?' Division

This Division comprises 2 clusters, each containing 6 of the 12 learning styles. Here we have the classic yin/yang polarity difference expressed on the mental level. The outflow and the inflow. Exhalation and inhalation. Active and receptive.

These two clusters hold diametrically opposed views about the nature of information and how it should be used. There is always tension between polar opposites. They stand at 180° to each other. It can be a face-off, a showdown. There is one side and there is the other. If we are not together, we are opponents.

The 'Information is to be shared, immediately' Family

Sharers: Scout, Buzz, Rex, ProCon, Flash, Boffin

With a natural belief that information is made to be shared, that's exactly what these folks are going to do. As soon as they have some, they give it away. If they read it, hear it, think it up, see it on TV or dream it, Sharers tell it all. The mental flow in these minds is upward and outward. Incoming ideas get down to about neck level before they are passed on. Overhear a bit of conversation? Repeat it. See the morning edition's headline? Shout it from the rooftops.

This Family of minds practises outgoing spontaneity. They actively go out in pursuit of information. And they are self-expressive, pouring forth their mental energies unreservedly, either by direct action or by social or verbal expression.

A sibling from the opposite camp may call this one a blabbermouth and wonder why on earth his brother had to go and tell everything to their parents. 'Why didn't he just stop and think? It was confidential! He was not supposed to say anything to anyone, ever, especially to the parents. I wouldn't have.'

The ' Information is to be held and cherished for a while' Family

Containers: Steady, Sponge, Details, Sherlock, Exec, Sonar

With a natural belief that information is made to be held and cherished for a while, then that's exactly what these folks are going to do. As soon as they have some, they tuck it away in a safe recess within the mind and look after it, or perhaps forget it. If they read it, hear it, think it up, see it on TV or dream it, members of this Family incorporate it. The mental flow in these minds is downward and inward. Incoming ideas are incorporated deeply into the feelings or into the cells of the body itself and are passed on only at some appropriate time. Overhear a bit of conversation? Conceal it. See the morning edition's headline? Keep it to yourself for a while. Consider it. Decide what it means to you. Interact with it. Make it your own. Maybe talk about it sometime, maybe not.

This Family of minds practises containment and timing. In their receptive mode, they attract information to themselves. They are self-expressive, sharing thoughts and ideas at the 'right time' after a period of containing their mental energies within.

A sibling from the opposite camp may call this one withholding and secretive and wonder why on earth her sister didn't speak up and tell what she had overheard. 'If only I had known the parents were planning a surprise birthday party for me, I would have worn my best jeans. Certainly it was not confidential! Why does she always have to make a secret of everything? I wouldn't have.'

B: The 'How shall I APPROACH this information?' Division

This Division comprises 3 Family clusters, each containing 4 of the 12 learning styles. Here minds are grouped according to what they do when they see some new information coming around the corner or over the far horizon. Before even knowing what it is, a mind will naturally treat an idea like a long-lost friend or an archenemy, with compassion, indifference, or hostility. The approach can carry a smile, a smirk or a big stick. This is fundamental, well before learning or rejecting occurs.

In the *Approach* Division, minds come together into Families based on their degree of inquisitiveness – open and evident curiosity versus an apparent initial lack of interest. In what frame of mind does one approach new information: to challenge it, change it, or reject it? While one of these Family clusters can become downright giddy with delight in the presence of new information, another might pull the covers up over its collective head or even build a stout stone wall to keep it at bay. Some minds enthusiastically charge at the new, while others retreat.

The 'Let's get on to the next topic' Family
The Initiators: Scout, Sponge, ProCon and Exec

Four of our twelve learning styles belong to this Family. That's one in three of us. The Initiator Family shares the natural tendency to power forward mentally. As soon as one piece of new information has been taken in, these minds are driven to move on to another, and then to another. One topic of conversation stimulates another. One mental activity leads on to more. Fuelled by its own mental process, the Initiator mind pushes forward relentlessly. Great, it says! What's next?

The common ground here is the forward motion. While some Initiators might resemble an unstoppable Roman phalanx, others move like an inchworm and still others flow gracefully like a river. One of these four learning styles organizes as it goes; another burns its way across the mental terrain. New information feeds the forward motion whether the mind creeps along cautiously, flows across the plane or makes progress by forming discrete packets of ideas.

These minds thrive on creating original material out of nothing. Initiators start fresh ideas, new lines of thought and novel ways of viewing things. They are motivated to initiate discussions and conversations, but while some step forward into verbal exchange, others moderate the impulse to do so. They 'mindstorm', generating a stack of solutions to any problem, a pile of answers to any question. This phase comes naturally. But, then they lose interest and want to hand over for others to implement. Starting is their natural strength – not completing.

Does it sound like there may be some restlessness here? Initiator children are not happy staying with a single mental task past its very personally defined end point. They run out of enthusiasm and become bored. You may observe your little Initiator moving on from one activity to another, with materials from several projects or pieces from multiple games strewn around the room. And if you are not an Initiator yourself, you might tend to misunderstand the drive and instead focus on the clutter.

Strategies can be developed to help this Family cluster fit into the real world where other children are sharing the same space, assignments must be turned in, projects completed and deadlines met. Hints are offered in Sections 2 and 4.

The 'Once an idea is in there, well, it's in there' Family

The Sustainers: Steady, Rex, Sherlock and Boffin

Four of our twelve learning styles belong to this Family. Collectively they are the long-term memory people of the world. Like the proverbial elephant, they are very, very good at remembering – once they have actually learned something. But don't be fooled. These children can appear to have taken up information. They can use it as if they have accepted it. They can convince others that this is so. But in truth they never did embrace the idea; they rejected it. You might hear your child say something like 'Gosh Dad, I totally forgot what you said about coming home early tonight.' Be suspicious whenever a Sustainer claims to have forgotten something. The idea never went in. These minds are like steel traps. Once a piece of information has gained entry, it tends to stay in there for the long term.

Mentally they have consistency, persistence and continuity – and they express these qualities on behalf of the larger group. Their thinking is not influenced by passing fads or fashions, or by what others think. They hold fast to their own ideas and opinions. Sustainers know a lot about mental commitment. They don't give up. They don't change their minds for the sake of it. If you offer your Sustainer child a bribe of ice cream before bed tomorrow night, if he would just stop making that awful noise with the pan lids (this instant!), he'll be right there the following evening, belly up to the table, at the appointed time… waiting…waiting…for the promised ice cream.

Because thought carries on and on and on (toward infinity?), members of this Family stop, look and listen carefully before capturing a new idea. They will consider something new, possibly long and hard, before adopting it. For this reason, others may see these folks as mentally stubborn or resistant. Well, yes. But it's their job. It's their contribution to the rest of us. Where would we be if nobody sustained long-term thinking in areas such as investment banking, architecture and building techniques, quality furniture manufacture or which side of the road to drive on?

They hesitate, before actually taking up new information, until it is validated from within, until it proves itself in some way. The four Family members are distinct in this regard, with four very different modes of validation. But once learned, ideas stay for the long run. Of course these children will be careful, concerned and restrained mentally. They know those ideas will still be with them years, decades, lifetimes from now. If they are important enough to learn, they are important enough to retain. Why change your mind after all that effort to ensure that a new idea is worthy, appealing, powerful, or unusual enough to gain access to one's mind in the first place? If you have put a new thought through its paces and it has passed the qualifying test, why reject it just because time has passed? It's not dusty, rusty or decaying around the edges. Thoughts are made to last the tests of time. Otherwise, why adopt them?

Sustainers are proud of their staying power and are puzzled when others view them as fixed, stubborn or stuck in the mud. It does not feel that way from the inside. Holding an unpopular view is not new to them – they are like that even as small children. Parents are well aware of the dialogue: Oh yes you will…Oh no I won't! In addition to persistence and perseverance, they have great mental courage and will 'stick to their guns' in the face of multiple Goliaths.

Learning is a matter of choice for the Sustainer Family. Even your little children will decide which ideas are acceptable to them and which are not. New information has to prove itself in one of the usual four ways. As school children they puzzle teachers who cannot be certain if they are 'smart', despite the good grades, because sometimes they learn nothing at all. Sustainer students may excel in some courses and fail utterly in others. But, nobody will ever force members of this Family to learn something against their will, decision or desire. Teachers, parents, caregivers, older siblings, team leaders, spouses, etc. might as well save their breath. If a Sustainer fixes itself against a thought (or even an entire body of knowledge) a team of wild horses will not change it. This is not failure on the part of a teacher and should not be taken personally! Don't bother forcing the issue, it will not work. However, some tips about honouring the person's Family grouping are offered in Section 4.

The 'What else is there to learn?' Family
The Adaptors: Buzz, Details, Flash and Sonar

Four of the twelve learning styles belong to this Family. The Adaptors are forever curious, always interested in something new. They are wide open to new information, without hesitation, resistance or filtration. As an Adaptor Family mind approaches the New, it does so with its little arms flung wide open. They love it – they thrive on it.

But, once the newest mountain of data has been scooped up and taken in, these minds cannot just let it be. They set about moving the ingredients around, reconstituting, reforming, reconnecting bits to other seemingly disconnected bits. This is the process of mental synthesis – of creating something very new and quite different from the original raw materials by stirring and blending. These minds extend thought.

Adaptor Family minds retain thoughts and ideas, keeping them right on the front burner, only for the duration of a project or while the information is in active or ongoing use. When there is no immediate need to hold on to some information, and often even when there is, these minds jettison it – off into the ether. Thus cleansed, the Adaptor mind is ready for the next mountain of interesting facts, ideas, etc. Adult Adaptors are apt to cast away the name of the author whose book they finished reading just the previous day, or perhaps its title. They may easily drop information like your phone number or your birthday, or a luncheon engagement, or where you were going to meet. They are sometimes late for appointments because some other very interesting and mentally stimulating situation presented itself just as they were on the way out the door – like a phone call. And the children are just apprentice adult Adaptors.

It is for this reason that Adaptor Family members have earned such an unfortunate reputation for forgetfulness. These folks are not strong in the area of long-term memory, and they take a lot of abuse about it, from members of other Family clusters.

They have different mental strengths. There are very good at short-term memory – some very short. They can be lively conversation-alists as they tend to know something about almost everything. Besides that, they can truly enjoy being told the same joke over and over again – as they will have forgotten it in the meantime.

Mentally life is always exciting and new. There is so much to learn, to read, to watch, to talk about, to forget and reread, rewatch, repeat. There are so many mental ingredients to stir together and see what comes out.

In summary, each Family cluster within the *Approach* Division has its mental strengths and its job to do on behalf of the larger community. We cannot get along without any one of these Families.

The Initiators' principle task is to instigate new ideas and lines of thought – they are good at it. There are no better original and creative 'brainstormers' anywhere. On the down side, they are not good at completing. They get bored and quite naturally move on to greener mental pastures.

The Sustainers' main strengths are tenacity, persistence and persever-ance. Unflappable, they preserve and contain thought over the long term on behalf of those who are mentally free to dash off to the new and different. On the down side, members of other Family clusters find these folks to be mentally stubborn, inflexible, and downright resistant to new ideas. They simply will not be pushed, cajoled or coerced.

The Adaptors, quite naturally and by example, inform the other Families when it's time to change and move on to other possibilities. Their strength is in coping with (working with and developing) large amounts of information over short periods of time. But they can appear unstable to the others, as the slightest breeze could change their thinking.

C: The 'What is my MODE of taking in this information?' Division

This Division comprises 4 clusters, each containing 3 of the 12 learning styles. It groups minds according to the actual mode of uptake.

Regardless of our particular mental antics when presented with new information, there is a point at which we actually do learn something new. Information, ideas, data which we didn't possess at one minute, becomes 'ours' the next. We have taken it in. Learning, however, is private business; the inner activity of that moment does not show on the surface. It occurs in our deepest recesses.

Of course, some people will express a visible outer response to a moment of learning – a wry smile, an uplifted eyebrow, a wahoop. It may reflect the learning moment, but it is not the learning. The aha moment ('Eureka! I've got it!') itself is not visible. For this reason it's open to all sorts of personal projection and interpretation. For example, this is what makes it easy to assume that learning is the same for all of us. Just because you cannot see the process happening, don't be fooled into thinking that the complex inner dynamic in your head is the same as in everyone else's head. It is not. Our modes of taking in new information are just as person-specific as our styles of approaching it, as discussed in the preceding Division. We do this differently.

Four primarily distinct ways of taking in new information can be grouped into Family clusters. Each is comprised of three different learning styles, so cluster members bear a resemblance to each other but are not identical. Their common ground ends with the mode of information uptake. Otherwise they go their own separate ways, mentally.

A vivid naming system for these four Families parallels the four 'elements' of nature: Fire, Air, Water and Earth. The Family portraits below cover points like:

- What the Family mind needs to do to/with information in order to 'have it'
- How deeply a mind needs to integrate information in order to 'have it'
- What 'having it' means
- How long this might take – speed of uptake demystified

Fire Family:
Scout, Rex and Flash

If your child is one of these and you are not, you will have to go some to keep up.

These are the liveliest of minds! They can be extremely fast moving because they need to interact so minimally with new information in order to take it in. This Family breathes in information without needing to alter it in any way. No processing is necessary, no analysis, no filtering, no grounding, no repetition, no conceptualization, no mind-maps, no drawings. Nothing. They look, they breathe, they have it – all in a flash! Ideas are inhaled, they are inspired, not in small pieces but fully developed. Learning occurs on the intuitive level.

Fire minds can burn with enthusiasm – sometimes with the rapid-fire flare of a shooting star, igniting suddenly and extinguishing quickly, and sometimes with the thermonuclear perseverance of the sun. Fire Family children identify strongly with their own thoughts and beliefs. These are positive, optimistic, active learners, who are sparked by ideas.

When speaking their minds, which they do, Fire Family members can really light up a conversation or nicely warm up a room full of people. But they can also scorch others like a raging forest fire. Their verbal delivery can be full of vitality, charged with energy and larger than life itself. With even a single Fire mind in your household you are likely to have your fill of boasting, arguing, shouting or competing.

Fire children do not place excessive demands upon a learning environment, as long as it's at least as large as the great outdoors and is not restraining. What is critically important is movement. When the body is in gear and is moving, the mind can too. Your Fire Family child might take in new information most easily while out for a walk, riding a pedal bike or an exercise bike, acting out the information or having a swim. Adult Fire Family members, who need clear thinking and an active brain, have been known to go for a drive, have a quick stroll to the water cooler or take a computer along on a train trip. Almost any kind of movement serves to quick-start mental activity. Conversely, the

Fire mind seems to close down when the body is stationary. Your request that a Fire Family child sit down and look tidy may soothe your nerves but will not improve the child's learning ability.

This presents an obvious dilemma in both the classroom and the living room where different and sometimes conflicting learning requirements coexist. That quandary does not alter the children's learning needs. Section 4 offers suggestions and activities for real-world applications.

Air Family:
Buzz, ProCon and Boffin

In order to take up new information and make it their own, members of this Family need to do a little bit more than the Fire Family, but not much more. Rather than just breathing it in intuitively, these minds have to grasp the idea behind the new material. They need to give it a structure and shape it into a concept. No concept, no learning. They will not take in what does not make sense – to them. For some Air Family members, new material has to fit with their currently held ideas, for example their concepts of what's interesting, of what's fair, of what benefits society or humanity.

Your Air child is a logical, rational thinker who can treat thoughts and ideas as if they were tangible. Either within themselves or with each other, Air Family members bat ideas around like tennis balls. They can rapidly build and dismantle conceptual structures. They like to talk things over, either within their own heads, with a computer or with other people. Some talk out loud to themselves, considering it among the best of possible conversations. Some talk to pets, plants, or road signs. They love words, especially newly invented conceptual words. It would have been Air Family adults who created 'downsizing', 'skill set' and 'New Labour'. Air minds deal and trade in concepts.

Their decisions, as well as their presentations, are based on logic and reason. Forget about an emotional appeal; the Air Family prefers intellectual detachment. An idea is a 'good' idea if it's new and makes sense conceptually, and they will only consider taking up 'good' ideas. They have a lot to go at.

The Air Family can learn readily from the written and spoken word. They easily take in information from books, lectures and conversations without needing to process it any further. Don't be fooled into thinking that all minds learn effectively in this way, despite the fact that this belief forms the basis of much modern educational theory. It's really just the Air Family, one in four of us, that learns effortlessly from the 'chalk and talk' teaching method. Members of the Air Family perpetuate this idea throughout the teaching profession, which they heavily populate.

The Water Family:

Sponge, Sherlock and Sonar

Following along, in order to learn something new, members of this Family have to draw information even more deeply into themselves than either Fire or Air Families. Water minds absorb information from the environment – just as sponges take up fluid – and then filter it through their feelings. Envision a clam at ease on the ocean floor, unconcerned, shell open, ocean water flowing in, ocean water flowing out, freely absorbing what it will from the current. In like manner Water minds absorb information from the environment. It swims or glides in, gaining access through the emotions, the intuition or the instincts. And what's taken in produces a personal emotional response, which is intertwined with learning, even if the information is purely factual.

They rely upon the link between mind and feelings not only to learn but to evaluate the merit of ideas and to make decisions – a good idea is one that feels right. Unlike other kinds of minds the newness, logic or practicality of an idea just does not matter.

Water Family minds are highly visual by nature and learning is facilitated by pictures, colour, diagrams, graphics, even videos. In fact they learn only through visual imagery. When presented with bare words or concepts, their learning process requires an additional step of translation. They have to give shape to the images behind the words, and then take in the impressions they have created. A Family trait is rich, active imaginations.

The optimal learning environment for the Water Family is one that feels safe. In fact these minds close down in a threatening environment just as quickly as a Fire mind does when told to sit down and be still. Words are like little brush strokes and Water minds can sense the whole picture from surprisingly few lines. But this is sensitive business and if the mind is upset by fear, loud noise, bullying, challenge, etc., then those big emotional responses overpower the subtle vibration associated with the new information and learning does not happen. As learning is based on the delicate feeling response to new information, emotional sensitivity is the key. An environment which conveys emotional safety and security is essential to these learners, at whatever age and whether at home or outside.

The three learning styles which comprise the Water Family experience unique but collective issues in the classroom. Their learning requirements are usually not recognized or catered for in the traditional educational setting. Consequently, a high percentage of young people who leave school feeling very badly about both their experience and themselves are members of this Family.

The Earth Family:
Steady, Details and Exec

Members of the Earth Family need to do still more to make new information their own. They must integrate it right down to the physical cellular level. These are 'hands-on' learners who have to get involved with information to really take it in. They need to try it out for themselves – do it, taste it, touch it, practise it, dramatize it, organize it, analyse it, structure it, digest it, or dig it into the earth and let it compost. To the Earth Family an idea is a good idea if it is practical and can be applied to real life. Otherwise, why bother? Earth minds evaluate an idea's merit by its usefulness. They opt for workable techniques, bringing an idea down and containing it, giving it form, structure and a home in the world of firm practicality. Earth minds tend to value the natural world and its dynamics (rules) for providing a reliable standard.

For example, to your Earth Family child the benefits of learning to read might not be self-evident. Rather than pointing out the conceptual or emotional benefits of reading, like enjoyment and enrichment, you might focus on the practical advantages of the skill, like reading the numbers on money, phone numbers, or maps. The same holds true with arithmetic. Earth minds can best practise fractions with application to measuring cups and recipes, steel tapes and nail sizes. Learning becomes easier when applied as a hands-on experience in tangible situations.

These grounded, responsible thinkers may be unimpressed by abstraction, daydreaming or flights of fancy, preferring a solid surface of fact. Their thinking is rooted, deep-seated, solid, real, sound, sensible, tangible, reasonable and pragmatic.

The Earth Family's learning dynamic often requires real time and cannot be pushed. Remember that new ideas are being integrated at a cellular level. These minds are most comfortable when allowed to process information in their own time. Asking them to hurry up and learn (or turn in the report, or provide feedback, or answer the question) is like asking your intestines to hurry up and digest lunch. Learning will happen in its own time and not a moment before.

Your Earth Family child will not often leap to conclusions or voice instant opinions like the Fire or Air Family. These minds really do prefer to give a considered response; they want to get it right and are uncomfortable with off-the-cuff replies. If they give in to the pressure and come up with the goods to please you, chances are they will suffer the next day. Their response was offered too soon, it was half-baked, hasty, partially broken down, not suitably structured. It was not the final product. It was imperfect or incorrect. They don't feel good about themselves. And you don't have what you wanted either.

In the classroom, Earth Family students are responsible and mentally very well behaved. (Please, do not confuse behaviour with mental work.) They may require more time than others as it often takes longer to ground an idea into the body than to fit it into a concept. They would benefit from having more time for assignments – to consider, to assess, to digest, to revise, to repeat, to recopy notes, etc. These students will strive toward perfection; things have to be right, no matter how long it might take to get there.

Application

To Real Life and Your Family

Hints, tips, games and strategies

Celebrating similarity and difference – moving toward mutual respect and understanding

To help your children claim their best and most natural mental strengths, the first step is to know what they are. You need to understand what makes their minds tick – all the way down to your toes. You, as a parent, need to take it in. Unless your own learning style places you in the Air Family, this information is not just another pretty idea. Don't leave it on the intellectual shelf. Truly accepting your child's learning style, with all its implications, is the single most difficult step along the path toward harmony in family relationships. If you can do it, if you will to do it, the rest is easy. And it's fun.

Let's look at some of the things that can stand in your way. First of all, there are many culturally rooted attitudes about smart and dumb that can cloud your perspective about your own children's learning dynamics.

Statements abound about what is or is not 'rocket science' or who is or is not capable in that field. 'Astrophysics' and 'brain surgery' are competitors. We all hear derogatory descriptions of people such as 'a few cards short of a full deck' or 'thick as two short planks'. And there is the all time favourite about 'my son (or daughter), the doctor'. All parents want to have smart children, special children. However, if you are committed to having a budding neurosurgeon in the family, but instead have an incipient world-class musician, you could be unhappy about your child's mental strengths. It's incomprehensible to the rest of us, unfortunate for the child, but true.

You might ask if the mental strengths attributed to your child really are strengths. Who values them – society, education authorities? Do you value them? If you do not value them, then your child will not value them either, and, over time, will lose touch with them. There is no doubt, talents and capabilities will deteriorate, becoming rusty from lack of use.

Everyone knows that speed of uptake is an indication of a smart person, right? No, no a thousand times over, no. Speed of uptake is a quality of the Fire Family. But we are staring down the Goliath of accepted educational theories here. If you have a hard time valuing the 'not fast' learning methods of your Earth Family child, for example, have a look instead at the depth to which that child incorporates new material, and test that for worth and value.

So here is our *first step*. Even if your children's mental dynamics are very different from yours and from those of others whom you hold in high regard, find the place within yourself from which you can view the most positive side of their minds and look there for essential value. Just shift your point of view. Try this, even if you would have preferred a different kind of child with different mental qualities. We all have unique strengths to contribute to the group and the ones we have are no less valuable than the ones in current vogue. These qualities are a natural part of your child's makeup. They are honest and genuine.

Here's a story about a family of three. The father's learning style is the rapid-fire, restless Flash, The Pioneer, always ready to explore what's over a distant hill or around the next corner. The mother is Buzz, The Curious, lover of new information and nearly as fast moving as Flash. Both are Adaptor Family members, quick to open up to any new ideas, nearly as quick to forget them and move on to another fascinating notion.

Their only child is as different from his parents as is possible, having been born into the Initiator and Earth Families as Exec, The Achiever. Well, what do you think they made of his natural aptitude for down-to-earth practical thought applied carefully (and profitably) to real life? Right, boring! They did not recognize or accept the value of their son's mental assets until they were grandparents. And, even now, they are not convinced.

The *second step* is to launch yourself enthusiastically into the adventure of discovering who your children are – as individuals. After reviewing the relevant Profiles in Section 2, listen for them to reveal their own inner truths. Find within yourself the joy of perceiving why their minds do what they do, rather than what you wish they would do.

'Oh, so that's why you gave up your guitar lessons.
The teacher was not stylish enough for you to learn from him.'

Now, really, your average parent might not see this as a potential moment of deep bonding with a child. But the parent of Steady, The Vault can stand firmly on the knowledge that a child with this learning style (and this learning style alone – do not let any of the other 11 'get away' with this) naturally selects only new ideas that are personally appealing and only from sources that are attractive as well.

This could be one of those points of pivotal significance in young

Steady's life. So, what do you do now? As parent, you hold all the cards. The ball is in your court. He means it. He cannot learn guitar from an instructor who lacks style. This is his truth, even though it may not be yours. Careful, now. They say the closer you are to a person, the more your behaviour toward them lacks respect. How do you, as the parent, respect the child's learning needs right then, right in that uncomfortable moment? How do you avoid putting in motion a steamroller of events that leads ultimately to a breakdown in communication at some point down the road?

You could try the *third step*, and lead with support, for example:

'Well, son, I never thought of guitar lessons in that way, myself. You should have seen some of my early guitar instructors – a scruffy lot, but excellent teachers nonetheless. Tell me more about this. Does it apply to all teachers or all music teachers or just guitar teachers? This is very interesting. How do you know when a teacher has style? I wonder if we mean the same thing by style…'

as opposed to the sad alternative, one which guarantees the child will disconnect from that which is most genuine:

'Child, after all the money we have spent on those guitar lessons, don't give me this style rubbish. I have never heard such nonsense, and I'll not listen to it now. You will practise before going to bed tonight and you will attend your lesson tomorrow. Your recital is only a few weeks away. And you will smile and show us some appreciation.'

Your expression of support helps your children identify their own particular mental qualities as being unique, natural, special and valued by you. Thus fortified they can claim their birthright of self-confidence, self-esteem, and joyous learning. People of any age who are comfortable in the knowledge of what they need for effective information handling, can make sure those needs are met. They can simply ask – for something to be repeated (Exec), for time to consider a response (Details), for more discussion (ProCon), for less discussion (Sherlock), for movement and action (Scout), etc. The specific learning needs and mental strengths of each of the 12 learning style groups are detailed as individual Profiles in Section 2.

Step four involves some introspection on the parent's part. Repeat steps *one* through *three* for yourself instead of your children. The Tables at the end of the book allow you to assign your own learning style also. In fact, you might even be able to discover your parents' learning styles and let the larger picture develop. View learning through the generations – construct your own Family Learning Tree.

You may already know exactly how your own mind ticks, exactly what you need in order to easily take in new information. You may rest comfortably with your own mental strengths, able to contribute them easily to society. You may be well aware of how your mind comes across to others. Or, alternatively, you may have disconnected from your own natural and normal way of handling information at some point between early childhood and yesterday. Many of us would rather contort our minds into pretzel shapes than potentially suffer criticism and judgement – just for being ourselves. Without recognizing it, you may still be trying to imitate the mental dynamics of an early school-teacher, who never knew about your personal learning needs, or your beloved grandfather, who years before had copied the style of his great uncle. *Step four* is an attempt to put the parent back on track with what is naturally strong and authentic in themselves. That's the part of you that needs to connect with the child's inner truth. How else could your efforts toward mutual respect within your family possibly succeed?

Strategies for Improving Family Interactions

These ideas can be applied to any relationship that carries tension – between you and your children, between you and your own parents, between parents or among children.

It will be helpful to recall that:

Tension inevitably develops at the meeting point of differing mental styles. It's natural.

That does not mean the tension has to escalate to world war proportions. It does not mean someone has to run off to the bedroom in tears, slamming doors along the way. It does not mean one person becomes a family scapegoat. Tension can be creatively resolved, right there in the moment, before it hardens into mutual long-term pain. And celebrate difference, don't just endure it or condemn it. Those with different learning styles have different points of view and therefore do not share the same blind spots. If one totally misses a particular point, the other may see it in stark relief. Similarity in thinking may make life easier, but difference, along with the tension it produces, generates space for creative solutions.

Here is another idea to share with your family, in as many ways as it takes to get the message across: *Although it may seem that another family member is 'getting at you' or is intentionally unpleasant, it could simply be that friction exists between the two natural but dissimilar mental styles.*

What one says is not what the other hears. Frustration or anger develops. They cannot talk to each other and that difficulty spills over into other parts of life. This is resolvable.

The first step is accepting that valid, natural difference exists, with neither being right nor wrong. Willingness to look through the other person's eyes and listen through their ears, to walk a mile in their mental moccasins is the second step. And learning to do so is the third. Many of the games, tricks and strategies which follow are aimed at offering just that experience among family members. How do things look from over there? What's going on in your head? Did what I just said frighten you, amuse you, encourage you? You just couldn't possibly have thought I intended to hurt your feelings, could you? Why didn't you say that in the first place? We are both good guys even if we are different!

Now let's turn to areas of ease and conflict, of similarity and difference, and find ways to resolve tensions which stem from mental diversity. Look at the learning styles of the two people in question and see if they belong to any of the same Family Groupings within the Divisions identified in Section 3. The more Family relationships the better, as they show areas of mental compatibility or like-mindedness. Let's consider the two extremes.

Extreme Similarity

Two people who meet each other within identical Families of all three Divisions have exactly the same learning style. (This does not mean they have identical minds or identical interests, an idea which is developed in Part II, Section 6.) Neither has to search for the best or most appropriate way to put something. Understanding just exists. Neither feels judged, stupid, slow or unpleasantly challenged. If one needs pictures in order to learn a new piece of information, the other will naturally supply them. If one likes to shout a newly learned fact from the highest hilltop, the other will pick it up, slip into their own hiking boots and head for high ground. There is mental accord; the minds are in sync, tuned to the same primary frequency. But it is also likely that they may be too similar and share the same blind spots. There is a one-in-twelve chance of this relationship.

Extreme Difference

On the other extreme are people whose minds meet in no Family groupings at all. This can be a difficult relationship as there is no natural common ground, but only difference in every aspect of thinking, learning and communicating. Just knowing this fact can explain quite a bit. It clarifies that both people are having a problem, not just one. Each may think the 'fault' lies with the other person who is obtuse, or stupid, or uncooperative, or withholding, or revealing, or deceptive, or too loud, or indecisive, or stubborn. But, it does not. The one thing they do share is the uneasy feeling of awkwardness with each other, and admitting this is the first step toward resolution. This relationship contains the greatest potential for creative problem-solving. These two minds view life through such different lenses that, taken together, they cover all the bases. If one misses something, the other certainly won't. The strategies offered below for harmonizing within every Division will be required in this case. For any given learning style, there are four other specific learning styles with which to form this abrasive relationship.

> **Judy, the mother**, and Jenny, one of her daughters, have exactly the same learning style, Buzz, The Curious. Their mental compatibility is nothing short of remarkable. Both read books, newspapers and magazines. Both attend courses, play bridge and watch TV. Chatting and laughing, they compare notes with each other several times a day, in person, by phone and email. They are more like twins than mother and daughter. This is 'extreme similarity'.

But, as Sherlock, The Detective, the elder daughter, Veronica, is positioned in 'extreme difference' to her mother and sister. Not only did she feel very left out in childhood, but she couldn't fathom how her sister could talk to their mother, or why she would ever want to. Even the word 'talk' had a completely different meaning to them – to Buzz ideas were light, logical and fun, easy come easy go, while to Sherlock ideas were powerful and intense, captured for the long term.

This story has a happy ending, but only because Veronica embraced these principles and put her remarkable mental commitment behind a solution. She truly understands the depth of difference between her own and Jenny's mental requirements well enough that these two women currently enjoy a thriving business partnership. Resolution with her mother has not been quite as successful, yet.

Between these extremes of easy mental exchange and serious inhibition is a wide field in which minds have some specific areas of similarity to each other. Such common ground serves as the cornerstone of potential harmony and can be integrated into positive tension-busting strategies.

This should be easy and fun for you and your family. If you have not done so already, consult the Assessment Tables beginning on page 163 and make a note of the individual learning styles and their Family group memberships within each of the three Divisions for the adults and each of your children. To help out, there is a simple worksheet for you to fill in on page 162. If, within any of the three Divisions, you have listed names beside more than one Family cluster, then your home might not be a zone of pure bliss. Just look below for specific strategies to help resolve the inevitable tensions which can develop at the meeting point of different mental styles.

A. The Two Families of the Reaction Division

Sharers and Containers

One area of difference which is single-handedly responsible for more hurt feelings, misunderstandings and mistrust than any other is within Division A: *Reaction* to New Information.

Sharers

Half of us believe it exists to be shared – right now! When ideas are learned or invented, they tumble straight from the mouth without restraint.

Containers

The other half is sure information should be contained, at least for a while. Their ideas seem to sink below the surface and sometimes never reappear.

The first group distrusts anything that is not 'out in the open' and cannot understand 'hiding' and 'concealing'. Meanwhile, the second group constantly feels betrayed by the first, who blab their 'private thoughts' all over town.

What to do? Neither of these polar-opposite Family groupings realizes the impact of their words. Whether they are Sharers or Containers, they know only their own response and it's always the other person's 'fault'. However, by taking one giant step backwards, we can all see both sharing and containing as purely natural impulses, which are usually unrecognized. Both Family groupings are unaware of what they do. The hurt they can cause is unintentional. Prove this to yourself! One morning tell something particularly interesting, either real or invented, to all members of your family – something like a recent local sighting of Santa, a 35-pound potato or a suspected UFO. In the evening, pick a convenient time and ask who told the story to others outside your family. It's illuminating! You might be amazed. This kind of group activity can demonstrate to everyone that malice is simply not intended when people either share or contain information. The two reactions are purely natural.

Although neither of these leopards will easily change its spots, simply realizing that we naturally fall into two camps and talking about the difference really helps. Each needs to hear the other's experience. Believe me, both will be very surprised. The stand-off becomes less personal, the grievance easier to accept and forgive. Certainly between these two Family clusters permission can ultimately be granted for people to be themselves and handle information as they do, naturally.

If there is a desire to get along better, they can begin to adapt – with particular pieces of information and in specific situations. For example, try clearly telling a Sharer that something is private and you would rather not have it repeated. You may meet with: Oh? OK. Don't see why not, but OK. When you do not ask for this, your words just might appear in next week's newspaper or on a community noticeboard – innocently. Similarly, as long as it's not an actual secret, a certain piece of information or an answer to a specific question can be coaxed from the mind of a Container for the sake of harmony.

Two sisters were having a very hard time with each other. Tears and frustrated anger were common. Realizing the conflict resulted purely from a natural mental difference between the girls, their mother invented a game. It worked – they were quickly reconciled. While Susan (the Sharer) practised 'not telling' unimportant facts, Helen (the Container) gained experience in 'telling' by freely reporting inconsequential items.

The mother and two daughters talked, joked and made up stories about sharing ideas right away versus containing them for a while.

A Sharer Mother reports that trying to hold back in order to say something to her Container son, at the 'right time', is really foreign territory to her. It has taken 23 years for her to see how necessary it is.

If you have a majority of one type represented in your family and only one of the other, be careful about exclusion, finger pointing or ganging up on the singleton.

B. The Three Families of the Approach Division

Sustainers, Adaptors and Initiators

The interaction among three is quite different from that between two. The two Families of the *Reaction* Division form a potentially adversarial dynamic, a black or white, either/or situation. Three is not quite as simple. Although not in the shape of a classic stand-off, contacts among these three Families provide tremendous scope for misunderstanding, suspicion, criticism, lack of respect and accusations of all sorts.

To function smoothly a family, a community or a society clearly needs all three kinds of mental strengths – initiating, sustaining and adapting. But we may need three people to supply them, because our minds do not naturally excel in all three areas, much as we might fantasize to the contrary. That includes your children, sorry. Some marvellous archetypal but fictional characters, like James Bond, may express mental capability in all three areas, with each evolved to a very high degree. Mere mortals like the rest of us may have some access to each of the three modes of approach (an idea which is more fully developed in Part II, Section 6), but with a controlling predominance toward one. Our primary learning style belongs to only one Family grouping within each of the three Divisions. This makes us all valuable – we are complemented by each other's mental strengths.

But, discord can arise from the difference in what minds do naturally. A person with one mental mode seems to think everyone else should have it also, that if he is right and you are different, then you are not right. When a different style is encountered the criticism starts to flow. The exasperated Sustainer jeers at the Adaptor: You have no memory at all, do you! The deflated Adaptor retaliates defensively with indictments of rigidity. Each one's strength has been perceived by the other as a weakness. *So much pain results from our lack of appreciation and respect for mental difference.* This can be resolved.

There is an additional problem. Although society places tremendous value on the fine mental qualities of each of these three Families, it ridicules their unavoidable flip sides. The Initiator's driving originality is criticized for lack of follow-through. The Sustainer's steadfast, persevering mind is held up as inflexible. The Adaptor's open acceptance of the new is belittled as wishy-washy. The highs and lows – the best and worst. It all depends on the circumstances and the viewer's lens as to which side is seen, how it's interpreted, and if it's valued.

- There is praise for initiating or brainstorming new ideas.
- There is praise for good long-term memory and an ability to follow a project through to completion.
- There is praise for adaptability and flexibility in thinking.

So let's consciously recognize and applaud the natural strengths of each of these Three Families of *Approach*. Stress-busting strategies involve sidestepping the criticism and trying out the other person's valid point of view as a route to understanding it. Relationships are transformed when family members, who are hung up in conflict, stop expecting others to be clones of themselves and start refocusing on the positive within each other's natural mental dynamics. Role playing and other activities which engage both adults and children can be very effective. Here are some recommendations for celebrating similarity and difference among Initiators, Sustainers and Adaptors. Suggestion: if your family is small, why not recruit others to join in.

A Family Game – Spot The *Approach*
The natural world is a great teacher. It gives us an arena in which to play and learn openly. We do not tend to judge or criticize minerals, plants and animals for their natural ways of being. They are part of nature, not separate from it.

It's always fun to watch animals. Although it's their outward behaviour which we observe, we can pretend that it results from mental activity, their drives, choices, interests, logic and commitments. And based on what we see, we can assign them to Family groupings within the *Approach* Division. (We know that human behaviour does not necessarily run parallel to thinking, but this is a game and we're pretending.)

By using examples from the animal world, adults and children can easily understand the ideas of natural difference, that all mental styles are fine, one is not better than another. However, it becomes clear that particular mental styles are more successfully applied to certain tasks. We see the immense power of natural mental drive. And we can be unbiased viewers.

Why not keep an ongoing list of family observations and add any new sightings to it. This can be a great activity on car trips, while watching TV or DVDs, or just schmoozing around your local area.

Sustainers

We would assign to this Family those animals that do the same thing for a very long time, as if they were totally committed to it. For example, explorers have observed entire flocks of penguins standing around on the ice, moving only very slowly from foot to foot, for months on end, each with an egg on its feet. If those travellers had been playing 'Spot The *Approach*', is there any question to which category they would have assigned penguins? True, it has to do with survival; the eggs would freeze in no time if flat on the ice. No more penguins. But it is exactly the point – that is just how important an idea can be to your Sustainer child. Ideas can be experienced as survival issues.

Migrating birds display the same intense commitment. They are going to do whatever it takes to reach their warm-weather nests and, in the other direction, their cold-weather roosts – whatever it takes. Swallows even leave the final brood behind and set off as a flock, to cover the very long but familiar route, with apparent confidence that the fledglings will follow when they are strong enough.

Sustainers are committed – for as long as necessary, but no longer.

The parent penguin is free to resume normal life, movement, fishing, playing, etc. as soon as the egg hatches. It does not substitute a rock for the former egg and keep standing there. The migrating birds endure the rigors of their journey, but only until they arrive. They do not overshoot the mark and keep flying and flying around the earth.

Cats are well known for luxuriating in the sunshine – possibly all day. But they eventually finish and walk away. Even the relentless winds of hurricanes, tornados and gales eventually end, leaving calm seas and light breezes. How many more can you add to the list?

Nature could pass a few pointers on to the parent of a Sustainer child.

The idea to which s/he may be totally committed can lose its hold in time.

Prepare your child to anticipate that the 'egg might hatch' and to notice with acceptance when it has.

Does every idea have to carry this intense weight? Is every thought worth the same struggle?

Assist your child to select the battles. Every notion is not as important as the future of the species.

This game can help other family members to respect the task involved here, to understand the power of the natural mental drive. They may not have to stand all winter with an egg on their feet. But maybe their brother does.

Observing and talking about animals that are assigned to this Family might help your Sustainer child realize how his mind affects other people and that there may be some options – for the sake of getting along.

An adult Sustainer (Sherlock, The Detective) has suggested another example of extreme persistence in the natural world as a way to help parents and siblings understand this mind and the actual extent of its steadfastness. Rocks. He says they are patient, persistent, committed and not prone to erratic change. When questioned about their natural dynamic, he said they are returning to the dust from which they came. He tells me that all the rocks he knows are smaller than they were when he was a child. They all wait, he says, with one eye half-open, watching for their big chance. And they apparently shriek in delight when being built into or falling from the top of a stone wall, when tumbling over each other as an ocean wave recedes down the beach or when tenderly picked up by a geologist. So the real hint here is to observe the sideways, offbeat humour lurking beneath the surface of your Sustainer child.

Adaptors

To spot the Adaptor Family in the natural world, look for animals that are in ceaseless, perhaps random motion or those that change direction frequently or that start and stop suddenly. Those who are up and down trees or back and forth across plains would also qualify.

Butterflies and songbirds are constantly on the move. They never stop or rest for long before they are off again. Many small garden birds dash endlessly between the cover of a shrub and a bird table or feeder. European blackbirds and American robins fit several Adaptor criteria with their amusing characteristic 'walk'. They run across the ground, screech to a halt, wait as if listening, and run off again, stop again, etc.

Chipmunks and all varieties of squirrels – reds, greys and flying – incessantly rush around, on the ground, in the trees, along the limbs, traversing the tree ways, across rooftops, down along the roads, disappearing into holes in the ground. They appear to be always busy, always on the move.

Roadrunners, well that says it all.

Ducks are most adaptable creatures! They swim in the water, fly in the air and walk on the earth. And when the weather gets cold, they simply move to a warmer location.

Chameleons change their skin colour to blend with the background.

They adapt for survival by becoming invisible. Who do you think originated the idea for camouflage colours?

There is a start. Can some of your family members add to this list?

All these animals do the moving-around task very well. It's their job. It wouldn't suit a penguin. And it's unlikely that a duck would stand for months protecting an egg from the cold.

Because of our different strengths and gifts, when taken together, we have an assortment of contributions to offer to our diversified world. Each and every one is valuable – people, animals, plants and minerals.

Initiators

To spot Initiator Family members in the natural world, look for expressions of movement in a forward direction, always and purposefully forward – toward whatever is new. Of course, with the Initiator mind, information is the fuel which feeds the forward movement.

Observe a brook, a creek or a river. It never even hesitates in its forward motion. Plunk a large rock, or even yourself, into a stream and the water simply diverts around the obstacle and just keeps flowing along. Nothing can stop a moving glacier. It rolls over trees, boulders, and even entire communities that stand in its path. It's the same with an active lava flow. Think of Pompeii.

An inchworm moves steadily forward. If it encounters an obstacle, it shifts its course just enough and carries on purposefully, in another straight line. The children might enjoy moving like an inchworm. You might too!

Time marches on, they say. So do clocks, watches, calendars, the seasons, the planets of our solar system, our age and all our other means of recording time.

Can you and your family add to this list?

Observing Initiator Family members in the natural world might shed some light on why it's so difficult for an Initiator child (or adult) to complete a project. The natural mental drive is to begin another one. Try pointing out new facets of an ongoing project as a strategy to whip up flagging enthusiasm.

A variation of – Spot the *Approach*

Extend your search for pure examples of the different mental *Approach* Families beyond the natural world to the human realm and our creations. Look to songs, literature, films, real people, historical figures, current politicians, celebrities and your friends.

Sustainers

A children's story, *The Little Engine Who Could*, features a steep hill climb by a little steam engine who chanted all the way up 'I think I can, I think I can'. The 'hatching moment' came as it crested the hill and changed the song to 'I thought I could! I thought I could!'

The persevering North American pioneers demonstrated an unswerving commitment to the arduous journey across dangerous and unfamiliar land, unsure of what they would find. They too recognized when the 'egg hatched'. They were not habituated to travel. They did not keep going endlessly, all the way to the Pacific Ocean. At some point they knew they had reached the right place. They stopped the dedication to travel and put down roots. This might be a great role-play exercise for your family.

Public figures who are Sustainer Family members and who clearly express its natural mental dynamic are George Bush and his son, George W Bush, Hillary Clinton, Bill Clinton, Sir Richard Branson, Sir Winston Churchill and Oprah Winfrey.

Adaptors

Think about the way falling snow looks when swirled by a gust of wind. The erratic movement in all different directions appears to have neither rhyme nor reason.

A kaleidoscope, with its constantly changing patterns of shape and colour, will give you and your children another glimpse of the Adaptor Family.

Many current dance styles, with their unexpected changes in direction, speed, leaps and twirls, also convey this theme.

An adult Adaptor Family member describes her way of moving through life 'like a person possessed'. We know she has accomplished more than a dozen ordinary people but at a frenetic pace.

Public figures whose minds place them in the Adaptor Family are: Woody Allen, Paul McCartney, Napoleon Bonaparte, Elton John and Marie Curie.

Initiators

This theme can be seen in the steady advance of an old-style army, with interlocking shields forming a solid wall of protection in front of them. Both Greeks and Romans called this military formation a phalanx. You and your family might enjoy sensing the power of forward movement. Try standing in a row, substituting pan lids for shields and move steadily onward, as a group.

Runners also express persistent forward motion. At a hurdle, they simply leap over it and carry on running. Similarly, rally drivers must alter direction according to the course but they keep right on going.

If you have ever watched a demonstration of, or tried for yourself, a movement called Tai Chi walking, you would discover another direct expression of the Initiator Family. Find it on the Internet and teach it to your children.

Firecrackers and explosions also have many Initiator qualities.

Lewis Carroll, who wrote *Alice in Wonderland*, is an Initiator Family member. Funny that Alice expresses the same mental traits.

Public figures whose mental processes include them in the Initiator Family are: Tony Blair, Albert Einstein, Bill Gates, Queen Elizabeth II, Bob Geldof and Bert Munro (whose story is told in the film *The World's Fastest Indian*).

A Family Game – What would it be like if we were all the same?
Here are some suggestions to use as a framework to increase awareness of the driving mental forces within the three Family groups by taking their natural traits to an extreme. They are meant to be explorations with very loose rules, involving more flow than hard structure. The intention of the activities is to foster mutual understanding. Employ them as seed ideas or guidelines. Apply them in a wide variety of ways, depending on your own imagination and the nature of the conflict at hand. They can be used in short bursts, if necessary, to intervene at moments of high mutual criticism and low mutual respect. Either use these ideas as points of discussion, perhaps appropriate with older children, or invent your own activities based upon them. Choose whichever of the following best suits the Family Grouping assignments of those whose conflict you wish to help resolve. The behavioural aspects involved here do not comment on your children's behaviour, but are used to amplify and dramatize their inner mental dynamics.

All Initiators – No Sustainers or Adaptors

What would home life be like if everything always moved forward and nothing ever stopped or grew? Talk about or assign a task for all to accomplish using this one rule – allow only creative forward movement. Applaud all novel ideas, imaginative conversations, original topics, inventive activities. Keep shifting gears and going forward to explore innovative lines of thought, fresh interests, unusual games, ingenious lessons, different friends, new playmates. Initiators dash off to The Next. Stopping or going backwards or in circles or repeating previous ideas is not permitted. Neither are rest breaks. This uses extreme Initiator activities to demonstrate a point. It is the process that's important, not the accomplishment.

All Sustainers – No Initiators or Adaptors

What would home life be like if nothing ever changed or moved creatively forward, if everything always carried on just as it was, with no new beginnings and no alterations? Little children would always be little children and would not grow older or bigger. If you couldn't read at the start of the game, you would never learn. If you were hungry or thirsty at the outset, you always would be. Your very favourite or least favourite colour would never change. Sustainers themselves do not forget and have difficulty when others do. They wait – they do not scurry off into other thoughts. Better set your kitchen timer for this one or the game itself would never be able to end.

All Adaptors – No Sustainers or Initiators

Play with the idea that nothing brand new ever begins, nor does anything ever reach completion. What would life be like in your home? The rule here allows for change only. Adaptors love new information – the more, the better. You don't have to keep it. If you don't want it, just toss it away. But at least consider it. Old things can be adapted into new ones, which can then undergo further development. Adaptors rush around making something new out of the old. It's an endless spiralling process.

Modify this to suit your own specific family needs. If tension has resulted from a 'dominant' *Approach* Family mind, try an exercise that demonstrates to the others what it would be like if that energy were missing altogether. Talk about or create role-play activities involving the pertinent scenario:

- No Initiators, only Sustainers and Adaptors
- No Sustainers, only Initiators and Adaptors
- No Adaptors, only Initiators and Sustainers

This really points out in vivid living colour the beneficial contribution made by each *Approach* Family. And in addition to planting seeds of mutual awareness, mutual respect and greater acceptance of each other, this kind of role-play can bolster self-acceptance, self-awareness and self-worth within the one who had acted out as 'dominant'.

> **Both parents were Sustainers**, enormously skilled at persever-ance. All three of their children were Initiators. The parents despaired of their children's lack of staying power. 'Not one of them ever finishes anything they start.' The children, now adults, can chuckle about it today, but it was not easy for any of them to give themselves permission to reconnect with their natural mental strengths.

A variation of – What would it be like if we were all the same? It's a little more advanced and really develops a skill at viewing through another person's point of view.

The endless continuous story

Hold a 'talking stick'. It can be anything from a toothpick to a tree limb in terms of size and manufacture. It does not matter. What is important is that only the person holding it can speak. The rest are silent until the talking stick is passed on.

Start making up a story – with a plot and characters and a setting. After a time hand the talking stick over to someone else who is to continue the story from where you left off, but with their own script, direction, sub-plots and new characters. However, you and each succeeding custodian of the talking stick must tell the story as if it were entirely dominated by only one Family of *Approach* – Initiator, Sustainer or Adaptor, whichever had been decided upon. The talking stick is passed among the players with the same rules – whoever holds the talking stick continues to unfold the story and cannot stop speaking.

As an even more advanced alternative, the person passing the stick can change the *Approach* assignment, for example from a Sustainer story to one dominated and told by an Initiator. Then the next person continues unfolding the story, its plot, new characters, etc. through the lens of the new assignment.

These simple exercises carry tremendous potential benefits. Both adults and children can opt to compromise as they realize the impact of their thoughts, ideas and resultant ways of being on the others with whom they share space. For the sake of improved relationships, each person might make concessions. Sustainers can pause to consider choices before making mental commitments. Initiators can come to realize that some projects need completing, some deadlines need meeting. Adaptors can knuckle down and stay focused in specific areas.

A report with a happy ending: An Adaptor child who thrives on the mental stimulation from social contact with friends, heard her Sustainer parent voice his opinion that communication is very seriously overrated and he just doesn't see the point. In fact once, when he spotted a cell phone on the road, it gave him great pleasure to take aim and run his car over it!

However, a rare moment of brutal honesty occurred during an *Approach* Family exercise and the Adaptor child came to envy the parent his deep satisfaction with long-term mental commitments and at the same time the Sustainer parent found himself actually admiring the child's winged mental agility.

C. The Four Families of the Mode of Uptake Division

Fire, Air, Water and Earth

There is a level of compatibility among members of any particular element Family. They seem to innately understand quite a lot about each other. For example, a group of Air Family members may happily spend the afternoon tossing concepts back and forth, and two or more from the Earth group will get on well together, experiencing rapport on a practical level. However, in relationships with members of other element Families, an Earth mind might tend to ruffle some feathers by frequently mentioning the rules of the game or pointing out that an opponent actually did step over the sideline, that another child's uniform is not as clean as it could be, that you were 12 minutes late collecting him, or in fact that the teacher didn't look too well today.

Tensions which build up between any of these four Families are often related to uptake time, the comparative length of time it takes each mind to 'get it'. This, in turn, is proportional to how each Family acts upon new information in order to take it in. On the two extremes, we have the Fire Family members who simply breathe in new ideas, intact and fully developed, with no processing required and the Earth Family members who must integrate new ideas right into the cellular structure of their bodies. Clearly, the interface between them could be stressful to both, with Earth feeling pushed by Fire and Fire feeling held back by Earth.

> **Fran (Flash, The Pioneer – Fire)** and son Alan (Details, The Analyst – Earth) 'have serious communication problems'. She finds it soul-destroying to offer him her very best ('expand, enlarge, extend!') and for him to clam up and withdraw. Alan has now stopped sharing his plans during their early stages, when she could still make a valuable contribution. He does not disclose an idea until it's complete. She is equally unhappy about his treatment of situations that need resolving between them. He insists on stepping back and getting the facts together. Basically, she says, he sits on it. She wants to jump in with both feet and sort the issue out on the spot, before it takes hold.
>
> Essentially, their clash is one of inspiration versus practicality.

Her risk taking, spontaneity and play-it-by-ear attitude conflict with his details, planning and proper timing. She feels like a forest fire coming at his Earth. He feels like a sand bucket aimed at her Fire. Sadly, neither knows they are both good guys.

Resolution can be approached by understanding and respecting one's own and each other's natural learning styles.

Discussions, activities and games which allow both children and adults to look through each other's eyes and perceive each other's reality can really help. As a starting point let's recall that every learning style is just right; one is neither better nor worse than another. The only error is in disconnecting from one's own natural mental strengths and trying to be like someone else.

Here are a few ways for adults and children to learn more about these four *Mode of Uptake* Family groups.

A Family Activity – Look to Nature

Why of course, these are elements of nature! Observe them, along with your child, in as many ways as possible and talk about all the many expressions. For example, water can fall around us in torrents or as a light mist. Air can have the fragrance of spring or the chill of winter. This will foster in both of you an understanding of what it's like to have a mind named after that element. Any one of the countless manifestations of an element in nature can portray exactly how your child experiences the inside of his own head at a particular moment. And having learned to do so yourself, you can show your child how to shift gears among different expressions of his mental element. Empower him with choice.

Also, these observations can help clarify aspects of your parent/child relationship. For example, if you are a Water Family member and your child is Fire, you might work with images of how those two elements get along in nature. Fire can be extinguished by water. Water can be warmed by fire, heated up, brought to the boil and turned to steam. On some days, you might unknowingly affect your Fire child like a high-pressure hose, while on others, like a stagnant swamp. Similarly, the Fire child might sometimes resemble a forest fire out of control. But, you can opt for different expressions. Your two minds could decide to dance together like a country brook (Water) in the warming sunshine

(Fire) or like a graceful city fountain (Water) under coloured spotlights (Fire).

You both have choice. If the interaction is discordant, bring it to harmony with different but authentic expressions. When the elements are in accord in the natural world, the picture is like Camelot – with long pleasant sunny days and the necessary showers coming only at night. The family home does not need to be a venue for cyclones, droughts, landslides and lightning storms.

Fire

How many examples can you and your children identify? Hints: there are friendly fires like those in the fireplace or wood stove and unfriendly fires which blaze where they should not be. There are tiny fires like tea-light candles and much larger fires like blowtorches. The biggest fire of all is the sun in the sky. And, there are the stars. You might extend this into all the ways humans have created and invented 'artificial' fire.

Recall that Fire Family minds function through the intuition. They are quick on the uptake as information requires no further processing or integrating. As many kinds of fire rapidly consume fuel and move on, Fire minds are frequently more than ready to leap to the next topic. Can you spot which fire examples from the above list appear to be different by not leaping about?

What would it be like if a Fire Family member turned the size of the mental flame down too low? The result might be a lack of spirit, enthusiasm, spunk, flare or zest for life. Boring!

This is how many Fire Family members view other people.

And what if the flame were turned way up high? Blasts of intuition! The mind might burn to ignition, too fast, too much, too hot, too big, too many, too arrogant, too loud, too bossy...

This is how many Fire Family members seem to other people.

Who is in charge of the size of the flame? Who makes the choices? How many other examples can you and your children think of? Act them out; write them down; talk about them. Ask each other: What would the world be like if nobody's mind worked like this, or everyone's?

Air

Look to nature for as many examples of air as you and your children can identify. Hints: There is still air, moving air and turbulent air. Thin air at high altitudes and thick air at sea level. Warm air and cold air. Wet air and dry air. Humid air and prickly hot air. Snowy, rainy, sleety, air. Smelly air. Don't forget all the ways we already control and contain air – air conditioners, fans, balloons, perfume, etc.

Air Family minds deal in concepts and logic. Just as air moves around and fills all available space, Air Family minds move information around. They chat, converse, debate and discuss. Logic and conscious-ness are everywhere. Intelligence occupies all space.

Imagine the effects of Air pressure turned down too low. There would be no motive to move ideas around, to talk, to let others know what's going on. The mind would not form ideas into concepts and share them.
This is how many Air Family members view other people.

And if the Air pressure were turned up too high, we might observe: all talk, all words and chatter, ungrounded, distant, cold, mentally dispas-sionate, blowing hot and cold, windy, lightheaded.
This is how many Air Family members seem to other people.

How many other examples can you and your children think of? Act them out; write them down; talk about them. Think about what the world would be like if nobody's mind worked like this, or everyone's.

Water

Nature has many examples of water. Some of it moves and some is still. Some is very deep and some is shallow. Some is underground, some on the surface and some falls from a great height. Some water is liquid, some is solid and some is vapour. Can you and your children provide examples of all these and other types of water? Don't forget the bath, the sauna and the whirlpool.

All liquid water fills the container which holds it, having no rigid structure of its own. Both a riverbed and a glass bottle are containers for holding water. Is there any water that does not need a container?

Water Family minds experience a natural link between the mind and the feelings. The emotions are reflected in the thinking. The flowing quality of water is like the flowing quality of feeling. Water is an age-old symbol of the feeling realms.

If the Water pressure is turned down too low, thoughts can wither like dead leaves on a vine. Ideas lack nurturing and become dry or brittle. The flow stops. The mind might turn in upon itself, becoming withdrawn and reflecting nothing back to the environment. Silence.

This is how many Water Family members view other people.

If there is too much Water or too high a pressure, the mind could become excessively fluid, overemotional, overly reflective or responsive, excessively worried, needy or drifty, looking outside itself for containment.

This is how many Water Family members seem to other people.

How many other examples can you and your children think of? Act them out; write them down; talk about them. What do you feel the world would be like if nobody's mind worked like this, or everyone's?

Earth

Earth is the physical ground on which we stand. It supports us. It's fundamental. It's material. It's tangible. And we absolutely take its stability for granted… until it erupts with a quake or a volcano. Some earth is called rich, and is excellent for growing food crops, and some is called poor, like sand. Some earth is solid bedrock, like granite. Some is highly structured crystals like diamonds and quartz. All the metals, the minerals and the chemical elements are of the earth. Can you and your children name any of them?

The minds of the Earth Family think along stable, practical lines. Ideas have both substance and reliability. They can be applied to the real, tangible world, put to work, put to the test. Earth minds deal with limits of all sorts – time, financial, speed, linguistic, structural, etc. They analyse and organize the rules and procedures.

What could we expect in a situation of too little earth, of the Earth pressure being turned down? Thinking could become ungrounded, impractical, unstructured, undisciplined, flaky or irresponsible. Deadlines could be ignored. Important provisions could run out.

This is how many Earth Family members view other people.

An overexpression of Earth might be: bound by rules, procedures or precedents, flat, stultifying, slow, uninspired, boring, a bucket of sand, feet of clay, pedantic.

This is how many Earth Family members seem to other people.

How many other examples can you and your children think of? Act them out; write them down; talk about them. Think about and discuss what the world would be like if nobody's mind worked like this, or everyone's.

A Family Activity – Look to the balance of the elements in nature. The beautiful spring day – perfect temperature (fire), light breezes (air), puffy white clouds (air and water), sunshine (fire) nicely warming the earth (earth) and bringing forth the grass, bulbs and flowers. The previous night's showers (water) cleansed their petals and leaves. Everything is clean and sparkly and in harmony. Lovely.

If any one of the four elements is either lacking or excessive, this pretty picture of balance and harmony is undermined. For example, if much less than the normal amount of rain falls, drought results. The earth is scorched by the sun. Crops fail, leading to food shortages. The parched earth turns to dust, which swirls up into the air. Pollution.

On the other hand, if much more than the normal rain falls, floods result. The earth is eroded by rushing water. Landslides follow. Sunlight is blocked by clouds. Trees and crops suffer or are destroyed. These are familiar news stories as extreme conditions happen on different parts of the earth.

What might result from other element imbalances in nature? Too much air? Not enough fire?

Our planet does not do well with either the absence or the excess of any of the four elements. All are critically important. Each is profoundly valuable. It's just the same with people of different learning styles. These climatic conditions, ranging from unpleasant to catastrophic, parallel family relationships with ongoing conflict, tension, judgement, criticism and scorn for members of other Element Families, just because they have a different mode of information uptake.

A Family Activity – Look to our bodies

Here is another way to view the critical importance of balance among the four elements. The stakes are high – if they get too far out of balance, we don't survive. Fortunately, within our bodies the element groups do not tend to judge each other for doing what comes naturally.

Earth: we appear to be made of the solid substance of *earth*... organic (carbon-containing) molecules, inorganic minerals, trace chemical elements, all joining in the formation of bone, muscle, connective tissue, soft tissue, membranes, eyelashes, toenails, etc.

Water: but we are made up of 50 to 78 per cent *water*. (Young children, who are more emotional than intellectual, are at the higher end of the spread.) Our blood, lymph and other fluids flow in response to a variety of rhythms.

Air: we cannot survive without breathing *air* for more than a few minutes. Oxygen feeds all our body's functions, especially the brain. Oxygen in, carbon dioxide out. The movement of air (blood gases) within the body is critical to health.

Fire: we are powered by *fire*. All the biochemical reactions which support our life are absorbing and releasing heat all the time.

A Family Activity – Look to the Metaphors in the Language
Your family might have some fun with this game. Keep an ear out for these snappy descriptive phrases or invent new ones. They so colourfully describe a mind's inner workings. Have an ongoing list and see how many can be added.

Fire: flash in the pan, a bright light, warms up a conversation, a bolt out of the blue, a shooting star of an idea, a burning passion, a rising star, a spark of an idea.

Air: airy fairy, up in the air, airhead, blowing hot and cold, ungrounded, windy, lightheaded, featherweight.

Water: still waters run deep, muddy the waters, go with the flow, don't push the river, a tidal wave of words, gentle as the morning dew.

Earth: solid as a rock, feet on the ground, salt of the earth, hard as nails.

A Family Activity – The Element Game
Older children and adults might really enjoy this more advanced activity. Arrange your family and any invited guests in a height spiral with Fire Family members standing on low stools, the Air Family standing on the floor next to them, the Water Family seated on chairs and the Earth Family seated on floor cushions. Leave extra space for any missing element groups by setting out stools, chairs and cushions. Arrange the participants in a semicircle, not in a straight line, so that everyone can see each other as well as any vacant places. The difference

in height from the high ones standing on stools to the low ones sitting on the floor gives the impression of a spiral shape.

This game packs a wallop. It's a powerful visual and experiential arrangement that conveys why tension exists in some family relationships. The spiral has to do with the relative depth to which new information is integrated, which in turn relates to speed of uptake. From the highest position to the lowest, each successive Family group has to become increasingly more involved with information in order to take it in. Those minds which are fastest on the uptake are the least involved. And as we move through the spiral, getting closer to the earth, the process of learning requires more and more from the learner. Fast is not better than slow, nor vice versa.

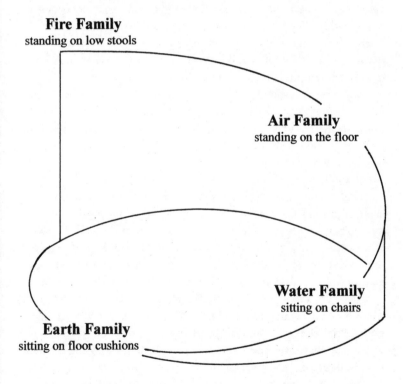

Fire Family
standing on low stools

Air Family
standing on the floor

Water Family
sitting on chairs

Earth Family
sitting on floor cushions

Review the descriptions of the different element Families (Part I Section 3) so participants can hear about their own mental strengths and learning requirements and those of the others. Each person can identify with and claim their position within the spiral pattern. Talk about the spiral and what it means. Find out how everyone is thinking or feeling about their position within it. Remind everyone that each element grouping is as necessary and important within your family and society as it is in nature, where the absence of even a single element can lead to catastrophe.

Now here's the interesting part. Suggest that each person move from where they are into the position in the spiral to which they are the most drawn. Encourage everyone to arrange themselves where they would like to be. The view and the feeling will be very different from there! Participants should shift gears and come around behind the point of view of their newly adopted element Families. For example, someone newly positioned in the Water Family could explore what it's like to define a 'good idea' as one that feels right and for someone newly positioned in Air a 'good idea' is one that is interesting.

Have on hand a few cards listing some simple questions which rearranged participants would answer – from the point of view of their newly adopted group position. A question like: If we were going to host a neighbourhood party over the weekend, what would you like to contribute? New Earth Family people would have to reach for a practical answer, like making sure there were enough paper plates or food for all the guests, despite the fact that it would not be their true and natural reply. It gives an inside look through the viewpoint of another person, which in turn builds bridges of understanding.

The discussion might turn to what encourages and what discourages each of the newly adopted Families. It's not the natural Family members asking for what they need – it's one step removed. The New Fire people can suggest, for example, what they think would support them (flashcards, quick, unexpected questions, freedom to move around more – like can I get off this stool now?) and the Real Fire people could add their comments. The New Fire people could suggest what they think extinguishes their flame. That could lead to an interesting discussion and some deep insights.

Suggest that everyone move again, but this time to the element Family position they are least drawn to. As you might imagine, the reasons why someone is least attracted to a certain kind of mind can bring all sorts of issues to the forefront of discussion. Each learning style is important, all are valuable. Please recall that we are dealing with mental dynamics, not egos, personalities or behaviour.

Ask what life on earth might be like if every single person belonged to the Fire Family. What if nobody did? What would be missing? Ask the same question about the Air, the Water and the Earth.

This is all about experiencing each other's reality and genuine learning requirements. It's a way to discover that other family members are just being themselves when it might seem they are being difficult. It's a way to crack open new possibilities of understanding both self and others. It's a giant step toward mutual respect and active encouragement of others, in the specific way they most need it.

Achieving harmony may be an *ongoing process*, of which the first step may be simply to agree that we all think, learn and communicate differently.

Case Studies

Here's a glimpse of what we have seen: the funny, the touching, the absolutely traumatic, the total misses, the happy endings. This is the Mercury Model in real people's lives.

1. Jane (Details, The Analyst – Earth, Adaptor)

Jane felt constantly pushed by life. She never seemed to have enough time to fulfil her family's requests, which were beginning to feel like demands. She and her husband were active partners in their busy veterinary clinic and parents of two school-age daughters. Well, no wonder! Oddly enough, both girls and their father all shared the same learning style: Flash, The Pioneer – Fire, Adaptor. Jane couldn't win. Given her natural tendency to meticulously analyse incoming information in practical terms, both her husband's and her children's rapid-fire mental enthusiasms and sudden leaps were overwhelming – from fascinating school projects to torn sports uniforms, from on-the-spot business decisions to animal treatment instructions.

However, she could and did learn to strategize, and in a way that did not threaten to extinguish the others' natural creative flames. One very successful component of her plan was to reassess all the mental and physical 'filing boxes' into which she placed incoming information, pending analysis. She learned to tuck away less material 'for future reference' by more quickly dispatching everything that was truly inconsequential. No more hesitation about junk mail/emails, less hesitation about articles, journals, magazines or recipes. And, all the remaining new material was reframed in pleasurable rather than oppressive ways. It added hours onto her week. Well done!

2. Sharon (Steady, The Vault – Earth, Sustainer)

Sharon requested help concerning her relationship with her 14-year-old son (Sponge, The Sensitive – Water, Initiator). 'He would come with his homework assignment and ask for help. I was so touched by the request and really wanted to help, but within a few minutes his eyes appeared to glaze over and he would say, "That's OK Mum, thanks anyway. I'm sure I can figure it out."' She would be heartbroken each time it happened.

The child's mind is highly visual. Learning is facilitated by pictures, colour, diagrams, graphics and videos. His mind absorbs information from the environment like a sponge takes up fluid, and filters it through his feelings. He has an emotional response even to factual information – he always will.

Sharon, on the other hand, has a strongly grounded mind. For her, learning requires hands-on, active involvement with the new material. Like so many people, she explained things to her son in the way she would need them explained to her. But, her practical teaching approach overpowered his mental sensitivity. He ran away.

Sharon completely understood the stylistic differences between the Earth Family and the Water Family and simply changed her approach. She offered him what he needed rather than what she would have needed herself. It worked! She only wished she had had the information years earlier.

3. Sharon's elder son (Sherlock, The Detective – Water, Sustainer)

Sharon's son caused her considerable concern. 'If I had known when I was bringing up this child, what I know now that he is nearly 18, it would have really helped. I always thought he was intentionally hiding things from me. And recently I began to wonder if he were on drugs. But all along it was just natural features of his learning style. What a relief!'

4. Patricia's nephew Len (Sponge, The Sensitive – Water, Initiator)

Len was having a very hard time with life and seemed on the verge of a breakdown. She talked to him about his learning style Profile and he was consoled. Len's words: 'With the Profile, I feel less isolated, as if someone really knows me.' His mother also read his Profile and thought she needed to translate the phrase 'One picture paints a thousand words', explaining it in more detail. He replied, 'Yes, Mum, I got it the first time – I always do.'

5. Bert's younger son Robert (Sonar, The Intuitive – Water, Adaptor)

When Robert was 11, his father was a psychologist and an NLP Practitioner who worked as a training consultant specializing in Learning to Learn. Through other assessments, he had identified the boy as 'musical, visually oriented, dreamy, a creative right-brain thinker'. But Bert had not observed the 'absorptive' quality of his son's learning dynamic. This fell into place like a missing puzzle piece. Within a week Robert was enjoying his dad's company with homework. They began using quite different language like 'imagination' and 'big picture'. Bert realized he had been looking, in generic terms, for what makes an effective learner but the models he had previously used had missed out the individual. He decided to stop trying to load 'his map of the world' onto his young son. This is a happy ending: At the age of 20, Robert is at university – studying installation art, 3-dimensional sculpture work creating atmospheres, situations, impressions. Perfect!

6. Bert's elder son John (Exec, The Organizer – Earth, Initiator)

Bert's elder son's story also has a happy ending. The father had looked at this model for his two sons and 'came away with a deeper appreciation for the enormous differences between their natural styles of learning'. He found the descriptions of his children's learning styles to be 'accurate with clear correlations to conventional assessments'. At that time John, aged 14 had been identified by conventional means as a 'left-brain logical, analytical' lad. Bert knew John was OK with the world and its ways. Now aged 23 John has completed his university course and is a trainee with a law firm. Also perfect! Had Bert expected (demanded?) the same from each of his boys and encouraged them from a single view of 'success' he would not now be the father of two creatively fulfilled young men.

7. Zoe (Sherlock, The Detective – Water, Sustainer)
and Crystal (Rex, The Dignified – Fire, Sustainer)

The mother is Zoe and the then 16-year-old daughter is Crystal. Both mother and daughter are Sustainers, each with a massively strong will, and each expecting the other to bow to it. Oh, the clashes! The Mercury Model was a revelation to Zoe and has helped her understand the issues which arise every time either of them speaks. They have come to recognize that they have different ways of thinking about things. They are committed to keeping their differences separate from their personal emotional bond, the shining light which has carried them through many years of 'mutual intractability'. Although it has never been smooth, they have never given up on each other. Crystal is now 25.

Their strategy is based on a perpetual positive intention to do enjoyable and creative projects together. It usually starts with tension and either they figure out how to work together or it ends in misconception and misunderstanding, which is eventually released over time. It's best when they decide to put one of them in charge – the one who originally conceived the project. If they arrive at an impasse, they try to remember that two chiefs can work together as long as they are coming from the same place. This either leads to a fight for control or offers the potential for a solution. And what does each want? Recognition of the value of what she has to offer.

Zoe's hints for others in a similar situation:

1. Maintain an appreciation of each other's strengths and inherent value.
2. Set aside judgement about right/wrong or how things should/should not be done.
3. Each needs to present things in a way the other can process (visual for water) and then be patient with each other during the processing, which can take some time.
4. Remember that different points of view can be a strength in any joint project.

8. Ann's son (Scout, The Trailblazer – Fire, Initiator)

Ann reported an incident that was amusing to her but deadly serious to her third son. The lad was very angry at her one morning when his sports uniform was not ready for the game. In her own defence she pointed out that he had not mentioned the match to her the previous afternoon when he'd brought home his dirty clothes. 'Mum' he said 'I showed you the schedule of our games my first week back to school. I told you once. I am not telling you every time.'

Ann understood her son's natural mental dynamics very well and for years strongly advocated for him in the schools. She recognized his need for activity and independence in order to stay interested and attentive in the classroom and she repeatedly recommended this approach to teachers. All he needed, she told them, was to occasionally stand up and take charge, to seize the initiative and spearhead a project of his own. One teacher (and only one) listened and tried it. He was a transformed boy! Student and teacher stopped butting heads, finally.

Part II

Variations and Background

Modifying Factors

Other Voices in Our Heads

As you have seen, the Mercury Model introduces and describes 12 fundamentally different styles of thinking, learning and communicating, pointing out that every mind resonates at one of 12 vibrations. As useful and helpful as this information may be, it does not tell the entire story. People are more individual than that. The whole of humanity does not fit into tidy classifications and we chafe against even the idea that we should do so. The first Part of this book represents the Mercury Model in a tremendously simplified form.

For the sake of completeness and for those readers who abhor the potential 'pigeon-holing' of classifications, let's look more deeply.

Subtones and individual mental uniqueness

Two minds which share the same primary tone learning style pulse at the same frequency, but they are probably not exactly the same. It is unusual, in fact a special case, for a mind to express as an absolutely pure example of one of the 12 learning styles. Usually people have additional mental influences, termed 'subtones', which contribute subtlety to the mind's overall makeup.

The scope for individual mental uniqueness is immense. A mind can be like:

- a clear solo note
- a simple musical chord involving one or two subtones combining with the primary tone
- a complex chord comprised of any combination of up to nine possible subtones.

More is neither better nor worse. It is the absence or presence of subtones and in specific combinations that relate to our mental uniqueness. We each have our own mind to enjoy and its qualities to contribute to the larger group.

A subtone makes its particular nature available to the overall mental makeup. For example, a subtone can supply Sustainer-style traits of persistence or stubbornness to a basically Adaptor mind, or an Earth-style practicality to an Air Family member. Subtone activity can give the appearance that a particular mind belongs to more than one Family within a Division, even though it does not. These additional factors can contribute not only proficiencies and virtues, but blind spots and shortcomings as well.

Like a primary tone learning style, each subtone is inherently neutral, being neither good nor bad. But any of them can at certain times behave very well or misbehave badly. Some subtones harmonize nicely with a primary tone learning style, supporting it with a similar viewpoint or mode. They naturally get along well together, figuratively producing a pleasant sounding chord. But, other subtones may be very, very different from each other or from a primary learning style, presenting a relationship dynamic inside one's head just as challenging as those sometimes encountered with other people. They spar with each other and vie for supremacy of world view or style. There can be an inner struggle, even if both are on their best behaviour.

This is critical to note: The primary tone – the basic learning style as it has been described in this book – runs the show; it's the boss. Subtones are employees. They stand in the same relationship as a team does to the team leader, an orchestra to its conductor, an athletic team to its coach, soldiers to their commanding officer, the crew to their captain. In each case the main man always has the final word. Despite the fierceness of a subtone's possible insistence about taking in some specific new information, the primary tone makes the final decision. It has the power of veto and ultimately plays the hand.

Here is an example: A Sonar, The Intuitive child will approach new ideas with relish, gleefully swimming around in the big pool of all information, absorbing freely of its bounty. If his mind also has a Sustainer subtone (Rex), he could have an uncharacteristic but excellent long-term memory for some items – those that have contributed to shaping his personal identity. But, most things will sink below the surface of specificity sooner or later and will be 'forgotten'.

On the other hand, a Rex, The Dignified child will approach new ideas with reserve, spontaneously perceiving which, if any, might be learned, taken to heart and kept there over the long term, adding important components to his personal identity. If his mind also has an Adaptor subtone (Sonar), it might sometimes drift toward the romantic, the poetic or the gentle, selectively searching for worthy new ideas.

The complexity of subtone analysis puts it beyond the scope of this book. The author will gladly provide information about 'in-depth' Profiles on request.

How it actually ticks

Another factor which is supplemental to the information provided thus far, and which perhaps is more important for adults than for children, relates to the wide gulf that can exist between how the mind actually works, on the one hand, and what we *wish* it would do for us on the other – the *attitude* we have about our mind, how we *think* it should function. Although this gulf can easily be identified and explored with more in-depth analysis, it's beyond the scope of intention here. This book deals with the actual mental dynamics themselves, not one's expectations.

Learning Versus Behaviour

Another area of potential confusion is the widespread blurring of the line between mental activity and behaviour. This can be tricky as behaviour is evident, even to the casual observer, while thinking and learning are not. Which part of the child are we describing? This book does not present insights about a child's behaviour. The mind is its own place.

Through Your Eyes

Here are a few pitfalls to very carefully avoid:

- mistaking the child's behavioural style for the learning style
- mistaking the child's other psychological/physical qualities (emotion, shyness, boldness, insecurity, poor hearing or vision, need to be liked or accepted, etc.) for learning style
- wishing for the child to have a different learning style, to make the adult's own life easier or to assert their own values
- conveying standards of acceptable performance which are incompatible with the child's natural mode.

The Mercury Model

What It Is and Where It Comes From

This Section is not for everyone. You do not have to involve yourself with it unless you want to. If you are quite happy with what you already know about the Mercury Model and you are ready to try it out on yourself, your family and friends, then just turn to the Assessment Tables on page 163 and go for it.

However, many readers' learning styles require an answer to this question. If your mind needs background material, all the details or the 'big picture', or if you simply enjoy new information, please read on. This Section is for you.

Let's look at the Model through two very different lenses – loosely, the art and the science: neither pure, both applied. Firstly

> *The Mercury Model blends the mythic and the archetypal.*

It assesses and describes our unique mental makeup by evaluating how we each experience the *mythic theme* of the ancient god Mercury, highly skilled in learning and communicating, as that theme is cast and costumed within the *archetypal pattern* Mercury expresses in our individual life.

And, secondly

> *The Mercury Model is a journey into the New Physics of thought.*

The New Physics looks at the energy fields or vibrations which underpin everything that exists in familiar 4-dimensional time/space. There is a subtle energy principle which is observable in all things 'mercurial'. That includes my mind, your mind, your children's minds and the spaces in between.

Do you wonder what that means? Then, please read on…

Traditional Wisdom

It all started a very long time ago in the dim recesses of history. Imagine those ancient times before television and street lighting, when our earliest ancestors might have given top billing to the starry night sky as the greatest show on earth. How else would they have occupied themselves during a long night?

With regular viewing it wouldn't have taken them too long to differentiate between planets and fixed stars. The five inner planets, Mercury, Venus, Mars, Jupiter and Saturn, all easily visible to the naked eye, move across the sky against an unchanging backdrop of the fixed stars. Interestingly, the word planet is said to come from the Greek *planasthi* meaning 'to wander'. Of course, we now know that planets are strictly confined to prescribed orbits around the sun. They are not really at liberty to wander; they have only a limited right to roam.

The fixed stars appear to be unmoving. Our early ancestors linked them into small groups, connecting the dots to form patterns, and then applied suitably descriptive names. Many are familiar to us today. Apparently, different cultures assigned the same stars to other clusters, generating a variety of meaningful images. These star clusters are the constellations.

Unrestricted by a materialist world view, and having never seen a big-screen Hollywood production, our ancestors looked up and identified stage settings, lead characters and storylines which have endured the test of time. Can you visualize parents telling their children the stories of the stars, linking the dots of light for them, pointing out the pictures and the patterns? Imagine generation after generation of parents repeating these stories, building what we now call an oral tradition.

Here are some examples. One northern constellation that never drops beneath the horizon, which is always present, all night, every night, is huge Orion, The Hunter. Children may have been told, and would later tell their own children, that The Hunter, big, reliable and armed, would perpetually look out for them and look after them from high above. The Warrior could provide an eternal example of courage,

Orion, The Hunter

fearlessness and strength. The Scales might serve as a reminder of justice and fair play. Polaris, the Pole Star, is positioned at the motionless centre, with all the other constellations of the night sky endlessly circling around it, like the peaceful and pivotal eye of the storm, a whirling dervish or a community flagpole. The stories undoubtedly conveyed comfort, warnings and guidance on how to live one's life, the moral principles of that age.

You will notice that the planets carry the names of ancient gods and goddesses, the big celebrities of those days. It was the elite, the larger-than-life immortals, who wandered hither and thither among the constellations of the night sky.

Jupiter was there hurling lightning bolts, his familiar calling card, a blast of insight to attract someone's attention. With evidence like that, who would not believe him to be top god. The attractive Venus, goddess of love, harmony and beauty, could grace any constellation into which she wandered or could incite the locals to battle. Of course, Mercury was there managing the messages, carrying bits of communication among the others. A quick, youthful, androgynous, prankster he was the ultimate in thinking, learning and communicating, the recognized master of instant messaging.

The planets were assigned top billing as the prime movers, the central characters, the mega-celebrities of the nocturnal drama. Each 'wanderer' came to personify the qualities and mythic themes that stood behind the god it represented. And although the names may have differed, the basic themes ran right through different cultures. For example, Venus was a Roman name, but she was called Aphrodite by the Greeks, Inanna by the Sumerians, Morning and Evening Star by the Mesopotamians, and simply the Goddess elsewhere.

Now what about the stage settings – where did our ancestors place the drama? Why, in the constellations, within the fixed star patterns created by linking the light dots. The cast of mythic heroes and heroines wandered, each at his or her own pace, through the star clusters which lay along their paths. They had experiences there: fell in love, engaged in conflict or combat, expressed creatively, ate their children or inherited untold wealth. Depending upon the star picture of the constellation, they were nurtured and helped, assisted others, ordered beheadings or were betrayed. The dramatic events depended upon the interpretation our ancestors had given to the constellation, how they saw and related to the connected dot patterns.

We find the levels of meaning they assigned to the star patterns went way beyond the personal. Neither ordinary nor commonplace, the ideas had universal scope. We would refer to them as *archetypal*. Let me clarify that term. The constellations identified and named by our distant forebears carry archetypal meaning for us. They represent or are examples of the big, familiar classic unifying ideas or standards that are evident throughout human history and also in individual lives. Archetypes have long-term continuity – themes conveyed by drawings discovered on cave walls still find expression today in musical patterns, in literature, art and film. These are notions we tend to understand without a great deal of explanation. For example, most of us instantly know when we encounter the unmistakably nurturing energy of a woman who is an archetypal 'Earth Mother'. Similarly, without needing an explanation, we recognize the disciplined, authoritative, highly organized feel of a high-powered chief executive – a 'Suit'. We can learn to quickly identify archetypal behaviour patterns whenever we see them, in individuals, in a country's national stereotypes or on our favourite TV series. Some examples are: The Lightweight or Butterfly, The Heavyweight or Bully, The Poet, The Scientist, The Courtesan, The Warrior/Soldier, The Compassionate One or The Victim.

Perhaps these big themes have always lived within our shared humanity or race memory, even from the beginning.

*Possibly the archetypes sprang fully developed from
the hearts of our predecessors and were projected onto
the shapes they saw in the starry night skies, where
they found correspondence and representation.*

From there, having entered the oral tradition, the archetypes passed to
us through the generations as stories.

But, the stellar patterns not only provided a structure to help our
ancestors organize their universe and beliefs, they also became long-
term storage vaults for the messages and the mythologies of their
cultures. The stories were placed by repetition in the night sky for safe-
keeping. The storage must have been reliable and sufficient. They are
still there. Stellar patterns still supply a visual key through the ages to
the universal truths of the human condition; archetypes still reside in
the stars. And the wandering planets still represent the mythic themes
of the ancient gods.

Modern people, possibly oblivious to the similarities, tend to dismiss
the richness held in these ancient safety-deposit boxes, having created
their own more up-to-date repositories for similar kinds of information.
Oddly enough the same big themes reoccur in our modern stories today.
TV programmes, films, plays, literature, dance and music itself as well
as music videos and concerts all present characters we might recognize
as The Hunter, The Warrior and The Scales if we looked into it.

And now back to our predecessors. Sooner or later some astute ancestor
of yours or mine would have tried to look for the practical applications
of the night-time observations – to bring the sky down to earth.

For example, someone first noticed that when the position of sunset
in its yearly trek toward the north began to fall back toward the south,
then the long summer days would soon give way to long cold winter
nights – time to migrate.

And at some point long ago an independent-minded farmer first
realized a successful harvest by anticipating, awaiting and then planting
according to primetime seed-sowing indicators in the night sky. Today
some still follow these old ways and call it planting by the moon. Also,
there would have been a first time when star-gazing coastal families
correctly foresaw an extremely high tide and took appropriate safety
measures.

*Those far distant ancestors had begun to observe
correlations between celestial bodies above and events
in their lives.*

They made the first entries in humanity's oldest database, the ancient
empirical database, the body of observations, subsequently accumulated
and recorded by the intellectuals of every culture on the planet, which
correlate planetary positions and movements above with the natural and
human worlds on earth below.

*They were the parents of modern astronomy and
astrology.*

During the intervening centuries the study they initiated has been for-
malized as we have matured both philosophically and technologically. The
early nomadic and agrarian observers were joined by philosophers and
scholars. In time, the once unified field of study diverged – astronomy
now involves itself with celestial observation, measurement and specu-
lation about origins while astrology correlates positions of celestial bodies
with events on earth, seeking interpretation and meaning.

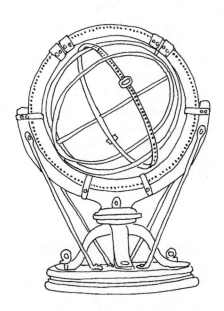

The work by Pythagoras in the 6th century BC is still the basis of the philosophy of astrology. Plato (ca.428–348 BC) then built a great deal of astrological theory on the foundation supplied by Pythagoras. Surfing through the centuries, we find many other respected scholars who made their contribution. A notable example was Ptolemy, who lived in Alexandria in the 2nd century and had the vast resources of its famous library available to him. He produced texts which summarized all the astrological work of the Mesopotamians and Greeks and which were the authoritative references on the sky for the next 1,500 years.

In medieval times many scholars were also astrologers. In the 13th century Thomas Aquinas wrote about correlations between planetary positions and human nature, during times when astrology was interwoven in the fabric of Christianity. Kepler and Galileo were both astrological advisers at court. Despite the ebb and flow of popular opinion, astrology has always enjoyed a most illustrious following. We have refined our methods of observation and measurement since the early days. Today we need not even venture outdoors, let alone hope for a cloudless night, as we now have computer-generated reference material listing precise positions of the sun, moon and planets of our solar system as well as a wealth of supporting information.

Modern astrologers have the legacy of this ancient database, accumulated over the centuries by all major cultures of the world. It provides both a foundation and a springboard for continuing research along current lines. Today's astrologers rarely advise on the likely outcome of a joust but then their ancient counterparts were seldom consulted about stock-trading trends.

The extensive body of empirical knowledge is available to support any field in which the understanding of individual human qualities is beneficial: management training, human resource development, education, psychology and counselling, health, personal growth, career and marriage guidance. Now it can benefit your family through the *Mercury Model*.

The New Physics

Shifting now to the somewhat more scientific lens, the *Mercury Model* is a journey into the New Physics of thought.

The New Physics will ultimately result in a full-scale scientific paradigm shift, not unlike the one which resulted from Einstein's insights into relativity and Schrödinger's recognition of the mathematics of quantum mechanics. The New Physics is currently a groundswell of innovative rethinking about energy. It provides an alternative vision of a host of topics through a totally different perspective: matter has an energetic component, but the space between material objects does as well.

> *We are energetic beings who live in a sea of*
> *interconnected, pulsing vibrations.*

While certain practical applications of this thinking already make our modern world go around (i-Pods, BlackBerry and Bluetooth wireless technologies), some are still considered fringe in certain circles, but life-saving or life-enhancing in others. Many look to the New Physics to explain what has previously baffled us. This includes energy medicine and alternative therapies like homeopathy and acupuncture, mind/body/ spirit work such as meditation, intention and prayer, the Zero Point Field work and all its top-notch research, and certainly astrology. The revolution is just around the corner.

We cannot see energy. We can, however, observe its effects. During his interaction with the famous apple Sir Isaac Newton observed the effects of gravity. The apple fell, but the gravitational force itself was invisible. Our senses cannot detect the energy of magnetism, but we have all learned that opposite magnetic poles attract each other while the same poles repel. And although we cannot see, hear, smell, taste or feel the energetic radiation called gamma rays, we certainly know about their very powerful effects. Radiotherapists focus and direct beams of them at cancerous tumours.

We have come to understand these energies, gravity, magnetism and radioactivity, by seeing how they behave. We now accept them, no longer doubting their existence just because they are invisible to our ordinary senses. This was not always the case. As we continue to push against the frontiers of knowledge, we will certainly discover other types of energies. And if history is repetitive, it is likely that the new ones will not meet with open-hearted acceptance – initially.

Essential Mercury – a subtle energy

Here is a concept, not in ordinary use at the moment – the subtle energy principle. Like other energies, an energy principle is not visible to our ordinary senses, but we can demonstrate its existence by observing its behaviour. An energy principle is the subtle version of a particular theme; it is the essence common to all expressions of that theme, and themes are dynamic processes. Consider, for example, the action of alternating tension and relaxation or the lively activities of solidification or attraction. An unexpressed energy principle is as vague or tenuous as gravity when it has nothing to act upon. Gravity came to life and expressed itself visibly when Newton's apple fell, but it was still a force prior to that instant. Similarly, a subtle energy principle becomes obvious only when it proclaims itself or 'comes to rest' by interacting with matter. Then we can see hints of its existence – energetically expressing a particular theme through the variety of different vehicles in which it settles. We can come to know the underlying principle by spotting its theme, by observing where and how it expresses in nature, and by glimpsing it in as many ways as possible. We have to peer at it.

To view the *Mercury Model* through the lens of the New Physics, I wish to introduce the subtle energy principle which underpins this book, and name it *Essential Mercury* or *EM* for short. To search for evidence of the elusive *EM*, let us consider 'all things mercurial', the multitude of containers in which it finds expression.

Certainly we could start with the metallic element called mercury. All metals are physical forms which provide suitable grounding points for particular subtle energies. We could examine mercury's chemical behaviour and physical properties, its colour and appearance, the locations and the chemical forms in which it naturally occurs, the uses we have found for it in society, etc. Defining the vehicle in which the energy principle is 'comfortable' informs us about its essential nature.

In our search for evidence of *EM* we could consider the planet called Mercury. Each planet in our solar system bears a symbolic correspondence with a metallic element, a musical note, a colour, a chakra point in our bodies, and more. Furthermore, we can identify suitable vehicles which provide grounding for *EM* among animals, in plants, in the realm of biochemistry and in ourselves.

Essential Mercury is the quintessence of the planet in orbit around our sun, and central to any meaning the planet has to either astronomers or astrologers. *EM* is even more transcendent than the mythic figure of the ancient god, his qualities or activities. Standing behind these evident and esoteric expressions, back behind planets and mythologies, *Essential Mercury* is a subtle energy principle which is universal, cosmic, immense and part of nature. All of its expressions include the key features of levity, agility and quickness.

Essential Mercury – where it proclaims itself

- Mercury the *planet* is the innermost wanderer in our solar system and the fastest moving, taking only 88 days to journey around the sun. Sometimes it even appears to go backward along its orbital path – three times a year for about three weeks per episode.
- Mercury the *element* is 'quicksilver', the only metal that is liquid at room temperature. As its nickname suggests it is always in motion, never stopping. It is so adventurous that if left alone in an uncovered container, it leaves, it evaporates into the atmosphere. If poured from a container, quicksilver breaks into tiny balls which dash about making contact with everything from dust to dog hair. Then, with just the slightest encouragement, it will coalesce again into a large pool. All the tiny silver balls reconnect, forming something akin to a multinational union, incorporating the dust and all. In chemical reactions it is often used as a catalyst, fostering 'communication' pathways between reactants. Mercury has a rapid response to temperature and pressure fluctuations and is useful in thermometers and barometers. As mercury is a metal, it conducts electricity, and is used in scientific and electronic equipment, even in fluorescent tubes.
- Mercury in *music* is quick, light and staccato. Its sounds have short wavelengths. All wind instruments capture Mercury's essential nature as they depend on the rhythm of breath. Striking examples are Vivaldi's recorder and oboe concerti.
- Mercury *animals* have swift disconnected movements exemplified by songbirds, squirrels, monkeys, crows, parrots and all flying insects and especially butterflies.
- Mercury in *literature* is seen in adventurous characters who convey youthful and light-hearted curiosity – 'I wonder what

today will bring!' Examples include the *puer aeternus* (eternal child) theme discussed by Carl Jung, Dorothy in *The Wizard of Oz*, *The Lion, The Witch and The Wardrobe*, *Peter Pan* and *Swallows and Amazons*.

- Mercury in *esoterica* is exemplified by The Fool card of the tarot deck, the astrological sign of Gemini, and the brow chakra at the third eye.
- Mercury in *us* has a special relationship with the brain, nervous system, lungs, oxygen and other blood gases, all the sensory organs, which are the information receptors. *EM* allows us to live, to breathe and to perceive.

Essential Mercury and the ancient god of communication
In ancient Greek mythology, Hermes was the handsome young messenger and herald of the gods. He alone had totally free mobility and access to both Zeus, his father on high, and to Pluto in the depth of the underworld. (Between the heights of the superconscious and the depths of the subconscious resides our conscious awareness.) With his swiftness and agility, portrayed by a winged helmet and sandals, the quicksilver-tongued Hermes guided writers, speakers, teachers, travellers, traders and tricksters.

Renamed Mercury by the Romans, he inherited the role – god of eloquence and manager of messages. This universal mythic theme is found in many cultures, going under different names, for example the Norse Woden, the Egyptian Thoth and the Indian Ganesh.

Essential Mercury and the astrological symbol
In astrology, the planet Mercury symbolizes all the mental dynamics: learning, thinking, sharing, receiving, processing and communicating information. It represents conscious intelligence, our own particular logic and our pattern of consciousness.

Mercury corresponds with the uniquely human powers of reflection and speech – our ability to plan, organize, name and categorize objects. It represents our need to be understood by another person, the urge to establish contact in true give-and-take information exchange.

Like the breath, the inflow is perception while the outflow is the urge to express our thoughts.

The fleet-footed courier of information has been represented artistically over the centuries, in stylized drawings, classic paintings and elegant sculptures. Even a simple feather has conveyed the image of thought taking flight.

Still evident today, the mercurial theme is symbolized on British Telecom public phone booths, an enduring emblem of the winged bearer of communications.

Essential Mercury and the Mercury Model

When it comes to exploring the New Physics, we do not have a firm foundation – yet. We are cautiously moving over the thin ice of the new. Without accepted laws or even well-phrased theories, but fully aware that something important is going on here, we can return to basic scientific practice and involve ourselves in empirical observation. If we cannot see, feel, taste or measure subtle energy directly, we can still observe it in action and watch its effects. We can follow in the well-positioned footsteps of post-Newtonian students of gravity and of Marie Curie's early students of ionizing radiation. Hopefully, we too can come to understand the energy by seeing how it behaves. We can collect data, take note of evident correlations and test them.

We cannot directly measure the subtle energy principle, *Essential Mercury*. But, we can experience it as it expresses through the planet, the metal, specific animals, music, literature, and ourselves.

The subtle energy principle called *Essential Mercury* comes to rest within and proclaims itself through every one of us. It must be one of our operating programs. *EM* contains features that are attributable to the human mind. As children and adults we perceive, learn, think and share information, exhibiting mercurial qualities. It's universal, but it's not uniform. We are different; we each have a learning style.

The observable fact is that one's learning style, the specific archetypal manner in which *EM* operates through a person, correlates with the zodiacal position of the planet Mercury at the person's birth. Further investigation reveals the presence and specific blend of subtones, which pinpoint individual mental uniqueness. Does *Essential Mercury* somehow enliven or vitalize the archetypal qualities filed in the stars over the centuries? It is quite possible for many people to use the Mercury Model and the benefits it offers to individuals and families without further consideration of its intricacies. Others are going to need to push against the outer boundary of current human knowledge to find out why and how it works.

The Big Picture

Part III

Identify a Learning Style

Worksheet

Your Family Learning Tree

Family member	Learning Style	Reaction	Approach	Mode of Uptake
Example: Mother	Exec, The Achiever	Container	Initiator	Earth

Reaction Division:
        Sharers:
        Containers:

Approach Division
        Initiators:
        Sustainers:
        Adaptors:

Mode of Uptake Division
        Fire:
        Air:
        Water:
        Earth:

Tensions to address:

Assessment Tables

Identify Primary Learning Styles

These Tables show the date and time in GMT (Greenwich Mean Time) when the planet Mercury passed from one zodiacal sign to another, when the ancient god Mercury changed his costume and his mood, and when the archetypal pattern behind the mercurial qualities shifted from one learning style to another. During the time between listings one learning style archetype prevails.

Using the Table for 1915 as an example, the learning style of anyone born between midnight on 1 January and 4:28 AM on 15 January is Exec, The Achiever.

Shifts from one learning style archetype to another occur on average about 14 times each year. To assign the learning style for a person born on one of those particular days, the time of birth has to be taken into account. This is not necessary for people born on the other 351 days per year.

Continuing to use 1915 as an example, a person born on 15 January, before 4:28 AM GMT, would have the learning style of Exec, The Achiever. However, if the birth occurred after 4:28 AM, we would be looking at Boffin, The Innovator. And Boffin, The Innovator would be the learning style for everyone born from then until 10:33 AM on 2 February.

1915

Date	Time	Style	Reaction	Approach	Uptake
Jan lst	0:00 AM	Exec – The Achiever	Container	Initiator	Earth
Jan 15th	4:28 AM	Boffin – The Innovator	Sharer	Sustainer	Air
Feb 2nd	10:33 AM	Sonar – The Intuitive	Container	Adaptor	Water
Feb 23rd	3:13 PM	Boffin – The Innovator	Sharer	Sustainer	Air
Mar 19th	8:46 AM	Sonar – The Intuitive	Container	Adaptor	Water
April 10th	7:22 PM	Scout – The Trailblazer	Sharer	Initiator	Fire
April 26th	9:40 PM	Steady – The Vault	Container	Sustainer	Earth
May 10th	11:47 PM	Buzz – The Curious	Sharer	Adaptor	Air
May 29th	10:34 AM	Sponge – The Sensitive	Container	Initiator	Water
Aug 4th	9:00 AM	Rex – The Dignified	Sharer	Sustainer	Fire
Aug 19th	4:38 AM	Details – The Analyst	Container	Adaptor	Earth
Sept 5th	9:02 AM	ProCon – The Diplomat	Sharer	Initiator	Air
Sept 28th	8:11 AM	Sherlock – The Detective	Container	Sustainer	Water
Oct 21st	1:13 AM	ProCon – The Diplomat	Sharer	Initiator	Air
Nov 11th	2:08 PM	Sherlock – The Detective	Container	Sustainer	Water
Dec 1st	9:18 AM	Flash – The Pioneer	Sharer	Adaptor	Fire
Dec 20th	11:14 AM	Exec – The Achiever	Container	Initiator	Earth

1916

Date	Time	Style	Reaction	Approach	Uptake
Jan 1st	0:00 AM	Exec – The Achiever	Container	Initiator	Earth
Jan 8th	1:22 AM	Boffin – The Innovator	Sharer	Sustainer	Air
Mar 15th	12:08 AM	Sonar – The Intuitive	Container	Adaptor	Water
April 2nd	11:00 AM	Scout – The Trailblazer	Sharer	Initiator	Fire
April 17th	11:00 AM	Steady – The Vault	Container	Sustainer	Earth
May 2nd	4:14 PM	Buzz – The Curious	Sharer	Adaptor	Air
July 10th	6:17 PM	Sponge – The Sensitive	Container	Initiator	Water
July 26th	1:42 AM	Rex – The Dignified	Sharer	Sustainer	Fire
Aug 10th	4:04 AM	Details – The Analyst	Container	Adaptor	Earth
Aug 29th	4:52 AM	ProCon – The Diplomat	Sharer	Initiator	Air
Nov 4th	12:25 PM	Sherlock – The Detective	Container	Sustainer	Water
Nov 23rd	3:40 AM	Flash – The Pioneer	Sharer	Adaptor	Fire
Dec 12th	7:13 AM	Exec – The Achiever	Container	Initiator	Earth

1917

Date	Time	Style	Reaction	Approach	Uptake
Jan 1st	0:00 AM	Exec – The Achiever	Container	Initiator	Earth
Jan 1st	5:07 PM	Boffin – The Innovator	Sharer	Sustainer	Air
Jan 18th	4:20 AM	Exec – The Achiever	Container	Initiator	Earth
Feb15th	3:20 AM	Boffin – The Innovator	Sharer	Sustainer	Air
Mar 8th	3:34 PM	Sonar – The Intuitive	Container	Adaptor	Water
Mar 25th	11:35 AM	Scout – The Trailblazer	Sharer	Initiator	Fire
April 9th	5:43 AM	Steady – The Vault	Container	Sustainer	Earth
June 14th	6:14 PM	Buzz – The Curious	Sharer	Adaptor	Air
July 3rd	10:27 AM	Sponge – The Sensitive	Container	Initiator	Water
July 17th	1:26 PM	Rex – The Dignified	Sharer	Sustainer	Fire
Aug 2nd	7:31 PM	Details – The Analyst	Container	Adaptor	Earth
Aug 26th	10:50 PM	ProCon – The Diplomat	Sharer	Initiator	Air
Sept 14th	11:41 AM	Details – The Analyst	Container	Sustainer	Water
Oct 10th	4:48 AM	ProCon – The Diplomat	Sharer	Initiator	Air
Oct 28th	5:23 AM	Sherlock – The Detective	Container	Sustainer	Water
Nov 15th	9:29 PM	Flash – The Pioneer	Sharer	Adaptor	Fire
Dec 5th	4:57PM	Exec – The Achiever	Container	Initiator	Earth

1918

Date	Time	Style	Reaction	Approach	Uptake
Jan 1st	0:00 AM	Exec – The Achiever	Container	Initiator	Earth
Feb 10th	9:24 AM	Boffin – The Innovator	Sharer	Sustainer	Air
Mar 1st	7:52 AM	Sonar – The Intuitive	Container	Adaptor	Water
Mar 17th	7:24 AM	Scout – The Trailblazer	Sharer	Initiator	Fire
April 2nd	1:15 PM	Steady – The Vault	Container	Sustainer	Earth
June 10th	1:22 AM	Buzz – The Curious	Sharer	Adaptor	Air
June 24th	11:50 PM	Sponge – The Sensitive	Container	Initiator	Water
July 9th	8:39 AM	Rex – The Dignified	Sharer	Sustainer	Fire
July 28th	1:27 AM	Details – The Analyst	Container	Adaptor	Earth
Oct 3rd	8:59 AM	ProCon – The Diplomat	Sharer	Initiator	Air
Oct 20th	4:47 PM	Sherlock – The Detective	Container	Sustainer	Water
Nov 8th	10:06 PM	Flash – The Pioneer	Sharer	Adaptor	Fire
Dec 1st	4:19 PM	Exec – The Achiever	Container	Initiator	Earth
Dec 15th	12:20 PM	Flash – The Pioneer	Sharer	Adaptor	Fire

1919

Date	Time	Style	Reaction	Approach	Uptake
Jan 1st	0:00 AM	Flash – The Pioneer	Sharer	Adaptor	Fire
Jan 13th	6:13 PM	Exec – The Achiever	Container	Initiator	Earth
Feb 3rd	7:27 PM	Boffin – The Innovator	Sharer	Sustainer	Air
Feb 21st	2:10 PM	Sonar – The Intuitive	Container	Adaptor	Water
Mar 9th	10:42 AM	Scout – The Trailblazer	Sharer	Initiator	Fire
May 16th	2:25 AM	Steady – The Vault	Container	Sustainer	Earth
June 2nd	11:06 AM	Buzz – The Curious	Sharer	Adaptor	Air
June 16th	8:44 AM	Sponge – The Sensitive	Container	Initiator	Water
July 2nd	2:02 AM	Rex – The Dignified	Sharer	Sustainer	Fire
Sept 9th	3:43 AM	Details – The Analyst	Container	Adaptor	Earth
Sept 25th	2:16 PM	ProCon – The Diplomat	Sharer	Initiator	Air
Oct 13th	7:25 AM	Sherlock – The Detective	Container	Sustainer	Water
Nov 2nd	7:07 PM	Flash – The Pioneer	Sharer	Adaptor	Fire

1920

Date	Time	Style	Reaction	Approach	Uptake
Jan 1st	0:00 AM	Flash – The Pioneer	Sharer	Adaptor	Fire
Jan 8th	5:55 AM	Exec – The Achiever	Container	Initiator	Earth
Jan 27th	1:49 PM	Boffin – The Innovator	Sharer	Sustainer	Air
Feb 13th	6:41 PM	Sonar – The Intuitive	Container	Adaptor	Water
Mar 2nd	7:25 PM	Scout – The Trailblazer	Sharer	Initiator	Fire
Mar 19th	4:15 PM	Sonar – The Intuitive	Container	Adaptor	Water
April 17th	6:06 PM	Scout – The Trailblazer	Sharer	Initiator	Fire
May 8th	11:55 PM	Steady – The Vault	Container	Sustainer	Earth
May 24th	12:32 AM	Buzz – The Curious	Sharer	Adaptor	Air
June 7th	3:02 AM	Sponge – The Sensitive	Container	Initiator	Water
June 26th	12:30 PM	Rex – The Dignified	Sharer	Sustainer	Fire
Aug 2nd	10:30 PM	Sponge – The Sensitive	Container	Initiator	Water
Aug 10th	9:10 AM	Rex – The Dignified	Sharer	Sustainer	Fire
Aug 31st	6:29 PM	Details – The Analyst	Container	Adaptor	Earth
Sept 16th	5:13 PM	ProCon – The Diplomat	Sharer	Initiator	Air
Oct 5th	9:27 AM	Sherlock – The Detective	Container	Sustainer	Water
Oct 30th	12:40 PM	Flash – The Pioneer	Sharer	Adaptor	Fire
Nov 10th	7:00 PM	Sherlock – The Detective	Container	Sustainer	Water
Dec 11th	4:37 AM	Flash – The Pioneer	Sharer	Adaptor	Fire
Dec 31st	11:22 AM	Exec – The Achiever	Container	Initiator	Earth

1921

Date	Time	Style	Reaction	Approach	Uptake
Jan 1st	0:00 AM	Exec – The Achiever	Container	Initiator	Earth
Jan 19th	2:28 AM	Boffin – The Innovator	Sharer	Sustainer	Air
Feb 5th	10:14 AM	Sonar – The Intuitive	Container	Adaptor	Water
April 14th	2:12 AM	Scout – The Trailblazer	Sharer	Initiator	Fire
May 1st	7:03 AM	Steady – The Vault	Container	Sustainer	Earth
May 15th	10:09 AM	Buzz – The Curious	Sharer	Adaptor	Air
May 31st	5:12 AM	Sponge – The Sensitive	Container	Initiator	Water
Aug 8th	7:42 AM	Rex – The Dignified	Sharer	Sustainer	Fire
Aug 23rd	1:54 PM	Details – The Analyst	Container	Adaptor	Earth
Sept 9th	2:37 AM	ProCon – The Diplomat	Sharer	Initiator	Air
Sept 29th	4:01 PM	Sherlock – The Detective	Container	Sustainer	Water
Dec 5th	12:28 AM	Flash – The Pioneer	Sharer	Adaptor	Fire
Dec 24th	6:45 AM	Exec – The Achiever	Container	Initiator	Earth

1922

Date	Time	Style	Reaction	Approach	Uptake
Jan 1st	0:00 AM	Exec – The Achiever	Container	Initiator	Earth
Jan 11th	4:58 PM	Boffin – The Innovator	Sharer	Sustainer	Air
Feb 1st	5:47 PM	Sonar – The Intuitive	Container	Adaptor	Water
Feb 9th	3:39 AM	Boffin – The Innovator	Sharer	Sustainer	Air
Mar 18th	6:32 AM	Sonar – The Intuitive	Container	Adaptor	Water
April 7th	10:22 AM	Scout – The Trailblazer	Sharer	Initiator	Fire
April 22nd	11:19 PM	Steady – The Vault	Container	Sustainer	Earth
May 7th	7:03 AM	Buzz – The Curious	Sharer	Adaptor	Air
June 1st	3:06 AM	Sponge – The Sensitive	Container	Initiator	Water
June 10th	9:54 PM	Buzz – The Curious	Sharer	Adaptor	Air
July 13th	8:04 PM	Sponge – The Sensitive	Container	Initiator	Water
July 31st	1:25 PM	Rex – The Dignified	Sharer	Sustainer	Fire
Aug 15th	8:59 AM	Details – The Analyst	Container	Adaptor	Earth
Sept 2nd	4:20 AM	ProCon – The Diplomat	Sharer	Initiator	Air
Oct 1st	9:08 AM	Sherlock – The Detective	Container	Sustainer	Water
Oct 5th	1:04 AM	ProCon – The Diplomat	Sharer	Initiator	Air
Nov 8th	10:32 PM	Sherlock – The Detective	Container	Sustainer	Water
Nov 27th	11:05 PM	Flash – The Pioneer	Sharer	Adaptor	Fire
Dec 17th	12:27 AM	Exec – The Achiever	Container	Initiator	Earth

1923

Date	Time	Style	Reaction	Approach	Uptake
Jan 1st	0:00 AM	Exec – The Achiever	Container	Initiator	Earth
Jan 4th	11:40 PM	Boffin – The Innovator	Sharer	Sustainer	Air
Feb 6th	5:08 PM	Exec – The Achiever	Container	Initiator	Earth
Feb 13th	11:24 PM	Boffin – The Innovator	Sharer	Sustainer	Air
Mar 13th	2:36 AM	Sonar – The Intuitive	Container	Adaptor	Water
Mar 30th	6:09 PM	Scout – The Trailblazer	Sharer	Initiator	Fire
April 14th	12:58 PM	Steady – The Vault	Container	Sustainer	Earth
May 1st	5:18 AM	Buzz – The Curious	Sharer	Adaptor	Air
July 8th	12:47 PM	Sponge – The Sensitive	Container	Initiator	Water
July 23rd	2:07 AM	Rex – The Dignified	Sharer	Sustainer	Fire
Aug 7th	1:33 PM	Details – The Analyst	Container	Adaptor	Earth
Aug 27th	10:30 PM	ProCon – The Diplomat	Sharer	Initiator	Air
Oct 4th	1:19 PM	Details – The Analyst	Container	Sustainer	Water
Oct 11th	10:23 PM	ProCon – The Diplomat	Sharer	Initiator	Air
Nov 2nd	2:47 AM	Sherlock – The Detective	Container	Sustainer	Water
Nov 20th	4:26 PM	Flash – The Pioneer	Sharer	Adaptor	Fire
Dec 10th	12:18 AM	Exec – The Achiever	Container	Initiator	Earth

1924

Date	Time	Style	Reaction	Approach	Uptake
Jan 1st	0:00 AM	Exec – The Achiever	Container	Initiator	Earth
Feb 14th	3:18 AM	Boffin – The Innovator	Sharer	Sustainer	Air
Mar 5th	5:53 AM	Sonar – The Intuitive	Container	Adaptor	Water
Mar 21st	3:37 PM	Scout – The Trailblazer	Sharer	Initiator	Fire
April 5th	4:23 PM	Steady – The Vault	Container	Sustainer	Earth
June 13th	1:42 AM	Buzz – The Curious	Sharer	Adaptor	Air
June 29th	1:22 PM	Sponge – The Sensitive	Container	Initiator	Water
July 13th	3:38 PM	Rex – The Dignified	Sharer	Sustainer	Fire
July 30th	4:48 PM	Details – The Analyst	Container	Adaptor	Earth
Oct 7th	4:12 AM	ProCon – The Diplomat	Sharer	Initiator	Air
Oct 24th	3:59 PM	Sherlock – The Detective	Container	Sustainer	Water
Nov 12th	12:08 PM	Flash – The Pioneer	Sharer	Adaptor	Fire
Dec 2nd	11:41 PM	Exec – The Achiever	Container	Initiator	Earth
Dec 31st	4:35 PM	Flash – The Pioneer	Sharer	Adaptor	Fire

1925

Date	Time	Style	Reaction	Approach	Uptake
Jan 1st	0:00 AM	Flash – The Pioneer	Sharer	Adaptor	Fire
Jan 14th	7:16 AM	Exec – The Achiever	Container	Initiator	Earth
Feb 7th	8:12 AM	Boffin – The Innovator	Sharer	Sustainer	Air
Feb 25th	4:53 PM	Sonar – The Intuitive	Container	Adaptor	Water
Mar 13th	12:36 PM	Scout – The Trailblazer	Sharer	Initiator	Fire
April 1st	3:21 PM	Steady – The Vault	Container	Sustainer	Earth
April 15th	11:09 PM	Scout – The Trailblazer	Sharer	Initiator	Fire
May 17th	1:32 AM	Steady – The Vault	Container	Sustainer	Earth
June 6th	3:23 PM	Buzz – The Curious	Sharer	Adaptor	Air
June 20th	11:07 PM	Sponge – The Sensitive	Container	Initiator	Water
July 5th	5:52 PM	Rex – The Dignified	Sharer	Sustainer	Fire
July 26th	11:46 AM	Details – The Analyst	Container	Adaptor	Earth
Aug 27th	6:46 AM	Rex – The Dignified	Sharer	Sustainer	Fire
Sept 11th	5:09 AM	Details – The Analyst	Container	Adaptor	Earth
Sept 29th	6:04 PM	ProCon – The Diplomat	Sharer	Initiator	Air
Oct 17th	3:52 AM	Sherlock – The Detective	Container	Sustainer	Water
Nov 5th	6:54 PM	Flash – The Pioneer	Sharer	Adaptor	Fire

1926

Date	Time	Style	Reaction	Approach	Uptake
Jan 1st	0:00	Flash – The Pioneer	Sharer	Adaptor	Fire
Jan 11th	7:27 AM	Exec – The Achiever	Container	Initiator	Earth
Jan 31st	10:04 AM	Boffin – The Innovator	Sharer	Sustainer	Air
Feb 17th	9:30 PM	Sonar – The Intuitive	Container	Adaptor	Water
Mar 6th	2:57 AM	Scout – The Trailblazer	Sharer	Initiator	Fire
May 13th	10:53 AM	Steady – The Vault	Container	Sustainer	Earth
May 29th	1:51 PM	Buzz – The Curious	Sharer	Adaptor	Air
June 12th	10:08 AM	Sponge – The Sensitive	Container	Initiator	Water
June 29th	5:01 AM	Rex – The Dignified	Sharer	Sustainer	Fire
Sept 5th	8:33 PM	Details – The Analyst	Container	Adaptor	Earth
Sept 21st	8:57 PM	ProCon – The Diplomat	Sharer	Initiator	Air
Oct 9th	9:58 PM	Sherlock – The Detective	Container	Sustainer	Water
Oct 31st	11:01 AM	Flash – The Pioneer	Sharer	Adaptor	Fire
Nov 28th	5:27 AM	Sherlock – The Detective	Container	Sustainer	Water
Dec 13th	8:38 PM	Flash – The Pioneer	Sharer	Adaptor	Fire

1927

Date	Time	Style	Reaction	Approach	Uptake
Jan 1st	0:00 AM	Flash – The Pioneer	Sharer	Adaptor	Fire
Jan 5th	1:58 AM	Exec – The Achiever	Container	Initiator	Earth
Jan 24th	1:13 AM	Boffin – The Innovator	Sharer	Sustainer	Air
Feb 10th	4:28 AM	Sonar – The Intuitive	Container	Adaptor	Water
April 17th	12:24 PM	Scout – The Trailblazer	Sharer	Initiator	Fire
May 6th	11:28 AM	Steady – The Vault	Container	Sustainer	Earth
May 21st	12:03 AM	Buzz – The Curious	Sharer	Adaptor	Air
June 4th	1:38 PM	Sponge – The Sensitive	Container	Initiator	Water
June 28th	7:33 PM	Rex – The Dignified	Sharer	Sustainer	Fire
July 14th	3:50 AM	Sponge – The Sensitive	Container	Initiator	Water
Aug 12th	3:43 AM	Rex – The Dignified	Sharer	Sustainer	Fire
Aug 28th	11:07 PM	Details – The Analyst	Container	Adaptor	Earth
Sept 14th	1:37 AM	ProCon – The Diplomat	Sharer	Initiator	Air
Oct 3rd	8:38 AM	Sherlock – The Detective	Container	Sustainer	Water
Dec 9th	9:26 AM	Flash – The Pioneer	Sharer	Adaptor	Fire
Dec 29th	1:48 AM	Exec – The Achiever	Container	Initiator	Earth

1928

Date	Time	Style	Reaction	Approach	Uptake
Jan 1st	0:00 AM	Exec – The Achiever	Container	Initiator	Earth
Jan 16th	1:35 PM	Boffin – The Innovator	Sharer	Sustainer	Air
Feb 3rd	10:22 AM	Sonar – The Intuitive	Container	Adaptor	Water
Feb 29th	6:26 AM	Boffin – The Innovator	Sharer	Sustainer	Air
Mar 18th	2:45 AM	Sonar – The Intuitive	Container	Adaptor	Water
April 11th	1:55 AM	Scout – The Trailblazer	Sharer	Initiator	Fire
April 27th	10:35 AM	Steady – The Vault	Container	Sustainer	Earth
May 11th	12:07 PM	Buzz – The Curious	Sharer	Adaptor	Air
May 28th	11:03 PM	Sponge – The Sensitive	Container	Initiator	Water
Aug 4th	8:00 PM	Rex – The Dignified	Sharer	Sustainer	Fire
Aug 19th	4:59 PM	Details – The Analyst	Container	Adaptor	Earth
Sept 5th	4:20 PM	ProCon – The Diplomat	Sharer	Initiator	Air
Sept 27th	6:12 PM	Sherlock – The Detective	Container	Sustainer	Water
Oct 24th	9:45 PM	ProCon – The Diplomat	Sharer	Initiator	Air
Nov 11th	9:05 AM	Sherlock – The Detective	Container	Sustainer	Water
Dec 1st	4:57 PM	Flash – The Pioneer	Sharer	Adaptor	Fire
Dec 20th	7:37 PM	Exec – The Achiever	Container	Initiator	Earth

1929

Date	Time	Style	Reaction	Approach	Uptake
Jan 1st	0:00 AM	Exec – The Achiever	Container	Initiator	Earth
Jan 8th	8:09 AM	Boffin – The Innovator	Sharer	Sustainer	Air
Mar 16th	1:07 AM	Sonar – The Intuitive	Container	Adaptor	Water
April 3rd	9:21 PM	Scout – The Trailblazer	Sharer	Initiator	Fire
April 19th	12:23 AM	Steady – The Vault	Container	Sustainer	Earth
May 3rd	9:34 PM	Buzz – The Curious	Sharer	Adaptor	Air
July 11th	9:07 PM	Sponge – The Sensitive	Container	Initiator	Water
July 27th	3:11 PM	Rex – The Dignified	Sharer	Sustainer	Fire
Aug 11th	2:48 PM	Details – The Analyst	Container	Adaptor	Earth
Aug 30th	6:01 PM	ProCon – The. Diplomat	Sharer	Initiator	Air
Nov 5th	7:29 PM	Sherlock – The Detective	Container	Sustainer	Water
Nov 24th	12:06 PM	Flash – The Pioneer	Sharer	Adaptor	Fire
Dec 13th	2:42 PM	Exec – The Achiever	Container	Initiator	Earth

1930

Date	Time	Style	Reaction	Approach	Uptake
Jan 1st	0:00 AM	Exec – The Achiever	Container	Initiator	Earth
Jan 2nd	10:25 AM	Boffin – The Innovator	Sharer	Sustainer	Air
Jan 23rd	12:30 AM	Exec – The Achiever	Container	Initiator	Earth
Feb 15th	3:08 PM	Boffin – The Innovator	Sharer	Sustainer	Air
Mar 9th	10:39 PM	Sonar – The Intuitive	Container	Adaptor	Water
Mar 26th	11:36 PM	Scout – The Trailblazer	Sharer	Initiator	Fire
April 10th	5:05 PM	Steady – The Vault	Container	Sustainer	Earth
May 1st	5:30 AM	Buzz – The Curious	Sharer	Adaptor	Air
May 17th	10:46 AM	Steady – The Vault	Container	Sustainer	Earth
June 14th	8:09 PM	Buzz – The Curious	Sharer	Adaptor	Air
July 4th	10:10 PM	Sponge – The Sensitive	Container	Initiator	Water
July 19th	2:44 AM	Rex – The Dignified	Sharer	Sustainer	Fire
Aug 4th	2:38 AM	Details – The Analyst	Container	Adaptor	Earth
Aug 26th	6:04 PM	ProCon – The Diplomat	Sharer	Initiator	Air
Sept 20th	2:13 AM	Details – The Analyst	Container	Adaptor	Earth
Oct 11th	4:45 AM	ProCon – The Diplomat	Sharer	Initiator	Air
Oct 29th	2:35 PM	Sherlock – The Detective	Container	Sustainer	Water
Nov 17th	5:31 AM	Flash – The Pioneer	Sharer	Adaptor	Fire
Dec 6th	8:57 PM	Exec – The Achiever	Container	Initiator	Earth

1931

Date	Time	Style	Reaction	Approach	Uptake
Jan 1st	0:00 AM	Exec – The Achiever	Container	Initiator	Earth
Feb 11th	12:27 PM	Boffin – The Innovator	Sharer	Sustainer	Air
Mar 2nd	5:28 PM	Sonar – The Intuitive	Container	Adaptor	Water
Mar 18th	7:31 PM	Scout – The Trailblazer	Sharer	Initiator	Fire
April 3rd	1:38 PM	Steady – The Vault	Container	Sustainer	Earth
June 11th	7:27 AM	Buzz – The Curious	Sharer	Adaptor	Air
June 26th	1:49 PM	Sponge – The Sensitive	Container	Initiator	Water
July 10th	7:56 PM	Rex – The Dignified	Sharer	Sustainer	Fire
July 28th	11:24 PM	Details – The Analyst	Container	Adaptor	Earth
Oct 4th	6:27 PM	ProCon – The Diplomat	Sharer	Initiator	Air
Oct 22nd	2:08 AM	Sherlock – The Detective	Container	Sustainer	Water
Nov 10th	4:27 AM	Flash – The Pioneer	Sharer	Adaptor	Fire
Dec 2nd	12:00 AM	Exec – The Achiever	Container	Initiator	Earth
Dec 20th	7:47 AM	Flash – The Pioneer	Sharer	Adaptor	Fire

1932

Date	Time	Style	Reaction	Approach	Uptake
Jan 1st	0:00 AM	Flash – The Pioneer	Sharer	Adaptor	Fire
Jan 14th	12:47 PM	Exec – The Achiever	Container	Initiator	Earth
Feb 5th	2:36 AM	Boffin – The Innovator	Sharer	Sustainer	Air
Feb 23rd	12:50 AM	Sonar – The Intuitive	Container	Adaptor	Water
Mar 9th	8:21 PM	Scout – The Trailblazer	Sharer	Initiator	Fire
May 15th	10:49 PM	Steady – The Vault	Container	Sustainer	Earth
June 2nd	11:05 PM	Buzz – The Curious	Sharer	Adaptor	Air
June 16th	10:30 PM	Sponge – The Sensitive	Container	Initiator	Water
July 2nd	8:16 AM	Rex – The Dignified	Sharer	Sustainer	Fire
July 27th	8:38 PM	Details – The Analyst	Container	Adaptor	Earth
Aug 10th	6:52 AM	Rex – The Dignified	Sharer	Sustainer	Fire
Sept 9th	7:20 AM	Details – The Analyst	Container	Adaptor	Earth
Sept 26th	1:15 AM	ProCon – The Diplomat	Sharer	Initiator	Air
Oct 13th	3:41 PM	Sherlock – The Detective	Container	Sustainer	Water
Nov 2nd	8:28 PM	Flash – The Pioneer	Sharer	Adaptor	Fire

1933

Date	Time	Style	Reaction	Approach	Uptake
Jan 1st	0:00 AM	Flash – The Pioneer	Sharer	Adaptor	Fire
Jan 8th	10:25 AM	Exec – The Achiever	Container	Initiator	Earth
Jan 27th	10:39 PM	Boffin – The Innovator	Sharer	Sustainer	Air
Feb 14th	5:06 AM	Sonar – The Intuitive	Container	Adaptor	Water
Mar 3rd	10:49 AM	Scout – The Trailblazer	Sharer	Initiator	Fire
Mar 25th	9:52 PM	Sonar – The Intuitive	Container	Adaptor	Water
April17th	3:27 PM	Scout – The Trailblazer	Sharer	Initiator	Fire
May 10th	7:42 AM	Steady – The Vault	Container	Sustainer	Earth
May 25th	2:27 PM	Buzz – The Curious	Sharer	Adaptor	Air
June 8th	2:12 PM	Sponge – The Sensitive	Container	Initiator	Water
June 27th	1:12 AM	Rex – The Dignified	Sharer	Sustainer	Fire
Sept 2nd	5:44 AM	Details – The Analyst	Container	Adaptor	Earth
Sept 18th	3:48 AM	ProCon – The Diplomat	Sharer	Initiator	Air
Oct 6th	3:04 PM	Sherlock – The Detective	Container	Sustainer	Water
Oct 30th	4:27 AM	Flash – The Pioneer	Sharer	Adaptor	Fire
Nov 16th	1:57 AM	Sherlock – The Detective	Container	Sustainer	Water
Dec 12th	3:44 AM	Flash – The Pioneer	Sharer	Adaptor	Fire

1934

Date	Time	Style	Reaction	Approach	Uptake
Jan 1st	0:00 AM	Flash – The Pioneer	Sharer	Adaptor	Fire
Jan 1st	6:40 PM	Exec – The Achiever	Container	Initiator	Earth
Jan 20th	11:44 AM	Boffin – The Innovator	Sharer	Sustainer	Air
Feb 6th	5:24 PM	Sonar – The Intuitive	Container	Adaptor	Water
April 15th	4:14 AM	Scout – The Trailblazer	Sharer	Initiator	Fire
May 2nd	6:45 PM	Steady – The Vault	Container	Sustainer	Earth
May 16th	11:43 PM	Buzz – The Curious	Sharer	Adaptor	Air
June 1st	8:22 AM	Sponge – The Sensitive	Container	Initiator	Water
Aug 9th	1:49 PM	Rex – The Dignified	Sharer	Sustainer	Fire
Aug 25th	2:18 AM	Details – The Analyst	Container	Adaptor	Earth
Sept 10th	11:29 AM	ProCon – The Diplomat	Sharer	Initiator	Air
Sept 30th	2:46 PM	Sherlock – The Detective	Container	Sustainer	Water
Dec 6th	6:42 AM	Flash – The Pioneer	Sharer	Adaptor	Fire
Dec 25th	2:59 PM	Exec – The Achiever	Container	Initiator	Earth

1935

Date	Time	Style	Reaction	Approach	Uptake
Jan 1st	0:00 AM	Exec – The Achiever	Container	Initiator	Earth
Jan 13th	1:20 AM	Boffin – The Innovator	Sharer	Sustainer	Air
Feb 1st	11:16 AM	Sonar – The Intuitive	Container	Adaptor	Water
Feb 15th	2:50 AM	Boffin – The Innovator	Sharer	Sustainer	Air
Mar 18th	9:53 PM	Sonar – The Intuitive	Container	Adaptor	Water
April 8th	6:40 PM	Scout – The Trailblazer	Sharer	Initiator	Fire
April 24th	12:29 PM	Steady – The Vault	Container	Sustainer	Earth
May 8th	5:20 PM	Buzz – The Curious	Sharer	Adaptor	Air
May 29th	7:26 PM	Sponge – The Sensitive	Container	Initiator	Water
June 20th	5:55 PM	Buzz – The Curious	Sharer	Adaptor	Air
July 13th	10:22 PM	Sponge – The Sensitive	Container	Initiator	Water
Aug 2nd	1:48 AM	Rex – The Dignified	Sharer	Sustainer	Fire
Aug 16th	8:39 PM	Details – The Analyst	Container	Adaptor	Earth
Sept 3rd	9:33 AM	ProCon – The Diplomat	Sharer	Initiator	Air
Sept 28th	3:52 PM	Sherlock – The Detective	Container	Sustainer	Water
Oct 12th	5:22 PM	ProCon – The Diplomat	Sharer	Initiator	Air
Nov 10th	1:24 AM	Sherlock – The Detective	Container	Sustainer	Water
Nov 29th	7:05 AM	Flash – The Pioneer	Sharer	Adaptor	Fire
Dec 18th	8:28 AM	Exec – The Achiever	Container	Initiator	Earth

1936

Date	Time	Style	Reaction	Approach	Uptake
Jan 1st	0:00 AM	Exec – The Achiever	Container	Initiator	Earth
Jan 6th	3:32 AM	Boffin – The Innovator	Sharer	Sustainer	Air
Mar 13th	6:40 AM	Sonar – The Intuitive	Container	Adaptor	Water
Mar 31st	5:08 AM	Scout – The Trailblazer	Sharer	Initiator	Fire
April 15th	1:45 AM	Steady – The Vault	Container	Sustainer	Earth
May 1st	1:30 AM	Buzz – The Curious	Sharer	Adaptor	Air
July 8th	8:47 PM	Sponge – The Sensitive	Container	Initiator	Water
July 23rd	3:39 PM	Rex – The Dignified	Sharer	Sustainer	Fire
Aug 7th	10:59 PM	Details – The Analyst	Container	Adaptor	Earth
Aug 27th	5:43 PM	ProCon – The Diplomat	Sharer	Initiator	Air
Nov 2nd	11:00 AM	Sherlock – The Detective	Container	Sustainer	Water
Nov 21st	12:39 AM	Flash – The Pioneer	Sharer	Adaptor	Fire
Dec 10th	6:40 AM	Exec – The Achiever	Container	Initiator	Earth

1937

Date	Time	Style	Reaction	Approach	Uptake
Jan 1st	0:00 AM	Exec – The Achiever	Container	Initiator	Earth
Jan 1st	4:44 PM	Boffin – The Innovator	Sharer	Sustainer	Air
Jan 9th	8:49 PM	Exec – The Achiever	Container	Initiator	Earth
Feb 14th	12:26 AM	Boffin – The Innovator	Sharer	Sustainer	Air
Mar 6th	2:06 PM	Sonar – The Intuitive	Container	Adaptor	Water
Mar 23rd	3:41 AM	Scout – The Trailblazer	Sharer	Initiator	Fire
April 7th	1:09 AM	Steady – The Vault	Container	Sustainer	Earth
June 13th	10:28 PM	Buzz – The Curious	Sharer	Adaptor	Air
July 1st	2:21 AM	Sponge – The Sensitive	Container	Initiator	Water
July 15th	4:11 AM	Rex – The Dignified	Sharer	Sustainer	Fire
July 31st	9:07 PM	Details – The Analyst	Container	Adaptor	Earth
Oct 8th	10:12 AM	ProCon – The Diplomat	Sharer	Initiator	Air
Oct 26th	1:14 AM	Sherlock – The Detective	Container	Sustainer	Water
Nov 13th	7:25 PM	Flash – The Pioneer	Sharer	Adaptor	Fire
Dec 3rd	11:51 PM	Exec – The Achiever	Container	Initiator	Earth

1938

Date	Time	Style	Reaction	Approach	Uptake
Jan 1st	0:00 AM	Exec – The Achiever	Container	Initiator	Earth
Jan 6th	10:16 PM	Flash – The Pioneer	Sharer	Adaptor	Fire
Jan 12th	10:30 PM	Exec – The Achiever	Container	Initiator	Earth
Feb 8th	1:17 PM	Boffin – The Innovator	Sharer	Sustainer	Air
Feb 27th	3:01 AM	Sonar – The Intuitive	Container	Adaptor	Water
Mar 15th	12:02 AM	Scout – The Trailblazer	Sharer	Initiator	Fire
April 1st	1:24 PM	Steady – The Vault	Container	Sustainer	Earth
April 23rd	2:02 PM	Scout – The Trailblazer	Sharer	Initiator	Fire
May 16th	5:46 PM	Steady – The Vault	Container	Sustainer	Earth
June 8th	12:32 AM	Buzz – The Curious	Sharer	Adaptor	Air
June 22nd	1:09 PM	Sponge – The Sensitive	Container	Initiator	Water
July 7th	3:21 AM	Rex – The Dignified	Sharer	Sustainer	Fire
July 26th	10:55 PM	Details – The Analyst	Container	Adaptor	Earth
Sept 3rd	3:40 AM	Rex – The Dignified	Sharer	Sustainer	Fire
Sept 10th	3:38 PM	Details – The Analyst	Container	Adaptor	Earth
Oct 1st	4:19 AM	ProCon – The Diplomat	Sharer	Initiator	Air
Oct 18th	12:43 PM	Sherlock – The Detective	Container	Sustainer	Water
Nov 6th	11:33 PM	Flash – The Pioneer	Sharer	Adaptor	Fire

1939

Date	Time	Style	Reaction	Approach	Uptake
Jan 1st	0:00 AM	Flash – The Pioneer	Sharer	Adaptor	Fire
Jan 12th	7:57 AM	Exec – The Achiever	Container	Initiator	Earth
Feb 1st	5:57 PM	Boffin – The Innovator	Sharer	Sustainer	Air
Feb 19th	8:09 AM	Sonar – The Intuitive	Container	Adaptor	Water
Mar 7th	9:14 AM	Scout – The Trailblazer	Sharer	Initiator	Fire
May 14th	1:43 PM	Steady – The Vault	Container	Sustainer	Earth
May 31st	2:45 AM	Buzz – The Curious	Sharer	Adaptor	Air
June 13th	11:01 PM	Sponge – The Sensitive	Container	Initiator	Water
June 30th	6:41 AM	Rex – The Dignified	Sharer	Sustainer	Fire
Sept 7th	4:58 AM	Details – The Analyst	Container	Adaptor	Earth
Sept 23rd	7:48 AM	ProCon – The Diplomat	Sharer	Initiator	Air
Oct 11th	5:20 AM	Sherlock – The Detective	Container	Sustainer	Water
Nov 1st	7:03 AM	Flash – The Pioneer	Sharer	Adaptor	Fire
Dec 3rd	8:22 AM	Sherlock – The Detective	Container	Sustainer	Water
Dec 13th	7:16 PM	Flash – The Pioneer	Sharer	Adaptor	Fire

1940

Date	Time	Style	Reaction	Approach	Uptake
Jan 1st	0:00 AM	Flash – The Pioneer	Sharer	Adaptor	Fire
Jan 6th	7:56 AM	Exec – The Achiever	Container	Initiator	Earth
Jan 25th	10:14 AM	Boffin – The Innovator	Sharer	Sustainer	Air
Feb 11th	2:01 PM	Sonar – The Intuitive	Container	Adaptor	Water
Mar 4th	10:09 AM	Scout – The Trailblazer	Sharer	Initiator	Fire
Mar 8th	12:55 AM	Sonar – The Intuitive	Container	Adaptor	Water
April 17th	4:56 AM	Scout – The Trailblazer	Sharer	Initiator	Fire
May 6th	9:14 PM	Steady – The Vault	Container	Sustainer	Earth
May 21st	1:59 PM	Buzz – The Curious	Sharer	Adaptor	Air
June 4th	10:29 PM	Sponge – The Sensitive	Container	Initiator	Water
June 26th	2:32 PM	Rex – The Dignified	Sharer	Sustainer	Fire
July 21st	1:39 AM	Sponge – The Sensitive	Container	Initiator	Water
Aug 11th	5:06 PM	Rex – The Dignified	Sharer	Sustainer	Fire
Aug 29th	11:11 AM	Details – The Analyst	Container	Adaptor	Earth
Sept 14th	11:34 AM	ProCon – The Diplomat	Sharer	Initiator	Air
Oct 3rd	12:14 PM	Sherlock – The Detective	Container	Sustainer	Water
Dec 9th	12:45 PM	Flash – The Pioneer	Sharer	Adaptor	Fire
Dec 29th	9:35 AM	Exec – The Achiever	Container	Initiator	Earth

1941

Date	Time	Style	Reaction	Approach	Uptake
Jan 1st	0:00 AM	Exec – The Achiever	Container	Initiator	Earth
Jan 16th	10:36 PM	Boffin – The Innovator	Sharer	Sustainer	Air
Feb 3rd	1:08 PM	Sonar – The Intuitive	Container	Adaptor	Water
Mar 7th	2:54 AM	Boffin – The Innovator	Sharer	Sustainer	Air
Mar 16th	12:26 PM	Sonar – The Intuitive	Container	Adaptor	Water
April 12th	7:19 AM	Scout – The Trailblazer	Sharer	Initiator	Fire
April 28th	11:09 PM	Steady – The Vault	Container	Sustainer	Earth
May 13th	12:50 AM	Buzz – The Curious	Sharer	Adaptor	Air
May 29th	5:32 PM	Sponge – The Sensitive	Container	Initiator	Water
Aug 6th	5:57 AM	Rex – The Dignified	Sharer	Sustainer	Fire
Aug 21st	5:18 AM	Details – The Analyst	Container	Adaptor	Earth
Sept 6th	11:58 PM	ProCon – The Diplomat	Sharer	Initiator	Air
Sept 28th	9:21 AM	Sherlock – The Detective	Container	Sustainer	Water
Oct 29th	8:51 PM	ProCon – The Diplomat	Sharer	Initiator	Air
Nov 11th	8:11 PM	Sherlock – The Detective	Container	Sustainer	Water
Dec 3rd	12:11 AM	Flash – The Pioneer	Sharer	Adaptor	Fire
Dec 22nd	3:54 AM	Exec – The Achiever	Container	Initiator	Earth

1942

Date	Time	Style	Reaction	Approach	Uptake
Jan 1st	0:00 AM	Exec – The Achiever	Container	Initiator	Earth
Jan 9th	3:24 PM	Boffin – The Innovator	Sharer	Sustainer	Air
Mar 17th	12:10 AM	Sonar – The Intuitive	Container	Adaptor	Water
April 5th	7:06 AM	Scout – The Trailblazer	Sharer	Initiator	Fire
April 20th	1:42 PM	Steady – The Vault	Container	Sustainer	Earth
May 5th	4:37 AM	Buzz – The Curious	Sharer	Adaptor	Air
July 12th	8:24 PM	Sponge – The Sensitive	Container	Initiator	Water
July 29th	4:24 AM	Rex – The Dignified	Sharer	Sustainer	Fire
Aug 13th	1:48 AM	Details – The Analyst	Container	Adaptor	Earth
Aug 31st	8:27 AM	ProCon – The Diplomat	Sharer	Initiator	Air
Nov 7th	1:44 AM	Sherlock – The Detective	Container	Sustainer	Water
Nov 25th	8:26 PM	Flash – The Pioneer	Sharer	Adaptor	Fire
Dec 14th	10:21 PM	Exec – The Achiever	Container	Initiator	Earth

1943

Date	Time	Style	Reaction	Approach	Uptake
Jan 1st	0:00 AM	Exec – The Achiever	Container	Initiator	Earth
Jan 3rd	8:27 AM	Boffin – The Innovator	Sharer	Sustainer	Air
Jan 27th	11:42 PM	Exec – The Achiever	Container	Initiator	Earth
Feb 15th	7:00 PM	Boffin – The Innovator	Sharer	Sustainer	Air
Mar 11th	4:59 AM	Sonar – The Intuitive	Container	Adaptor	Water
Mar 28th	11:19 AM	Scout – The Trailblazer	Sharer	Initiator	Fire
April 12th	4:56 AM	Steady – The Vault	Container	Sustainer	Earth
April 30th	3:56 PM	Buzz – The Curious	Sharer	Adaptor	Air
May 26th	10:22 AM	Steady – The Vault	Container	Sustainer	Earth
June 14th	12:46 AM	Buzz – The Curious	Sharer	Adaptor	Air
July 6th	9:05 AM	Sponge – The Sensitive	Container	Initiator	Water
July 20th	4:08 PM	Rex – The Dignified	Sharer	Sustainer	Fire
Aug 5th	10:33 AM	Details – The Analyst	Container	Adaptor	Earth
Aug 27th	12:36 AM	ProCon – The Diplomat	Sharer	Initiator	Air
Sept 25th	10:08 AM	Details – The Analyst	Container	Adaptor	Earth
Oct 11th	11:27 PM	ProCon – The Diplomat	Sharer	Initiator	Air
Oct 30th	11:37 PM	Sherlock – The Detective	Container	Sustainer	Water
Nov 18th	1:39 PM	Flash – The Pioneer	Sharer	Adaptor	Fire
Dec 8th	1:47 AM	Exec – The Achiever	Container	Initiator	Earth

1944

Date	Time	Style	Reaction	Approach	Uptake
Jan 1st	0:00 AM	Exec – The Achiever	Container	Initiator	Earth
Feb 12th	2:17 PM	Boffin – The Innovator	Sharer	Sustainer	Air
Mar 3rd	2:45 AM	Sonar – The Intuitive	Container	Adaptor	Water
Mar 19th	7:43 AM	Scout – The Trailblazer	Sharer	Initiator	Fire
April 3rd	5:29 PM	Steady – The Vault	Container	Sustainer	Earth
June 11th	11:46 AM	Buzz – The Curious	Sharer	Adaptor	Air
June 27th	3:40 AM	Sponge – The Sensitive	Container	Initiator	Water
July 11th	7:41 AM	Rex – The Dignified	Sharer	Sustainer	Fire
July 28th	11:44 PM	Details – The Analyst	Container	Adaptor	Earth
Oct 5th	3:17 AM	ProCon – The Diplomat	Sharer	Initiator	Air
Oct 22nd	11:33 AM	Sherlock – The Detective	Container	Sustainer	Water
Nov 10th	11:09 AM	Flash – The Pioneer	Sharer	Adaptor	Fire
Dec 1st	3:31 PM	Exec – The Achiever	Container	Initiator	Earth
Dec 23rd	11:21 PM	Flash – The Pioneer	Sharer	Adaptor	Fire

1945

Date	Time	Style	Reaction	Approach	Uptake
Jan 1st	0:00 AM	Flash – The Pioneer	Sharer	Adaptor	Fire
Jan 14th	3:04 AM	Exec – The Achiever	Container	Initiator	Earth
Feb 5th	9:20 AM	Boffin – The Innovator	Sharer	Sustainer	Air
Feb 23rd	11:25 AM	Sonar – The Intuitive	Container	Adaptor	Water
Mar 11th	6:45 AM	Scout – The Trailblazer	Sharer	Initiator	Fire
May 16th	3:21 PM	Steady – The Vault	Container	Sustainer	Earth
June 4th	10:30 AM	Buzz – The Curious	Sharer	Adaptor	Air
June 18th	12:27 PM	Sponge – The Sensitive	Container	Initiator	Water
July 3rd	3:39 PM	Rex – The Dignified	Sharer	Sustainer	Fire
July 26th	2:48 PM	Details – The Analyst	Container	Adaptor	Earth
Aug 17th	8:35 AM	Rex – The Dignified	Sharer	Sustainer	Fire
Sept 10th	7:21 AM	Details – The Analyst	Container	Adaptor	Earth
Sept 27th	12:08 PM	ProCon – The Diplomat	Sharer	Initiator	Air
Oct 15th	12:13 AM	Sherlock – The Detective	Container	Sustainer	Water
Nov 3rd	11:06 PM	Flash – The Pioneer	Sharer	Adaptor	Fire

1946

Date	Time	Style	Reaction	Approach	Uptake
Jan 1st	0:00 AM	Flash – The Pioneer	Sharer	Adaptor	Fire
Jan 9th	2:09 PM	Exec – The Achiever	Container	Initiator	Earth
Jan 29th	7:22 AM	Boffin – The Innovator	Sharer	Sustainer	Air
Feb 15th	3:43 PM	Sonar – The Intuitive	Container	Adaptor	Water
Mar 4th	9:26 AM	Scout – The Trailblazer	Sharer	Initiator	Fire
April 1st	6:44 PM	Sonar – The Intuitive	Container	Adaptor	Water
April 16th	2:54 PM	Scout – The Trailblazer	Sharer	Initiator	Fire
May 11th	2:29 PM	Steady – The Vault	Container	Sustainer	Earth
May 27th	4:13 AM	Buzz – The Curious	Sharer	Adaptor	Air
June 10th	2:00 AM	Sponge – The Sensitive	Container	Initiator	Water
June 27th	7:07 PM	Rex – The Dignified	Sharer	Sustainer	Fire
Sept 3rd	4:29 PM	Details – The Analyst	Container	Adaptor	Earth
Sept 19th	2:34 PM	ProCon – The Diplomat	Sharer	Initiator	Air
Oct 7th	9:21 PM	Sherlock – The Detective	Container	Sustainer	Water
Oct 30th	11:23 AM	Flash – The Pioneer	Sharer	Adaptor	Fire
Nov 20th	8:09 PM	Sherlock – The Detective	Container	Sustainer	Water
Dec 13th	12:03 AM	Flash – The Pioneer	Sharer	Adaptor	Fire

1947

Date	Time	Style	Reaction	Approach	Uptake
Jan 1st	0:00 AM	Flash – The Pioneer	Sharer	Adaptor	Fire
Jan 3rd	1:46 AM	Exec – The Achiever	Container	Initiator	Earth
Jan 21st	9:06 PM	Boffin – The Innovator	Sharer	Sustainer	Air
Feb 8th	1:31 AM	Sonar – The Intuitive	Container	Adaptor	Water
April 16th	4:31 AM	Scout – The Trailblazer	Sharer	Initiator	Fire
May 4th	6:03 AM	Steady – The Vault	Container	Sustainer	Earth
May 18th	1:33 PM	Buzz – The Curious	Sharer	Adaptor	Air
June 2nd	1:40 PM	Sponge – The Sensitive	Container	Initiator	Water
Aug 10th	5:40 PM	Rex – The Dignified	Sharer	Sustainer	Fire
Aug 26th	2:50 PM	Details – The Analyst	Container	Adaptor	Earth
Sept 11th	8:54 PM	ProCon – The Diplomat	Sharer	Initiator	Air
Oct 1st	3:26 PM	Sherlock – The Detective	Container	Sustainer	Water
Dec 7th	12:32 PM	Flash – The Pioneer	Sharer	Adaptor	Fire
Dec 26th	11:17 PM	Exec – The Achiever	Container	Initiator	Earth

1948

Date	Time	Style	Reaction	Approach	Uptake
Jan 1st	0:00 AM	Exec – The Achiever	Container	Initiator	Earth
Jan 14th	10:06 AM	Boffin – The Innovator	Sharer	Sustainer	Air
Feb 2nd	12:46 AM	Sonar – The Intuitive	Container	Adaptor	Water
Feb 20th	11:05 AM	Boffin – The Innovator	Sharer	Sustainer	Air
Mar 18th	8:14 AM	Sonar – The Intuitive	Container	Adaptor	Water
April 9th	2:26 AM	Scout – The Trailblazer	Sharer	Initiator	Fire
April 25th	1:38 AM	Steady – The Vault	Container	Sustainer	Earth
May 9th	4:38 AM	Buzz – The Curious	Sharer	Adaptor	Air
May 28th	10:50 AM	Sponge – The Sensitive	Container	Initiator	Water
June 28th	6:24 PM	Buzz – The Curious	Sharer	Adaptor	Air
July 11th	8:56 PM	Sponge – The Sensitive	Container	Initiator	Water
Aug 2nd	1:54 PM	Rex – The Dignified	Sharer	Sustainer	Fire
Aug 17th	8:44 AM	Details – The Analyst	Container	Adaptor	Earth
Sept 3rd	3:47 PM	ProCon – The Diplomat	Sharer	Initiator	Air
Sept 27th	7:19 AM	Sherlock – The Detective	Container	Sustainer	Water
Oct 17th	3:21 AM	ProCon – The Diplomat	Sharer	Initiator	Air
Nov 10th	2:19 AM	Sherlock – The Detective	Container	Sustainer	Water
Nov 29th	3:09 PM	Flash – The Pioneer	Sharer	Adaptor	Fire
Dec 18th	4:46 PM	Exec – The Achiever	Container	Initiator	Earth

1949

Date	Time	Style	Reaction	Approach	Uptake
Jan 1st	0:00 AM	Exec – The Achiever	Container	Initiator	Earth
Jan 6th	8:53 AM	Boffin – The Innovator	Sharer	Sustainer	Air
Mar 14th	9:52 AM	Sonar – The Intuitive	Container	Adaptor	Water
April 1st	4:02 PM	Scout – The Trailblazer	Sharer	Initiator	Fire
April 16th	2:55 PM	Steady – The Vault	Container	Sustainer	Earth
May 2nd	2:19 AM	Buzz – The Curious	Sharer	Adaptor	Air
July 10th	3:19 AM	Sponge – The Sensitive	Container	Initiator	Water
July 25th	5:20 AM	Rex – The Dignified	Sharer	Sustainer	Fire
Aug 9th	9:04 AM	Details – The Analyst	Container	Adaptor	Earth
Aug 28th	3:48 PM	ProCon – The Diplomat	Sharer	Initiator	Air
Nov 3rd	6:58 PM	Sherlock – The Detective	Container	Sustainer	Water
Nov 22nd	9:06 AM	Flash – The Pioneer	Sharer	Adaptor	Fire
Dec 11th	1:37 PM	Exec – The Achiever	Container	Initiator	Earth

1950

Date	Time	Style	Reaction	Approach	Uptake
Jan 1st	0:00 AM	Exec – The Achiever	Container	Initiator	Earth
Jan 1st	12:39 PM	Boffin – The Innovator	Sharer	Sustainer	Air
Jan 15th	7:08 AM	Exec – The Achiever	Container	Initiator	Earth
Feb 14th	7:12 PM	Boffin – The Innovator	Sharer	Sustainer	Air
Mar 7th	10:04 PM	Sonar – The Intuitive	Container	Adaptor	Water
Mar 24th	3:52 PM	Scout – The Trailblazer	Sharer	Initiator	Fire
April 8th	11:13 AM	Steady – The Vault	Container	Sustainer	Earth
June 14th	2:33 PM	Buzz – The Curious	Sharer	Adaptor	Air
July 2nd	2:57 PM	Sponge – The Sensitive	Container	Initiator	Water
July 16th	5:08 PM	Rex – The Dignified	Sharer	Sustainer	Fire
Aug 2nd	2:44 AM	Details – The Analyst	Container	Adaptor	Earth
Aug 27th	2:17 PM	ProCon – The Diplomat	Sharer	Initiator	Air
Sept 10th	6:41 PM	Details – The Analyst	Container	Sustainer	Water
Oct 9th	2:40 PM	ProCon – The Diplomat	Sharer	Initiator	Air
Oct 27th	10:36 AM	Sherlock – The Detective	Container	Sustainer	Water
Nov 15th	3:10 AM	Flash – The Pioneer	Sharer	Adaptor	Fire
Dec 5th	1:57 AM	Exec – The Achiever	Container	Initiator	Earth

1951

Date	Time	Style	Reaction	Approach	Uptake
Jan 1st	0:00 AM	Exec – The Achiever	Container	Initiator	Earth
Feb 9th	5:50 PM	Boffin – The Innovator	Sharer	Sustainer	Air
Feb 28th	1:04 PM	Sonar – The Intuitive	Container	Adaptor	Water
Mar 16th	11:53 AM	Scout – The Trailblazer	Sharer	Initiator	Fire
April 2nd	3:27 AM	Steady – The Vault	Container	Sustainer	Earth
May 1st	9:25 PM	Scout – The Trailblazer	Sharer	Initiator	Fire
May 15th	1:40 AM	Steady – The Vault	Container	Sustainer	Earth
June 9th	8:43 AM	Buzz – The Curious	Sharer	Adaptor	Air
June 24th	3:13 AM	Sponge – The Sensitive	Container	Initiator	Water
July 8th	1:39 PM	Rex – The Dignified	Sharer	Sustainer	Fire
July 27th	3:24 PM	Details – The Analyst	Container	Adaptor	Earth
Oct 2nd	2:25 PM	ProCon – The Diplomat	Sharer	Initiator	Air
Oct 19th	9:52 PM	Sherlock – The Detective	Container	Sustainer	Water
Nov 8th	4:59 AM	Flash – The Pioneer	Sharer	Adaptor	Fire
Dec 1st	8:41 PM	Exec – The Achiever	Container	Initiator	Earth
Dec 12th	11:32 AM	Flash – The Pioneer	Sharer	Adaptor	Fire

1952

Date	Time	Style	Reaction	Approach	Uptake
Jan 1st	12:39 PM	Flash – The Pioneer	Sharer	Adaptor	Fire
Jan 13th	6:44 AM	Exec – The Achiever	Container	Initiator	Earth
Feb 3rd	1:38 AM	Boffin – The Innovator	Sharer	Sustainer	Air
Feb 20th	6:55 PM	Sonar – The Intuitive	Container	Adaptor	Water
Mar 7th	5:10 PM	Scout – The Trailblazer	Sharer	Initiator	Fire
May 14th	2:43 PM	Steady – The Vault	Container	Sustainer	Earth
May 31st	3:26 PM	Buzz – The Curious	Sharer	Adaptor	Air
June 14th	12:22 PM	Sponge – The Sensitive	Container	Initiator	Water
June 30th	10:27 AM	Rex – The Dignified	Sharer	Sustainer	Fire
Sept 7th	12:02 PM	Details – The Analyst	Container	Adaptor	Earth
Sept 23rd	6:45 PM	ProCon – The Diplomat	Sharer	Initiator	Air
Oct 11th	1:05 PM	Sherlock – The Detective	Container	Sustainer	Water
Nov 1st	5:34 AM	Flash – The Pioneer	Sharer	Adaptor	Fire

1953

Date	Time	Style	Reaction	Approach	Uptake
Jan 1st	0:00 AM	Flash – The Pioneer	Sharer	Adaptor	Fire
Jan 6th	1:24 PM	Exec – The Achiever	Container	Initiator	Earth
Jan 25th	7:10 PM	Boffin – The Innovator	Sharer	Sustainer	Air
Feb 11th	11:57 PM	Sonar – The Intuitive	Container	Adaptor	Water
Mar 2nd	7:21 PM	Scout – The Trailblazer	Sharer	Initiator	Fire
Mar 15th	9:01 PM	Sonar – The Intuitive	Container	Adaptor	Water
April 17th	4:48 PM	Scout – The Trailblazer	Sharer	Initiator	Fire
May 8th	6:24 AM	Steady – The Vault	Container	Sustainer	Earth
May 23rd	3:58 AM	Buzz – The Curious	Sharer	Adaptor	Air
June 6th	8:23 AM	Sponge – The Sensitive	Container	Initiator	Water
June 26th	11:01 AM	Rex – The Dignified	Sharer	Sustainer	Fire
July 28th	2:09 PM	Sponge – The Sensitive	Container	Initiator	Water
Aug 11th	2:04 PM	Rex – The Dignified	Sharer	Sustainer	Fire
Aug 30th	10:59 PM	Details – The Analyst	Container	Adaptor	Earth
Sept 15th	9:45 PM	ProCon – The Diplomat	Sharer	Initiator	Air
Oct 4th	4:40 PM	Sherlock – The Detective	Container	Sustainer	Water
Oct 31st	3:49 PM	Flash – The Pioneer	Sharer	Adaptor	Fire
Nov 6th	9:36 PM	Sherlock – The Detective	Container	Sustainer	Water
Dec 10th	2:48 PM	Flash – The Pioneer	Sharer	Adaptor	Fire
Dec 30th	5:14 PM	Exec – The Achiever	Container	Initiator	Earth

1954

Date	Time	Style	Reaction	Approach	Uptake
Jan 1st	0:00 AM	Exec – The Achiever	Container	Initiator	Earth
Jan 18th	7:43 AM	Boffin – The Innovator	Sharer	Sustainer	Air
Feb 4th	6:03 PM	Sonar – The Intuitive	Container	Adaptor	Water
April 13th	11:34 AM	Scout – The Trailblazer	Sharer	Initiator	Fire
April 30th	11:26 AM	Steady – The Vault	Container	Sustainer	Earth
May 14th	1:57 PM	Buzz – The Curious	Sharer	Adaptor	Air
May 30th	4:13 PM	Sponge – The Sensitive	Container	Initiator	Water
Aug 7th	2:44 PM	Rex – The Dignified	Sharer	Sustainer	Fire
Aug 22nd	5:42 PM	Details – The Analyst	Container	Adaptor	Earth
Sept 8th	8:05 AM	ProCon – The Diplomat	Sharer	Initiator	Air
Sept 29th	4:06 AM	Sherlock – The Detective	Container	Sustainer	Water
Nov 4th	12:18 PM	ProCon – The Diplomat	Sharer	Initiator	Air
Nov 11th	10:25 AM	Sherlock – The Detective	Container	Sustainer	Water
Dec 4th	7:02 AM	Flash – The Pioneer	Sharer	Adaptor	Fire
Dec 23rd	12:10 PM	Exec – The Achiever	Container	Initiator	Earth

1955

Date	Time	Style	Reaction	Approach	Uptake
Jan 1st	0:00 AM	Exec – The Achiever	Container	Initiator	Earth
Jan 10th	11:05 PM	Boffin – The Innovator	Sharer	Sustainer	Air
Mar 17th	8:49 PM	Sonar – The Intuitive	Container	Adaptor	Water
April 6th	4:14 PM	Scout – The Trailblazer	Sharer	Initiator	Fire
April 22nd	2:57 AM	Steady – The Vault	Container	Sustainer	Earth
May 6th	1:05 PM	Buzz – The Curious	Sharer	Adaptor	Air
July 13th	2:44 PM	Sponge – The Sensitive	Container	Initiator	Water
July 30th	5:22 PM	Rex – The Dignified	Sharer	Sustainer	Fire
Aug 14th	1:08 PM	Details – The Analyst	Container	Adaptor	Earth
Sept 1st	12:06 PM	ProCon – The Diplomat	Sharer	Initiator	Air
Nov 8th	6:57 AM	Sherlock – The Detective	Container	Sustainer	Water
Nov 27th	4:34 AM	Flash – The Pioneer	Sharer	Adaptor	Fire
Dec 16th	6:06 AM	Exec – The Achiever	Container	Initiator	Earth

1956

Date	Time	Style	Reaction	Approach	Uptake
Jan 1st	0:00 AM	Exec – The Achiever	Container	Initiator	Earth
Jan 4th	9:16 AM	Boffin – The Innovator	Sharer	Sustainer	Air
Feb 2nd	1:16 PM	Exec – The Achiever	Container	Initiator	Earth
Feb 15th	6:34 AM	Boffin – The Innovator	Sharer	Sustainer	Air
Mar 11th	10:27 AM	Sonar – The Intuitive	Container	Adaptor	Water
Mar 28th	10:41 PM	Scout – The Trailblazer	Sharer	Initiator	Fire
April 12th	5:10 PM	Steady – The Vault	Container	Sustainer	Earth
April 29th	10:41 PM	Buzz – The Curious	Sharer	Adaptor	Air
July 6th	7:02 PM	Sponge – The Sensitive	Container	Initiator	Water
July 21st	5:35 AM	Rex – The Dignified	Sharer	Sustainer	Fire
Aug 5th	7:06 PM	Details – The Analyst	Container	Adaptor	Earth
Aug 26th	1:30 PM	ProCon – The Diplomat	Sharer	Initiator	Air
Sept 29th	9:40 PM	Details – The Analyst	Container	Sustainer	Water
Oct 11th	7:30 AM	ProCon – The Diplomat	Sharer	Initiator	Air
Oct 31st	8:19 AM	Sherlock – The Detective	Container	Sustainer	Water
Nov 18th	9:42 PM	Flash – The Pioneer	Sharer	Adaptor	Fire
Dec 8th	7:11 AM	Exec – The Achiever	Container	Initiator	Earth

1957

Date	Time	Style	Reaction	Approach	Uptake
Jan 1st	0:00 AM	Exec – The Achiever	Container	Initiator	Earth
Feb 12th	2:30 PM	Boffin – The Innovator	Sharer	Sustainer	Air
Mar 4th	11:34 AM	Sonar – The Intuitive	Container	Adaptor	Water
Mar 20th	7:48 PM	Scout – The Trailblazer	Sharer	Initiator	Fire
April 4th	11:37 PM	Steady – The Vault	Container	Sustainer	Earth
June 12th	1:40 PM	Buzz – The Curious	Sharer	Adaptor	Air
June 28th	5:08 PM	Sponge – The Sensitive	Container	Initiator	Water
July 12th	7:41 PM	Rex – The Dignified	Sharer	Sustainer	Fire
July 30th	1:44 AM	Details – The Analyst	Container	Adaptor	Earth
Oct 6th	11:08 PM	ProCon – The Diplomat	Sharer	Initiator	Air
Oct 23rd	8:50 PM	Sherlock – The Detective	Container	Sustainer	Water
Nov 11th	6:00 PM	Flash – The Pioneer	Sharer	Adaptor	Fire
Dec 2nd	11:19 AM	Exec – The Achiever	Container	Initiator	Earth
Dec 28th	5:55 PM	Flash – The Pioneer	Sharer	Adaptor	Fire

1958

Date	Time	Style	Reaction	Approach	Uptake
Jan 1st	0:00 AM	Flash – The Pioneer	Sharer	Adaptor	Fire
Jan 14th	10:03 AM	Exec – The Achiever	Container	Initiator	Earth
Feb 6th	3:21 PM	Boffin – The Innovator	Sharer	Sustainer	Air
Feb 24th	9:44 PM	Sonar – The Intuitive	Container	Adaptor	Water
Mar 12th	5:31 PM	Scout – The Trailblazer	Sharer	Initiator	Fire
April 2nd	7:20 PM	Steady – The Vault	Container	Sustainer	Earth
April 10th	12:35 PM	Scout – The Trailblazer	Sharer	Initiator	Fire
May 17th	1:53 AM	Steady – The Vault	Container	Sustainer	Earth
June 5th	8:59 PM	Buzz – The Curious	Sharer	Adaptor	Air
June 20th	2:20 AM	Sponge – The Sensitive	Container	Initiator	Water
July 4th	11:46 PM	Rex – The Dignified	Sharer	Sustainer	Fire
July 26th	10:08 AM	Details – The Analyst	Container	Adaptor	Earth
Aug 23rd	2:36 PM	Rex – The Dignified	Sharer	Sustainer	Fire
Sept 11th	1:10 AM	Details – The Analyst	Container	Adaptor	Earth
Sept 28th	10:45 PM	ProCon – The Diplomat	Sharer	Initiator	Air
Oct 16th	8:52 AM	Sherlock – The Detective	Container	Sustainer	Water
Nov 5th	2:36 AM	Flash – The Pioneer	Sharer	Adaptor	Fire

1959

Date	Time	Style	Reaction	Approach	Uptake
Jan 1st	0:00 AM	Flash – The Pioneer	Sharer	Adaptor	Fire
Jan 10th	4:47 PM	Exec – The Achiever	Container	Initiator	Earth
Jan 30th	3:41 PM	Boffin – The Innovator	Sharer	Sustainer	Air
Feb 17th	2:15 AM	Sonar – The Intuitive	Container	Adaptor	Water
Mar 5th	11:52 AM	Scout – The Trailblazer	Sharer	Initiator	Fire
May 12th	7:48 PM	Steady – The Vault	Container	Sustainer	Earth
May 28th	5:35 PM	Buzz – The Curious	Sharer	Adaptor	Air
June 11th	2:11 PM	Sponge – The Sensitive	Container	Initiator	Water
June 28th	4:31 PM	Rex – The Dignified	Sharer	Sustainer	Fire
Sept 5th	2:28 AM	Details – The Analyst	Container	Adaptor	Earth
Sept 21st	1:20 AM	ProCon – The Diplomat	Sharer	Initiator	Air
Oct 9th	4:02 AM	Sherlock – The Detective	Container	Sustainer	Water
Oct 31st	1:16 AM	Flash – The Pioneer	Sharer	Adaptor	Fire
Nov 25th	12:07 PM	Sherlock – The Detective	Container	Sustainer	Water
Dec 13th	3:42 PM	Flash – The Pioneer	Sharer	Adaptor	Fire

1960

Date	Time	Style	Reaction	Approach	Uptake
Jan 1st	0:00 AM	Flash – The Pioneer	Sharer	Adaptor	Fire
Jan 4th	8:24 AM	Exec – The Achiever	Container	Initiator	Earth
Jan 23rd	6:16 AM	Boffin – The Innovator	Sharer	Sustainer	Air
Feb 9th	10:13 AM	Sonar – The Intuitive	Container	Adaptor	Water
April 16th	2:22 AM	Scout – The Trailblazer	Sharer	Initiator	Fire
May 4th	4:45 PM	Steady – The Vault	Container	Sustainer	Earth
May 19th	3:27 AM	Buzz – The Curious	Sharer	Adaptor	Air
June 2nd	8:31 PM	Sponge – The Sensitive	Container	Initiator	Water
July 1st	1:08 AM	Rex – The Dignified	Sharer	Sustainer	Fire
July 6th	12:59 AM	Sponge – The Sensitive	Container	Initiator	Water
Aug 10th	5:49 PM	Rex – The Dignified	Sharer	Sustainer	Fire
Aug 27th	3:11 AM	Details – The Analyst	Container	Adaptor	Earth
Sept 12th	6:29 AM	ProCon – The Diplomat	Sharer	Initiator	Air
Oct 1st	5:17 PM	Sherlock – The Detective	Container	Sustainer	Water
Dec 7th	5:30 PM	Flash – The Pioneer	Sharer	Adaptor	Fire
Dec 27th	7:21 AM	Exec – The Achiever	Container	Initiator	Earth

1961

Date	Time	Style	Reaction	Approach	Uptake
Jan 1st	0:00 AM	Exec – The Achiever	Container	Initiator	Earth
Jan 14th	6:58 PM	Boffin – The Innovator	Sharer	Sustainer	Air
Feb 1st	9:39 PM	Sonar – The Intuitive	Container	Adaptor	Water
Feb 24th	8:31 PM	Boffin – The Innovator	Sharer	Sustainer	Air
Mar 18th	10:16 AM	Sonar – The Intuitive	Container	Adaptor	Water
April 10th	9:22 AM	Scout – The Trailblazer	Sharer	Initiator	Fire
April 26th	2:34 PM	Steady – The Vault	Container	Sustainer	Earth
May 10th	4:34 PM	Buzz – The Curious	Sharer	Adaptor	Air
May 28th	5:23 PM	Sponge – The Sensitive	Container	Initiator	Water
Aug 4th	1:15 AM	Rex – The Dignified	Sharer	Sustainer	Fire
Aug 18th	8:52 PM	Details – The Analyst	Container	Adaptor	Earth
Sept 4th	10:32 PM	ProCon – The Diplomat	Sharer	Initiator	Air
Sept 27th	12:16 PM	Sherlock – The Detective	Container	Sustainer	Water
Oct 22nd	2:29 AM	ProCon – The Diplomat	Sharer	Initiator	Air
Nov 10th	11:53 PM	Sherlock – The Detective	Container	Sustainer	Water
Nov 30th	10:54 PM	Flash – The Pioneer	Sharer	Adaptor	Fire
Dec 20th	1:04 AM	Exec – The Achiever	Container	Initiator	Earth

1962

Date	Time	Style	Reaction	Approach	Uptake
Jan 1st	0:00 AM	Exec – The Achiever	Container	Initiator	Earth
Jan 7th	3:08 PM	Boffin – The Innovator	Sharer	Sustainer	Air
Mar 15th	11:43 AM	Sonar – The Intuitive	Container	Adaptor	Water
April 3rd	2:32 AM	Scout – The Trailblazer	Sharer	Initiator	Fire
April 18th	4:10 AM	Steady – The Vault	Container	Sustainer	Earth
May 3rd	6:05 AM	Buzz – The Curious	Sharer	Adaptor	Air
July 11th	7:36 AM	Sponge – The Sensitive	Container	Initiator	Water
July 26th	6:50 PM	Rex – The Dignified	Sharer	Sustainer	Fire
Aug 10th	7:29 PM	Details – The Analyst	Container	Adaptor	Earth
Aug 29th	3:48 PM	ProCon – The Diplomat	Sharer	Initiator	Air
Nov 5th	2:20 AM	Sherlock – The Detective	Container	Sustainer	Water
Nov 23rd	5:31 PM	Flash – The Pioneer	Sharer	Adaptor	Fire
Dec 12th	8:51 PM	Exec – The Achiever	Container	Initiator	Earth

1963

Date	Time	Style	Reaction	Approach	Uptake
Jan 1st	0:00 AM	Exec – The Achiever	Container	Initiator	Earth
Jan 2nd	1:10 AM	Boffin – The Innovator	Sharer	Sustainer	Air
Jan 20th	4:56 AM	Exec – The Achiever	Container	Initiator	Earth
Feb 15th	10:08 AM	Boffin – The Innovator	Sharer	Sustainer	Air
Mar 9th	5:26 AM	Sonar – The Intuitive	Container	Adaptor	Water
Mar 26th	3:52 AM	Scout – The Trailblazer	Sharer	Initiator	Fire
April 9th	10:03 PM	Steady – The Vault	Container	Sustainer	Earth
May 3rd	4:14 AM	Buzz – The Curious	Sharer	Adaptor	Air
May 10th	7:56 PM	Steady – The Vault	Container	Sustainer	Earth
June 14th	11:20 PM	Buzz – The Curious	Sharer	Adaptor	Air
July 4th	3:00 AM	Sponge – The Sensitive	Container	Initiator	Water
July 18th	6:19 AM	Rex – The Dignified	Sharer	Sustainer	Fire
Aug 3rd	9:20 AM	Details – The Analyst	Container	Adaptor	Earth
Aug 26th	8:33 PM	ProCon – The Diplomat	Sharer	Initiator	Air
Sept 16th	8:17 PM	Details – The Analyst	Container	Adaptor	Earth
Oct 10th	4:44 PM	ProCon – The Diplomat	Sharer	Initiator	Air
Oct 28th	7:54 PM	Sherlock – The Detective	Container	Sustainer	Water
Nov 16th	11:07 AM	Flash – The Pioneer	Sharer	Adaptor	Fire
Dec 6th	5:17 AM	Exec – The Achiever	Container	Initiator	Earth

1964

Date	Time	Style	Reaction	Approach	Uptake
Jan 1st	0:00 AM	Exec – The Achiever	Container	Initiator	Earth
Feb 10th	9:30 PM	Boffin – The Innovator	Sharer	Sustainer	Air
Feb 29th	10:50 PM	Sonar – The Intuitive	Container	Adaptor	Water
Mar 16th	11:54 PM	Scout – The Trailblazer	Sharer	Initiator	Fire
April 2nd	12:57 AM	Steady – The Vault	Container	Sustainer	Earth
June 9th	3:45 PM	Buzz – The Curious	Sharer	Adaptor	Air
June 24th	5:17 PM	Sponge – The Sensitive	Container	Initiator	Water
July 9th	12:38 AM	Rex – The Dignified	Sharer	Sustainer	Fire
July 27th	11:35 AM	Details – The Analyst	Container	Adaptor	Earth
Oct 3rd	12:12 AM	ProCon – The Diplomat	Sharer	Initiator	Air
Oct 20th	7:11 AM	Sherlock – The Detective	Container	Sustainer	Water
Nov 8th	11:02 AM	Flash – The Pioneer	Sharer	Adaptor	Fire
Nov 30th	7:30 PM	Exec – The Achiever	Container	Initiator	Earth
Dec 16th	2:01 PM	Flash – The Pioneer	Sharer	Adaptor	Fire

1965

Date	Time	Style	Reaction	Approach	Uptake
Jan 1st	0:00 AM	Flash – The Pioneer	Sharer	Adaptor	Fire
Jan 13th	3:12 AM	Exec – The Achiever	Container	Initiator	Earth
Feb 3rd	9:02 AM	Boffin – The Innovator	Sharer	Sustainer	Air
Feb 21st	5:40 AM	Sonar – The Intuitive	Container	Adaptor	Water
Mar 9th	2:19 AM	Scout – The Trailblazer	Sharer	Initiator	Fire
May 15th	1:19 PM	Steady – The Vault	Container	Sustainer	Earth
June 2nd	3:47 AM	Buzz – The Curious	Sharer	Adaptor	Air
June 16th	2:04 AM	Sponge – The Sensitive	Container	Initiator	Water
July 1st	3:55 PM	Rex – The Dignified	Sharer	Sustainer	Fire
July 31st	11:23 AM	Details – The Analyst	Container	Adaptor	Earth
Aug 3rd	4:57 AM	Rex – The Dignified	Sharer	Sustainer	Fire
Sept 8th	5:14 PM	Details – The Analyst	Container	Adaptor	Earth
Sept 25th	5:49 AM	ProCon – The Diplomat	Sharer	Initiator	Air
Oct 12th	9:15 PM	Sherlock – The Detective	Container	Sustainer	Water
Nov 2nd	6:04 AM	Flash – The Pioneer	Sharer	Adaptor	Fire

1966

Date	Time	Style	Reaction	Approach	Uptake
Jan 1st	0:00 AM	Flash – The Pioneer	Sharer	Adaptor	Fire
Jan 7th	6:26 PM	Exec – The Achiever	Container	Initiator	Earth
Jan 27th	4:10 AM	Boffin – The Innovator	Sharer	Sustainer	Air
Feb 13th	10:17 AM	Sonar – The Intuitive	Container	Adaptor	Water
Mar 3rd	2:57 AM	Scout – The Trailblazer	Sharer	Initiator	Fire
Mar 22nd	2:34 AM	Sonar – The Intuitive	Container	Adaptor	Water
April 17th	9:31 PM	Scout – The Trailblazer	Sharer	Initiator	Fire
May 9th	2:48 PM	Steady – The Vault	Container	Sustainer	Earth
May 24th	5:59 PM	Buzz – The Curious	Sharer	Adaptor	Air
June 7th	7:11 PM	Sponge – The Sensitive	Container	Initiator	Water
June 26th	7:05 PM	Rex – The Dignified	Sharer	Sustainer	Fire
Sept 1st	10:35 AM	Details – The Analyst	Container	Adaptor	Earth
Sept 17th	8:19 AM	ProCon – The Diplomat	Sharer	Initiator	Air
Oct 5th	10:03 PM	Sherlock – The Detective	Container	Sustainer	Water
Oct 30th	7:38 AM	Flash – The Pioneer	Sharer	Adaptor	Fire
Nov 13th	3:03 AM	Sherlock – The Detective	Container	Sustainer	Water
Dec 11th	3:27 PM	Flash – The Pioneer	Sharer	Adaptor	Fire

1967

Date	Time	Style	Reaction	Approach	Uptake
Jan 1st	0:00 AM	Flash – The Pioneer	Sharer	Adaptor	Fire
Jan 1st	12:52 AM	Exec – The Achiever	Container	Initiator	Earth
Jan 19th	5:05 PM	Boffin – The Innovator	Sharer	Sustainer	Air
Feb 6th	12:38 AM	Sonar – The Intuitive	Container	Adaptor	Water
April 14th	2:38 PM	Scout – The Trailblazer	Sharer	Initiator	Fire
May 1st	11:26 PM	Steady – The Vault	Container	Sustainer	Earth
May 16th	3:27 AM	Buzz – The Curious	Sharer	Adaptor	Air
May 31st	6:02 PM	Sponge – The Sensitive	Container	Initiator	Water
Aug 8th	10:09 PM	Rex – The Dignified	Sharer	Sustainer	Fire
Aug 24th	6:17 AM	Details – The Analyst	Container	Adaptor	Earth
Sept 9th	4:53 PM	ProCon – The Diplomat	Sharer	Initiator	Air
Sept 30th	1:46 AM	Sherlock – The Detective	Container	Sustainer	Water
Dec 5th	1:41 PM	Flash – The Pioneer	Sharer	Adaptor	Fire
Dec 24th	8:33 PM	Exec – The Achiever	Container	Initiator	Earth

1968

Date	Time	Style	Reaction	Approach	Uptake
Jan 1st	0:00 AM	Exec – The Achiever	Container	Initiator	Earth
Jan 12th	7:19 AM	Boffin – The Innovator	Sharer	Sustainer	Air
Feb 1st	12:57 PM	Sonar – The Intuitive	Container	Adaptor	Water
Feb 11th	6:13 PM	Boffin – The Innovator	Sharer	Sustainer	Air
Mar 17th	2:45 PM	Sonar – The Intuitive	Container	Adaptor	Water
April 7th	1:01 AM	Scout – The Trailblazer	Sharer	Initiator	Fire
April 22nd	4:18 PM	Steady – The Vault	Container	Sustainer	Earth
May 6th	10:56 PM	Buzz – The Curious	Sharer	Adaptor	Air
May 29th	10:42 PM	Sponge – The Sensitive	Container	Initiator	Water
June 13th	10:26 PM	Buzz – The Curious	Sharer	Adaptor	Air
July 13th	1:30 AM	Sponge – The Sensitive	Container	Initiator	Water
July 31st	6:11 AM	Rex – The Dignified	Sharer	Sustainer	Fire
Aug 15th	12:53 AM	Details – The Analyst	Container	Adaptor	Earth
Sept 1st	4:59 PM	ProCon – The Diplomat	Sharer	Initiator	Air
Sept 28th	2:40 PM	Sherlock – The Detective	Container	Sustainer	Water
Oct 7th	10:25 PM	ProCon – The Diplomat	Sharer	Initiator	Air
Nov 8th	11:00 AM	Sherlock – The Detective	Container	Sustainer	Water
Nov 27th	12:47 PM	Flash – The Pioneer	Sharer	Adaptor	Fire
Dec 16th	2:11 PM	Exec – The Achiever	Container	Initiator	Earth

1969

Date	Time	Style	Reaction	Approach	Uptake
Jan 1st	0:00 AM	Exec – The Achiever	Container	Initiator	Earth
Jan 4th	12:18 PM	Boffin – The Innovator	Sharer	Sustainer	Air
Mar 12th	3:19 PM	Sonar – The Intuitive	Container	Adaptor	Water
Mar 30th	9:59 AM	Scout – The Trailblazer	Sharer	Initiator	Fire
April 14th	5:55 AM	Steady – The Vault	Container	Sustainer	Earth
April 30th	3:18 PM	Buzz – The Curious	Sharer	Adaptor	Air
July 8th	3:58 AM	Sponge – The Sensitive	Container	Initiator	Water
July 22nd	7:11 PM	Rex – The Dignified	Sharer	Sustainer	Fire
Aug 7th	4:21 AM	Details – The Analyst	Container	Adaptor	Earth
Aug 27th	6:50 AM	ProCon – The Diplomat	Sharer	Initiator	Air
Oct 7th	6:23 AM	Details – The Analyst	Container	Adaptor	Earth
Oct 9th	5:13 PM	ProCon – The Diplomat	Sharer	Initiator	Air
Nov 1st	4:53 PM	Sherlock – The Detective	Container	Sustainer	Water
Nov 20th	6:00 AM	Flash – The Pioneer	Sharer	Adaptor	Fire
Dec 9th	1:21 PM	Exec – The Achiever	Container	Initiator	Earth

1970

Date	Time	Style	Reaction	Approach	Uptake
Jan 1st	0:00 AM	Exec – The Achiever	Container	Initiator	Earth
Feb 13th	1:08 PM	Boffin – The Innovator	Sharer	Sustainer	Air
Mar 5th	8:10 PM	Sonar – The Intuitive	Container	Adaptor	Water
Mar 22nd	7:59 AM	Scout – The Trailblazer	Sharer	Initiator	Fire
April 6th	7:40 AM	Steady – The Vault	Container	Sustainer	Earth
June 13th	12:46 PM	Buzz – The Curious	Sharer	Adaptor	Air
June 30th	6:22 AM	Sponge – The Sensitive	Container	Initiator	Water
July 14th	8:06 AM	Rex – The Dignified	Sharer	Sustainer	Fire
July 31st	5:21 AM	Details – The Analyst	Container	Adaptor	Earth
Oct 7th	6:04 PM	ProCon – The Diplomat	Sharer	Initiator	Air
Oct 25th	6:16 AM	Sherlock – The Detective	Container	Sustainer	Water
Nov 13th	1:16 AM	Flash – The Pioneer	Sharer	Adaptor	Fire
Dec 3rd	10:14 AM	Exec – The Achiever	Container	Initiator	Earth

1971

Date	Time	Style	Reaction	Approach	Uptake
Jan 1st	0:00 AM	Exec – The Achiever	Container	Initiator	Earth
Jan 2nd	11:40 PM	Flash – The Pioneer	Sharer	Adaptor	Fire
Jan 14th	2:16 AM	Exec – The Achiever	Container	Initiator	Earth
Feb 7th	8:51 PM	Boffin – The Innovator	Sharer	Sustainer	Air
Feb 26th	7:57 AM	Sonar – The Intuitive	Container	Adaptor	Water
Mar 14th	4:46 AM	Scout – The Trailblazer	Sharer	Initiator	Fire
April 1st	2:11 PM	Steady – The Vault	Container	Sustainer	Earth
April 18th	9:47 PM	Scout – The Trailblazer	Sharer	Initiator	Fire
May 17th	3:32 AM	Steady – The Vault	Container	Sustainer	Earth
June 7th	6:45 AM	Buzz – The Curious	Sharer	Adaptor	Air
June 21st	4:25 PM	Sponge – The Sensitive	Container	Initiator	Water
July 6th	8:53 AM	Rex – The Dignified	Sharer	Sustainer	Fire
July 26th	5:03 PM	Details – The Analyst	Container	Adaptor	Earth
Aug 29th	8:57 PM	Rex – The Dignified	Sharer	Sustainer	Fire
Sept 11th	6:45 AM	Details – The Analyst	Container	Adaptor	Earth
Sept 30th	9:19 AM	ProCon – The Diplomat	Sharer	Initiator	Air
Oct 17th	5:49 PM	Sherlock – The Detective	Container	Sustainer	Water
Nov 6th	6:58 AM	Flash – The Pioneer	Sharer	Adaptor	Fire

1972

Date	Time	Style	Reaction	Approach	Uptake
Jan 1st	0:00 AM	Flash – The Pioneer	Sharer	Adaptor	Fire
Jan 11th	6:18 PM	Exec – The Achiever	Container	Initiator	Earth
Jan 31st	11:46 PM	Boffin – The Innovator	Sharer	Sustainer	Air
Feb 18th	12:53 PM	Sonar – The Intuitive	Container	Adaptor	Water
Mar 5th	4:59 PM	Scout – The Trailblazer	Sharer	Initiator	Fire
May 12th	11:45 PM	Steady – The Vault	Container	Sustainer	Earth
May 29th	6:46 AM	Buzz – The Curious	Sharer	Adaptor	Air
June 12th	2:56 AM	Sponge – The Sensitive	Container	Initiator	Water
June 28th	4:52 PM	Rex – The Dignified	Sharer	Sustainer	Fire
Sept 5th	11:36 AM	Details – The Analyst	Container	Adaptor	Earth
Sept 21st	12:11 PM	ProCon – The Diplomat	Sharer	Initiator	Air
Oct 9th	11:11 AM	Sherlock – The Detective	Container	Sustainer	Water
Oct 30th	7:27 PM	Flash – The Pioneer	Sharer	Adaptor	Fire
Nov 29th	7:46 AM	Sherlock – The Detective	Container	Sustainer	Water
Dec 12th	11:20 PM	Flash – The Pioneer	Sharer	Adaptor	Fire

1973

Date	Time	Style	Reaction	Approach	Uptake
Jan 1st	0:00 AM	Flash – The Pioneer	Sharer	Adaptor	Fire
Jan 4th	2:41 PM	Exec – The Achiever	Container	Initiator	Earth
Jan 23rd	3:23 PM	Boffin – The Innovator	Sharer	Sustainer	Air
Feb 9th	7:30 PM	Sonar – The Intuitive	Container	Adaptor	Water
April 16th	9:17 PM	Scout – The Trailblazer	Sharer	Initiator	Fire
May 6th	2:55 AM	Steady – The Vault	Container	Sustainer	Earth
May 20th	5:24 PM	Buzz – The Curious	Sharer	Adaptor	Air
June 4th	4:42 AM	Sponge – The Sensitive	Container	Initiator	Water
June 27th	6:42 AM	Rex – The Dignified	Sharer	Sustainer	Fire
July 16th	7:47 AM	Sponge – The Sensitive	Container	Initiator	Water
Aug 11th	12:21 PM	Rex – The Dignified	Sharer	Sustainer	Fire
Aug 28th	3:22 PM	Details – The Analyst	Container	Adaptor	Earth
Sept 13th	4:16 PM	ProCon – The Diplomat	Sharer	Initiator	Air
Oct 2nd	8:12 PM	Sherlock – The Detective	Container	Sustainer	Water
Dec 8th	9:29 PM	Flash – The Pioneer	Sharer	Adaptor	Fire
Dec 28th	3:14 PM	Exec – The Achiever	Container	Initiator	Earth

1974

Date	Time	Style	Reaction	Approach	Uptake
Jan 1st	0:00 AM	Exec – The Achiever	Container	Initiator	Earth
Jan 16th	3:56 AM	Boffin – The Innovator	Sharer	Sustainer	Air
Feb 2nd	10:42 PM	Sonar – The Intuitive	Container	Adaptor	Water
Mar 2nd	6:20 PM	Boffin – The Innovator	Sharer	Sustainer	Air
Mar 17th	8:11 PM	Sonar – The Intuitive	Container	Adaptor	Water
April 11th	3:20 PM	Scout – The Trailblazer	Sharer	Initiator	Fire
April 28th	3:10 AM	Steady – The Vault	Container	Sustainer	Earth
May 12th	4:55 AM	Buzz – The Curious	Sharer	Adaptor	Air
May 29th	8:03 AM	Sponge – The Sensitive	Container	Initiator	Water
Aug 5th	11:42 AM	Rex – The Dignified	Sharer	Sustainer	Fire
Aug 20th	9:04 AM	Details – The Analyst	Container	Adaptor	Earth
Sept 6th	5:48 AM	ProCon – The Diplomat	Sharer	Initiator	Air
Sept 28th	12:20 AM	Sherlock – The Detective	Container	Sustainer	Water
Oct 26th	11:21 PM	ProCon – The Diplomat	Sharer	Initiator	Air
Nov 11th	4:05 PM	Sherlock – The Detective	Container	Sustainer	Water
Dec 2nd	6:17 AM	Flash – The Pioneer	Sharer	Adaptor	Fire
Dec 21st	9:16 AM	Exec – The Achiever	Container	Initiator	Earth

1975

Date	Time	Style	Reaction	Approach	Uptake
Jan 1st	0:00 AM	Exec – The Achiever	Container	Initiator	Earth
Jan 8th	9:58 PM	Boffin – The Innovator	Sharer	Sustainer	Air
Mar 16th	11:50 AM	Sonar – The Intuitive	Container	Adaptor	Water
April 4th	12:28 PM	Scout – The Trailblazer	Sharer	Initiator	Fire
April 19th	5:20 PM	Steady – The Vault	Container	Sustainer	Earth
May 4th	11:55 AM	Buzz – The Curious	Sharer	Adaptor	Air
July 12th	8:56 AM	Sponge – The Sensitive	Container	Initiator	Water
July 28th	8:05 AM	Rex – The Dignified	Sharer	Sustainer	Fire
Aug 12th	6:12 AM	Details – The Analyst	Container	Adaptor	Earth
Aug 30th	5:20 PM	ProCon – The Diplomat	Sharer	Initiator	Air
Nov 6th	8:58 AM	Sherlock – The Detective	Container	Sustainer	Water
Nov 25th	1:44 AM	Flash – The Pioneer	Sharer	Adaptor	Fire
Dec 14th	4:10 AM	Exec – The Achiever	Container	Initiator	Earth

1976

Date	Time	Style	Reaction	Approach	Uptake
Jan 1st	0:00 AM	Exec – The Achiever	Container	Initiator	Earth
Jan 2nd	8:22 PM	Boffin – The Innovator	Sharer	Sustainer	Air
Jan 25th	1:34 AM	Exec – The Achiever	Container	Initiator	Earth
Feb 15th	7:03 PM	Boffin – The Innovator	Sharer	Sustainer	Air
Mar 9th	12:02 PM	Sonar – The Intuitive	Container	Adaptor	Water
Mar 26th	3:36 PM	Scout – The Trailblazer	Sharer	Initiator	Fire
April 10th	9:29 AM	Steady – The Vault	Container	Sustainer	Earth
April 29th	11:11 PM	Buzz – The Curious	Sharer	Adaptor	Air
May 19th	7:17 PM	Steady – The Vault	Container	Sustainer	Earth
June 13th	7:20 PM	Buzz – The Curious	Sharer	Adaptor	Air
July 4th	2:18 PM	Sponge – The Sensitive	Container	Initiator	Water
July 18th	7:35 PM	Rex – The Dignified	Sharer	Sustainer	Fire
Aug 3rd	4:41 PM	Details – The Analyst	Container	Adaptor	Earth
Aug 25th	8:52 PM	ProCon – The Diplomat	Sharer	Initiator	Air
Sept 21st	7:15 AM	Details – The Analyst	Container	Adaptor	Earth
Oct 10th	2:47 PM	ProCon – The Diplomat	Sharer	Initiator	Air
Oct 29th	4:55 AM	Sherlock – The Detective	Container	Sustainer	Water
Nov 16th	7:02 PM	Flash – The Pioneer	Sharer	Adaptor	Fire
Dec 6th	9:25 AM	Exec – The Achiever	Container	Initiator	Earth

1977

Date	Time	Style	Reaction	Approach	Uptake
Jan 1st	0:00 AM	Exec – The Achiever	Container	Initiator	Earth
Feb 10th	11:55 PM	Boffin – The Innovator	Sharer	Sustainer	Air
Mar 2nd	8:09 AM	Sonar – The Intuitive	Container	Adaptor	Water
Mar 18th	11:56 AM	Scout – The Trailblazer	Sharer	Initiator	Fire
April 3rd	2:46 AM	Steady – The Vault	Container	Sustainer	Earth
June 10th	9:07 PM	Buzz – The Curious	Sharer	Adaptor	Air
June 26th	7:07 AM	Sponge – The Sensitive	Container	Initiator	Water
July 10th	12:00 PM	Rex – The Dignified	Sharer	Sustainer	Fire
July 28th	10:15 AM	Details – The Analyst	Container	Adaptor	Earth
Oct 4th	9:16 AM	ProCon – The Diplomat	Sharer	Initiator	Air
Oct 21st	4:23 PM	Sherlock – The Detective	Container	Sustainer	Water
Nov 9th	5:20 PM	Flash – The Pioneer	Sharer	Adaptor	Fire
Dec 1st	6:43 AM	Exec – The Achiever	Container	Initiator	Earth
Dec 21st	7:15 AM	Flash – The Pioneer	Sharer	Adaptor	Fire

1978

Date	Time	Style	Reaction	Approach	Uptake
Jan 1st	0:00 AM	Flash – The Pioneer	Sharer	Adaptor	Fire
Jan 13th	10:07 PM	Exec – The Achiever	Container	Initiator	Earth
Feb 4th	3:54 PM	Boffin – The Innovator	Sharer	Sustainer	Air
Feb 22nd	4:11 PM	Sonar – The Intuitive	Container	Adaptor	Water
Mar 10th	12:10 PM	Scout – The Trailblazer	Sharer	Initiator	Fire
May 16th	8:20 AM	Steady – The Vault	Container	Sustainer	Earth
June 3rd	3:26 PM	Buzz – The Curious	Sharer	Adaptor	Air
June 17th	3:49 PM	Sponge – The Sensitive	Container	Initiator	Water
July 2nd	10:28 PM	Rex – The Dignified	Sharer	Sustainer	Fire
July 27th	6:10 AM	Details – The Analyst	Container	Adaptor	Earth
Aug 13th	6:40 AM	Rex – The Dignified	Sharer	Sustainer	Fire
Sept 9th	7:23 PM	Details – The Analyst	Container	Adaptor	Earth
Sept 26th	4:40 PM	ProCon – The Diplomat	Sharer	Initiator	Air
Oct 14th	5:30 AM	Sherlock – The Detective	Container	Sustainer	Water
Nov 3rd	7:48 AM	Flash – The Pioneer	Sharer	Adaptor	Fire

1979

Date	Time	Style	Reaction	Approach	Uptake
Jan 1st	0:00 AM	Flash – The Pioneer	Sharer	Adaptor	Fire
Jan 8th	10:33 PM	Exec – The Achiever	Container	Initiator	Earth
Jan 28th	12:49 PM	Boffin – The Innovator	Sharer	Sustainer	Air
Feb 14th	8:38 PM	Sonar – The Intuitive	Container	Adaptor	Water
Mar 3rd	9:32 PM	Scout – The Trailblazer	Sharer	Initiator	Fire
Mar 28th	11:01 AM	Sonar – The Intuitive	Container	Adaptor	Water
April 17th	12:48 PM	Scout – The Trailblazer	Sharer	Initiator	Fire
May 10th	10:03 PM	Steady – The Vault	Container	Sustainer	Earth
May 26th	7:44 AM	Buzz – The Curious	Sharer	Adaptor	Air
June 9th	6:32 AM	Sponge – The Sensitive	Container	Initiator	Water
June 27th	9:51 AM	Rex – The Dignified	Sharer	Sustainer	Fire
Sept 2nd	9:39 PM	Details – The Analyst	Container	Adaptor	Earth
Sept 18th	6:59 PM	ProCon – The Diplomat	Sharer	Initiator	Air
Oct 7th	3:55 AM	Sherlock – The Detective	Container	Sustainer	Water
Oct 30th	7:06 AM	Flash – The Pioneer	Sharer	Adaptor	Fire
Nov 18th	2:59 AM	Sherlock – The Detective	Container	Sustainer	Water
Dec 12th	1:34 PM	Flash – The Pioneer	Sharer	Adaptor	Fire

1980

Date	Time	Style	Reaction	Approach	Uptake
Jan 1st	0:00 AM	Flash – The Pioneer	Sharer	Adaptor	Fire
Jan 2nd	8:02 AM	Exec – The Achiever	Container	Initiator	Earth
Jan 21st	2:18 AM	Boffin – The Innovator	Sharer	Sustainer	Air
Feb 7th	8:07 AM	Sonar – The Intuitive	Container	Adaptor	Water
April 14th	3:58 PM	Scout – The Trailblazer	Sharer	Initiator	Fire
May 2nd	10:56 AM	Steady – The Vault	Container	Sustainer	Earth
May 16th	5:06 PM	Buzz – The Curious	Sharer	Adaptor	Air
May 31st	10:05 PM	Sponge – The Sensitive	Container	Initiator	Water
Aug 9th	3:31 AM	Rex – The Dignified	Sharer	Sustainer	Fire
Aug 24th	6:47 PM	Details – The Analyst	Container	Adaptor	Earth
Sept 10th	2:00 AM	ProCon – The Diplomat	Sharer	Initiator	Air
Sept 30th	1:16 AM	Sherlock – The Detective	Container	Sustainer	Water
Dec 5th	7:45 PM	Flash – The Pioneer	Sharer	Adaptor	Fire
Dec 25th	4:46 AM	Exec – The Achiever	Container	Initiator	Earth

1981

Date	Time	Style	Reaction	Approach	Uptake
Jan 1st	0:00 AM	Exec – The Achiever	Container	Initiator	Earth
Jan 12th	3:48 PM	Boffin – The Innovator	Sharer	Sustainer	Air
Jan 31st	5:35 PM	Sonar – The Intuitive	Container	Adaptor	Water
Feb 16th	7:48 AM	Boffin – The Innovator	Sharer	Sustainer	Air
Mar 18th	4:33 AM	Sonar – The Intuitive	Container	Adaptor	Water
April 8th	9:11 AM	Scout – The Trailblazer	Sharer	Initiator	Fire
April 24th	5:31 AM	Steady – The Vault	Container	Sustainer	Earth
May 8th	9:42 AM	Buzz – The Curious	Sharer	Adaptor	Air
May 28th	5:04 PM	Sponge – The Sensitive	Container	Initiator	Water
June 22nd	10:51 PM	Buzz – The Curious	Sharer	Adaptor	Air
July 12th	9:08 PM	Sponge – The Sensitive	Container	Initiator	Water
Aug 1st	6:30 PM	Rex – The Dignified	Sharer	Sustainer	Fire
Aug 16th	12:47 PM	Details – The Analyst	Container	Adaptor	Earth
Sept 2nd	10:40 PM	ProCon – The Diplomat	Sharer	Initiator	Air
Sept 27th	11:02 AM	Sherlock – The Detective	Container	Sustainer	Water
Oct 14th	1:56 AM	ProCon – The Diplomat	Sharer	Initiator	Air
Nov 9th	1:14 PM	Sherlock – The Detective	Container	Sustainer	Water
Nov 28th	8:52 PM	Flash – The Pioneer	Sharer	Adaptor	Fire
Dec 17th	10:21 PM	Exec – The Achiever	Container	Initiator	Earth

1982

Date	Time	Style	Reaction	Approach	Uptake
Jan 1st	0:00 AM	Exec – The Achiever	Container	Initiator	Earth
Jan 5th	4:49 PM	Boffin – The Innovator	Sharer	Sustainer	Air
Mar 13th	7:11 PM	Sonar – The Intuitive	Container	Adaptor	Water
Mar 31st	8:59 PM	Scout – The Trailblazer	Sharer	Initiator	Fire
April 15th	6:54 PM	Steady – The Vault	Container	Sustainer	Earth
May 1st	1:29 PM	Buzz – The Curious	Sharer	Adaptor	Air
July 9th	11:26 AM	Sponge – The Sensitive	Container	Initiator	Water
July 24th	8:48 AM	Rex – The Dignified	Sharer	Sustainer	Fire
Aug 8th	2:06 PM	Details – The Analyst	Container	Adaptor	Earth
Aug 28th	3:22 AM	ProCon – The Diplomat	Sharer	Initiator	Air
Nov 3rd	1:10 AM	Sherlock – The Detective	Container	Sustainer	Water
Nov 21st	2:28 PM	Flash – The Pioneer	Sharer	Adaptor	Fire
Dec 10th	8:04 PM	Exec – The Achiever	Container	Initiator	Earth

1983

Date	Time	Style	Reaction	Approach	Uptake
Jan 1st	0:00 AM	Exec – The Achiever	Container	Initiator	Earth
Jan 1st	1:32 PM	Boffin – The Innovator	Sharer	Sustainer	Air
Jan 12th	6:10 AM	Exec – The Achiever	Container	Initiator	Earth
Feb 14th	9:36 AM	Boffin – The Innovator	Sharer	Sustainer	Air
Mar 7th	4:24 AM	Sonar – The Intuitive	Container	Adaptor	Water
Mar 23rd	8:09 PM	Scout – The Trailblazer	Sharer	Initiator	Fire
April 7th	5:04 PM	Steady – The Vault	Container	Sustainer	Earth
June 14th	8:06 AM	Buzz – The Curious	Sharer	Adaptor	Air
July 1st	7:18 PM	Sponge – The Sensitive	Container	Initiator	Water
July 15th	8:57 PM	Rex – The Dignified	Sharer	Sustainer	Fire
Aug 1st	10:22 AM	Details – The Analyst	Container	Adaptor	Earth
Aug 29th	6:07 AM	ProCon – The Diplomat	Sharer	Initiator	Air
Sept 6th	1:59 AM	Details – The Analyst	Container	Adaptor	Earth
Oct 8th	11:44 PM	ProCon – The Diplomat	Sharer	Initiator	Air
Oct 26th	3:47 PM	Sherlock – The Detective	Container	Sustainer	Water
Nov 14th	8:56 AM	Flash – The Pioneer	Sharer	Adaptor	Fire
Dec 4th	11:22 AM	Exec – The Achiever	Container	Initiator	Earth

1984

Date	Time	Style	Reaction	Approach	Uptake
Jan 1st	0:00 AM	Exec – The Achiever	Container	Initiator	Earth
Feb 9th	1:50 AM	Boffin – The Innovator	Sharer	Sustainer	Air
Feb 27th	6:07 PM	Sonar – The Intuitive	Container	Adaptor	Water
Mar 14th	4:27 PM	Scout – The Trailblazer	Sharer	Initiator	Fire
Mar 31st	8:25 PM	Steady – The Vault	Container	Sustainer	Earth
April 25th	12:06 PM	Scout – The Trailblazer	Sharer	Initiator	Fire
May 15th	12:33 PM	Steady – The Vault	Container	Sustainer	Earth
June 7th	3:45 PM	Buzz – The Curious	Sharer	Adaptor	Air
June 22nd	6:39 AM	Sponge – The Sensitive	Container	Initiator	Water
July 6th	6:56 PM	Rex – The Dignified	Sharer	Sustainer	Fire
July 26th	6:49 AM	Details – The Analyst	Container	Adaptor	Earth
Sept 30th	7:44 PM	ProCon – The Diplomat	Sharer	Initiator	Air
Oct 18th	3:01 AM	Sherlock – The Detective	Container	Sustainer	Water
Nov 6th	12:09 PM	Flash – The Pioneer	Sharer	Adaptor	Fire
Dec 1st	4:32 PM	Exec – The Achiever	Container	Initiator	Earth
Dec 7th	8:52 PM	Flash – The Pioneer	Sharer	Adaptor	Fire

1985

Date	Time	Style	Reaction	Approach	Uptake
Jan 1st	0:00 AM	Flash – The Pioneer	Sharer	Adaptor	Fire
Jan 11th	6:25 PM	Exec – The Achiever	Container	Initiator	Earth
Feb 1st	7:43 AM	Boffin – The Innovator	Sharer	Sustainer	Air
Feb 18th	11:41 PM	Sonar – The Intuitive	Container	Adaptor	Water
Mar 7th	12:07 AM	Scout – The Trailblazer	Sharer	Initiator	Fire
May 14th	2:10 AM	Steady – The Vault	Container	Sustainer	Earth
May 30th	7:44 PM	Buzz – The Curious	Sharer	Adaptor	Air
June 13th	4:11 PM	Sponge – The Sensitive	Container	Initiator	Water
June 29th	7:34 PM	Rex – The Dignified	Sharer	Sustainer	Fire
Sept 6th	7:39 PM	Details – The Analyst	Container	Adaptor	Earth
Sept 22nd	11:13 PM	ProCon – The Diplomat	Sharer	Initiator	Air
Oct 10th	6:50 PM	Sherlock – The Detective	Container	Sustainer	Water
Oct 31st	4:44 PM	Flash – The Pioneer	Sharer	Adaptor	Fire
Dec 4th	8:16 PM	Sherlock – The Detective	Container	Adaptor	Earth
Dec 12th	11:05 AM	Flash – The Pioneer	Sharer	Adaptor	Fire

1986

Date	Time	Style	Reaction	Approach	Uptake
Jan 1st	0:00 AM	Flash – The Pioneer	Sharer	Adaptor	Fire
Jan 5th	8:42 PM	Exec – The Achiever	Container	Initiator	Earth
Jan 25th	12:33 AM	Boffin – The Innovator	Sharer	Sustainer	Air
Feb 11th	5:21 AM	Sonar – The Intuitive	Container	Adaptor	Water
Mar 3rd	7:22 AM	Scout – The Trailblazer	Sharer	Initiator	Fire
Mar 11th	4:37 PM	Sonar – The Intuitive	Container	Adaptor	Water
April 17th	12:33 PM	Scout – The Trailblazer	Sharer	Initiator	Fire
May 7th	12:33 PM	Steady – The Vault	Container	Sustainer	Earth
May 22nd	7:26 AM	Buzz – The Curious	Sharer	Adaptor	Air
June 5th	2:06 PM	Sponge – The Sensitive	Container	Initiator	Water
June 26th	2:13 PM	Rex – The Dignified	Sharer	Sustainer	Fire
July 23rd	9:51 PM	Sponge – The Sensitive	Container	Initiator	Water
Aug 11th	9:09 PM	Rex – The Dignified	Sharer	Sustainer	Fire
Aug 30th	3:28 AM	Details – The Analyst	Container	Adaptor	Earth
Sept 15th	2:28 AM	ProCon – The Diplomat	Sharer	Initiator	Air
Oct 4th	12:19 AM	Sherlock – The Detective	Container	Sustainer	Water
Dec 10th	12:34 AM	Flash – The Pioneer	Sharer	Adaptor	Fire
Dec 29th	11:09 PM	Exec – The Achiever	Container	Initiator	Earth

1987

Date	Time	Style	Reaction	Approach	Uptake
Jan 1st	0:00 AM	Exec – The Achiever	Container	Initiator	Earth
Jan 17th	1:08 PM	Boffin – The Innovator	Sharer	Sustainer	Air
Feb 4th	2:31 AM	Sonar – The Intuitive	Container	Adaptor	Water
Mar 11th	11:03 PM	Boffin – The Innovator	Sharer	Sustainer	Air
Mar 13th	10:23 PM	Sonar – The Intuitive	Container	Adaptor	Water
April 12th	8:23 PM	Scout – The Trailblazer	Sharer	Initiator	Fire
April 29th	3:39 PM	Steady – The Vault	Container	Sustainer	Earth
May 13th	5:30 PM	Buzz – The Curious	Sharer	Adaptor	Air
May 30th	4:21 AM	Sponge – The Sensitive	Container	Initiator	Water
Aug 6th	9:20 PM	Rex – The Dignified	Sharer	Sustainer	Fire
Aug 21st	9:36 PM	Details – The Analyst	Container	Adaptor	Earth
Sept 7th	1:52 PM	ProCon – The Diplomat	Sharer	Initiator	Air
Sept 28th	5:21 PM	Sherlock – The Detective	Container	Sustainer	Water
Nov 1st	2:16 AM	ProCon – The Diplomat	Sharer	Initiator	Air
Nov 11th	9:57 PM	Sherlock – The Detective	Container	Sustainer	Water
Dec 3rd	1:33 PM	Flash – The Pioneer	Sharer	Adaptor	Fire
Dec 22nd	5:40 PM	Exec – The Achiever	Container	Initiator	Earth

1988

Date	Time	Style	Reaction	Approach	Uptake
Jan 1st	0:00 AM	Exec – The Achiever	Container	Initiator	Earth
Jan 10th	5:28 AM	Boffin – The Innovator	Sharer	Sustainer	Air
Mar 16th	10:09 AM	Sonar – The Intuitive	Container	Adaptor	Water
April 4th	10:04 PM	Scout – The Trailblazer	Sharer	Initiator	Fire
April 20th	6:42 AM	Steady – The Vault	Container	Sustainer	Earth
May 4th	7:40 PM	Buzz – The Curious	Sharer	Adaptor	Air
July 12th	6:42 AM	Sponge – The Sensitive	Container	Initiator	Water
July 28th	9:19 PM	Rex – The Dignified	Sharer	Sustainer	Fire
Aug 12th	5:29 PM	Details – The Analyst	Container	Adaptor	Earth
Aug 30th	8:25 PM	ProCon – The Diplomat	Sharer	Initiator	Air
Nov 6th	2:57 PM	Sherlock – The Detective	Container	Sustainer	Water
Nov 25th	10:04 AM	Flash – The Pioneer	Sharer	Adaptor	Fire
Dec 14th	11:53 AM	Exec – The Achiever	Container	Initiator	Earth

1989

Date	Time	Style	Reaction	Approach	Uptake
Jan 1st	0:00 AM	Exec – The Achiever	Container	Initiator	Earth
Jan 2nd	7:41 PM	Boffin – The Innovator	Sharer	Sustainer	Air
Jan 29th	4:30 AM	Exec – The Achiever	Container	Initiator	Earth
Feb 14th	6:11 PM	Boffin – The Innovator	Sharer	Sustainer	Air
Mar 10th	6:07 PM	Sonar – The Intuitive	Container	Adaptor	Water
Mar 28th	3:16 AM	Scout – The Trailblazer	Sharer	Initiator	Fire
April 11th	9:36 PM	Steady – The Vault	Container	Sustainer	Earth
April 29th	7:53 PM	Buzz – The Curious	Sharer	Adaptor	Air
May 28th	10:59 PM	Steady – The Vault	Container	Sustainer	Earth
June 12th	8:56 AM	Buzz – The Curious	Sharer	Adaptor	Air
July 6th	12:55 AM	Sponge – The Sensitive	Container	Initiator	Water
July 20th	9:04 AM	Rex – The Dignified	Sharer	Sustainer	Fire
Aug 5th	12:54 AM	Details – The Analyst	Container	Adaptor	Earth
Aug 26th	6:14 AM	ProCon – The Diplomat	Sharer	Initiator	Air
Sept 26th	3:48 PM	Details – The Analyst	Container	Adaptor	Earth
Oct 11th	6:11 AM	ProCon – The Diplomat	Sharer	Initiator	Air
Oct 30th	1:53 PM	Sherlock – The Detective	Container	Sustainer	Water
Nov 18th	3:10 AM	Flash – The Pioneer	Sharer	Adaptor	Fire
Dec 7th	2:30 PM	Exec – The Achiever	Container	Initiator	Earth

1990

Date	Time	Style	Reaction	Approach	Uptake
Jan 1st	0:00 AM	Exec – The Achiever	Container	Initiator	Earth
Feb 12th	1:11 AM	Boffin – The Innovator	Sharer	Sustainer	Air
Mar 3rd	5:14 PM	Sonar – The Intuitive	Container	Adaptor	Water
Mar 20th	12:04 AM	Scout – The Trailblazer	Sharer	Initiator	Fire
April 4th	7:35 AM	Steady – The Vault	Container	Sustainer	Earth
June 12th	12:29 AM	Buzz – The Curious	Sharer	Adaptor	Air
June 27th	8:46 PM	Sponge – The Sensitive	Container	Initiator	Water
July 11th	11:48 PM	Rex – The Dignified	Sharer	Sustainer	Fire
July 29th	11:10 AM	Details – The Analyst	Container	Adaptor	Earth
Oct 5th	5:44 PM	ProCon – The Diplomat	Sharer	Initiator	Air
Oct 23rd	1:46 AM	Sherlock – The Detective	Container	Sustainer	Water
Nov 11th	12:06 AM	Flash – The Pioneer	Sharer	Adaptor	Fire
Dec 2nd	12:13 AM	Exec – The Achiever	Container	Initiator	Earth
Dec 25th	11:00 PM	Flash – The Pioneer	Sharer	Adaptor	Fire

1991

Date	Time	Style	Reaction	Approach	Uptake
Jan 1st	0:00 AM	Flash – The Pioneer	Sharer	Adaptor	Fire
Jan 14th	8:02 AM	Exec – The Achiever	Container	Initiator	Earth
Feb 5th	10:20 PM	Boffin – The Innovator	Sharer	Sustainer	Air
Feb 24th	2:35 AM	Sonar – The Intuitive	Container	Adaptor	Water
Mar 11th	10:40 PM	Scout – The Trailblazer	Sharer	Initiator	Fire
May 16th	10:45 PM	Steady – The Vault	Container	Sustainer	Earth
June 5th	2:24 AM	Buzz – The Curious	Sharer	Adaptor	Air
June 19th	5:40 AM	Sponge – The Sensitive	Container	Initiator	Water
July 4th	6:05 AM	Rex – The Dignified	Sharer	Sustainer	Fire
July 26th	1:00 PM	Details – The Analyst	Container	Adaptor	Earth
Aug 19th	9:40 PM	Rex – The Dignified	Sharer	Sustainer	Fire
Sept 10th	5:14 PM	Details – The Analyst	Container	Adaptor	Earth
Sept 28th	3:26 AM	ProCon – The Diplomat	Sharer	Initiator	Air
Oct 15th	2:01 PM	Sherlock – The Detective	Container	Sustainer	Water
Nov 4th	10:41 AM	Flash – The Pioneer	Sharer	Adaptor	Fire

1992

Date	Time	Style	Reaction	Approach	Uptake
Jan 1st	0:00 AM	Flash – The Pioneer	Sharer	Adaptor	Fire
Jan 10th	1:46 AM	Exec – The Achiever	Container	Initiator	Earth
Jan 29th	9:15 PM	Boffin – The Innovator	Sharer	Sustainer	Air
Feb 16th	7:04 AM	Sonar – The Intuitive	Container	Adaptor	Water
Mar 3rd	9:45 PM	Scout – The Trailblazer	Sharer	Initiator	Fire
April 3rd	11:52 PM	Sonar – The Intuitive	Container	Adaptor	Water
April 14th	5:35 PM	Scout – The Trailblazer	Sharer	Initiator	Fire
May 11th	4:10 AM	Steady – The Vault	Container	Sustainer	Earth
May 26th	9:16 PM	Buzz – The Curious	Sharer	Adaptor	Air
June 9th	6:27 AM	Sponge – The Sensitive	Container	Initiator	Water
June 27th	5:11 AM	Rex – The Dignified	Sharer	Sustainer	Fire
Sept 3rd	8:03 AM	Details – The Analyst	Container	Adaptor	Earth
Sept 19th	5:41 AM	ProCon – The Diplomat	Sharer	Initiator	Air
Oct 7th	10:13 AM	Sherlock – The Detective	Container	Sustainer	Water
Oct 29th	5:02 PM	Flash – The Pioneer	Sharer	Adaptor	Fire
Nov 21st	7:44 PM	Sherlock – The Detective	Container	Sustainer	Water
Dec 12th	8:05 AM	Flash – The Pioneer	Sharer	Adaptor	Fire

1993

Date	Time	Style	Reaction	Approach	Uptake
Jan 1st	0:00 AM	Flash – The Pioneer	Sharer	Adaptor	Fire
Jan 2nd	2:47 PM	Exec – The Achiever	Container	Initiator	Earth
Jan 21st	11:25 AM	Boffin – The Innovator	Sharer	Sustainer	Air
Feb 7th	4:19 PM	Sonar – The Intuitive	Container	Adaptor	Water
April 15th	3:18 PM	Scout – The Trailblazer	Sharer	Initiator	Fire
May 3rd	9:54 PM	Steady – The Vault	Container	Sustainer	Earth
May 18th	6:53 AM	Buzz – The Curious	Sharer	Adaptor	Air
June 2nd	3:54 AM	Sponge – The Sensitive	Container	Initiator	Water
Aug 10th	5:51 AM	Rex – The Dignified	Sharer	Sustainer	Fire
Aug 26th	7:06 AM	Details – The Analyst	Container	Adaptor	Earth
Sept 11th	11:18 AM	ProCon – The Diplomat	Sharer	Initiator	Air
Oct 1st	2:09 AM	Sherlock – The Detective	Container	Sustainer	Water
Dec 7th	1:04 AM	Flash – The Pioneer	Sharer	Adaptor	Fire
Dec 26th	12:47 PM	Exec – The Achiever	Container	Initiator	Earth

1994

Date	Time	Style	Reaction	Approach	Uptake
Jan 1st	0:00 AM	Exec – The Achiever	Container	Initiator	Earth
Jan 14th	12:25 AM	Boffin – The Innovator	Sharer	Sustainer	Air
Feb 1st	10:28 AM	Sonar – The Intuitive	Container	Adaptor	Water
Feb 21st	3:20 PM	Boffin – The Innovator	Sharer	Sustainer	Air
Mar 18th	12:04 PM	Sonar – The Intuitive	Container	Adaptor	Water
April 9th	4:30 PM	Scout – The Trailblazer	Sharer	Initiator	Fire
April 25th	6:27 PM	Steady – The Vault	Container	Sustainer	Earth
May 9th	9:08 PM	Buzz – The Curious	Sharer	Adaptor	Air
May 28th	2:52 PM	Sponge – The Sensitive	Container	Initiator	Water
July 2nd	11:27 PM	Buzz – The Curious	Sharer	Adaptor	Air
July 10th	12:41 PM	Sponge – The Sensitive	Container	Initiator	Water
Aug 3rd	6:09 AM	Rex – The Dignified	Sharer	Sustainer	Fire
Aug 18th	12:44 AM	Details – The Analyst	Container	Adaptor	Earth
Sept 4th	4:55 AM	ProCon – The Diplomat	Sharer	Initiator	Air
Sept 27th	8:51 AM	Sherlock – The Detective	Container	Sustainer	Water
Oct 19th	6:09 AM	ProCon – The Diplomat	Sharer	Initiator	Air
Nov 10th	12:46 PM	Sherlock – The Detective	Container	Sustainer	Water
Nov 30th	4:38 AM	Flash – The Pioneer	Sharer	Adaptor	Fire
Dec 19th	6:26 AM	Exec – The Achiever	Container	Initiator	Earth

1995

Date	Time	Style	Reaction	Approach	Uptake
Jan 1st	0:00 AM	Exec – The Achiever	Container	Initiator	Earth
Jan 6th	10:17 PM	Boffin – The Innovator	Sharer	Sustainer	Air
Mar 14th	9:35 PM	Sonar – The Intuitive	Container	Adaptor	Water
April 2nd	7:29 AM	Scout – The Trailblazer	Sharer	Initiator	Fire
April 17th	7:54 AM	Steady – The Vault	Container	Sustainer	Earth
May 2nd	3:18 PM	Buzz – The Curious	Sharer	Adaptor	Air
July 10th	4:58 PM	Sponge – The Sensitive	Container	Initiator	Water
July 25th	10:19 PM	Rex – The Dignified	Sharer	Sustainer	Fire
Aug 10th	12:13 AM	Details – The Analyst	Container	Adaptor	Earth
Aug 29th	2:07 AM	ProCon – The Diplomat	Sharer	Initiator	Air
Nov 4th	8:50 AM	Sherlock – The Detective	Container	Sustainer	Water
Nov 22nd	10:46 PM	Flash – The Pioneer	Sharer	Adaptor	Fire
Dec 12th	2:57 AM	Exec – The Achiever	Container	Initiator	Earth

1996

Date	Time	Style	Reaction	Approach	Uptake
Jan 1st	0:00 AM	Exec – The Achiever	Container	Initiator	Earth
Jan 1st	6:06 PM	Boffin – The Innovator	Sharer	Sustainer	Air
Jan 17th	9:17 AM	Exec – The Achiever	Container	Initiator	Earth
Feb 15th	2:44 AM	Boffin – The Innovator	Sharer	Sustainer	Air
Mar 7th	11:53 AM	Sonar – The Intuitive	Container	Adaptor	Water
Mar 24th	8:03 AM	Scout – The Trailblazer	Sharer	Initiator	Fire
April 8th	3:16 AM	Steady – The Vault	Container	Sustainer	Earth
June 13th	9:45 PM	Buzz – The Curious	Sharer	Adaptor	Air
July 2nd	7:36 AM	Sponge – The Sensitive	Container	Initiator	Water
July 16th	9:56 AM	Rex – The Dignified	Sharer	Sustainer	Fire
Aug 1st	4:17 PM	Details – The Analyst	Container	Adaptor	Earth
Aug 26th	5:17 AM	ProCon – The Diplomat	Sharer	Initiator	Air
Sept 12th	8:58 AM	Details – The Analyst	Container	Adaptor	Earth
Oct 9th	3:13 AM	ProCon – The Diplomat	Sharer	Initiator	Air
Oct 27th	1:01 AM	Sherlock – The Detective	Container	Sustainer	Water
Nov 14th	4:36 PM	Flash – The Pioneer	Sharer	Adaptor	Fire
Dec 4th	1:48 PM	Exec – The Achiever	Container	Initiator	Earth

1997

Date	Time	Style	Reaction	Approach	Uptake
Jan 1st	0:00 AM	Exec – The Achiever	Container	Initiator	Earth
Feb 9th	5:53 AM	Boffin – The Innovator	Sharer	Sustainer	Air
Feb 28th	3:54 AM	Sonar – The Intuitive	Container	Adaptor	Water
Mar 16th	4:13 AM	Scout – The Trailblazer	Sharer	Initiator	Fire
April 1st	1:45 PM	Steady – The Vault	Container	Sustainer	Earth
May 5th	2:21 AM	Scout – The Trailblazer	Sharer	Initiator	Fire
May 12th	10:25 AM	Steady – The Vault	Container	Sustainer	Earth
June 8th	11:25 PM	Buzz – The Curious	Sharer	Adaptor	Air
June 23rd	8:41 PM	Sponge – The Sensitive	Container	Initiator	Water
July 8th	5:28 AM	Rex – The Dignified	Sharer	Sustainer	Fire
July 27th	12:42 AM	Details – The Analyst	Container	Adaptor	Earth
Oct 2nd	5:38 AM	ProCon – The Diplomat	Sharer	Initiator	Air
Oct 19th	12:08 PM	Sherlock – The Detective	Container	Sustainer	Water
Nov 7th	5:42 PM	Flash – The Pioneer	Sharer	Adaptor	Fire
Nov 30th	7:11 PM	Exec – The Achiever	Container	Initiator	Earth
Dec 13th	5:26 PM	Flash – The Pioneer	Sharer	Adaptor	Fire

1998

Date	Time	Style	Reaction	Approach	Uptake
Jan 1st	0:00 AM	Flash – The Pioneer	Sharer	Adaptor	Fire
Jan 12th	4:20 PM	Exec – The Achiever	Container	Initiator	Earth
Feb 2nd	3:15 PM	Boffin – The Innovator	Sharer	Sustainer	Air
Feb 20th	10:22 AM	Sonar – The Intuitive	Container	Adaptor	Water
Mar 8th	8:28 AM	Scout – The Trailblazer	Sharer	Initiator	Fire
May 15th	2:10 AM	Steady – The Vault	Container	Sustainer	Earth
June 1st	8:07 AM	Buzz – The Curious	Sharer	Adaptor	Air
June 15th	5:33 AM	Sponge – The Sensitive	Container	Initiator	Water
June 30th	11:52 PM	Rex – The Dignified	Sharer	Sustainer	Fire
Sept 8th	1:58 AM	Details – The Analyst	Container	Adaptor	Earth
Sept 24th	10:12 AM	ProCon – The Diplomat	Sharer	Initiator	Air
Oct 12th	2:44 AM	Sherlock – The Detective	Container	Sustainer	Water
Nov 1st	4:02 PM	Flash – The Pioneer	Sharer	Adaptor	Fire

1999

Date	Time	Style	Reaction	Approach	Uptake
Jan 1st	0:00 AM	Flash – The Pioneer	Sharer	Adaptor	Fire
Jan 7th	2:03 AM	Exec – The Achiever	Container	Initiator	Earth
Jan 26th	9:32 AM	Boffin – The Innovator	Sharer	Sustainer	Air
Feb 12th	3:28 PM	Sonar – The Intuitive	Container	Adaptor	Water
Mar 2nd	10:50 PM	Scout – The Trailblazer	Sharer	Initiator	Fire
Mar 18th	9:06 AM	Sonar – The Intuitive	Container	Adaptor	Water
April 17th	10:09 PM	Scout – The Trailblazer	Sharer	Initiator	Fire
May 8th	9:22 PM	Steady – The Vault	Container	Sustainer	Earth
May 23rd	9:22 PM	Buzz – The Curious	Sharer	Adaptor	Air
June 7th	12:18 AM	Sponge – The Sensitive	Container	Initiator	Water
June 26th	3:39 PM	Rex – The Dignified	Sharer	Sustainer	Fire
July 31st	7:16 PM	Sponge – The Sensitive	Container	Initiator	Water
Aug 11th	4:25 AM	Rex – The Dignified	Sharer	Sustainer	Fire
Aug 31st	3:15 PM	Details – The Analyst	Container	Adaptor	Earth
Sept 16th	12:53 PM	ProCon – The Diplomat	Sharer	Initiator	Air
Oct 5th	5:12 AM	Sherlock – The Detective	Container	Sustainer	Water
Oct 30th	8:08 PM	Flash – The Pioneer	Sharer	Adaptor	Fire
Nov 9th	7:25 PM	Sherlock – The Detective	Container	Sustainer	Water
Dec 11th	2:09 AM	Flash – The Pioneer	Sharer	Adaptor	Fire
Dec 31st	6:48 AM	Exec – The Achiever	Container	Initiator	Earth

2000

Date	Time	Style	Reaction	Approach	Uptake
Jan 1st	0:00 AM	Exec – The Achiever	Container	Initiator	Earth
Jan 18th	10:21 PM	Boffin – The Innovator	Sharer	Sustainer	Air
Feb 5th	8:10 AM	Sonar – The Intuitive	Container	Adaptor	Water
April 13th	12:18 AM	Scout – The Trailblazer	Sharer	Initiator	Fire
April 30th	3:54 AM	Steady – The Vault	Container	Sustainer	Earth
May 14th	7:11 AM	Buzz – The Curious	Sharer	Adaptor	Air
May 30th	4:28 AM	Sponge – The Sensitive	Container	Initiator	Water
Aug 7th	5:43 AM	Rex – The Dignified	Sharer	Sustainer	Fire
Aug 22nd	10:12 AM	Details – The Analyst	Container	Adaptor	Earth
Sept 7th	10:23 PM	ProCon – The Diplomat	Sharer	Initiator	Air
Sept 28th	1:29 PM	Sherlock – The Detective	Container	Sustainer	Water
Nov 7th	7:29 AM	ProCon – The Diplomat	Sharer	Initiator	Air
Nov 8th	9:43 PM	Sherlock – The Detective	Container	Sustainer	Water
Dec 3rd	8:27 PM	Flash – The Pioneer	Sharer	Adaptor	Fire
Dec 23rd	2:04 AM	Exec – The Achiever	Container	Initiator	Earth

2001

Date	Time	Style	Reaction	Approach	Uptake
Jan 1st	0:00 AM	Exec – The Achiever	Container	Initiator	Earth
Jan 10th	1:27 PM	Boffin – The Innovator	Sharer	Sustainer	Air
Feb 1st	7:14 AM	Sonar – The Intuitive	Container	Adaptor	Water
Feb 6th	7:58 PM	Boffin – The Innovator	Sharer	Sustainer	Air
Mar 17th	6:06 AM	Sonar – The Intuitive	Container	Adaptor	Water
April 6th	7:15 AM	Scout – The Trailblazer	Sharer	Initiator	Fire
April 21st	8:09 PM	Steady – The Vault	Container	Sustainer	Earth
May 6th	4:54 AM	Buzz – The Curious	Sharer	Adaptor	Air
July 12th	10:48 PM	Sponge – The Sensitive	Container	Initiator	Water
July 30th	10:19 AM	Rex – The Dignified	Sharer	Sustainer	Fire
Aug 14th	5:05 AM	Details – The Analyst	Container	Adaptor	Earth
Sept 1st	12:38 AM	ProCon – The Diplomat	Sharer	Initiator	Air
Nov 7th	7:54 PM	Sherlock – The Detective	Container	Sustainer	Water
Nov 26th	6:25 PM	Flash – The Pioneer	Sharer	Adaptor	Fire
Dec 15th	7:56 PM	Exec – The Achiever	Container	Initiator	Earth

2002

Date	Time	Style	Reaction	Approach	Uptake
Jan 1st	0:00 AM	Exec – The Achiever	Container	Initiator	Earth
Jan 3rd	9:39 PM	Boffin – The Innovator	Sharer	Sustainer	Air
Feb 4th	4:20 AM	Exec – The Achiever	Container	Initiator	Earth
Feb 13th	5:21 PM	Boffin – The Innovator	Sharer	Sustainer	Air
Mar 11th	11:35 PM	Sonar – The Intuitive	Container	Adaptor	Water
Mar 29th	2:45 PM	Scout – The Trailblazer	Sharer	Initiator	Fire
April 13th	10:12 AM	Steady – The Vault	Container	Sustainer	Earth
April 30th	7:17 AM	Buzz – The Curious	Sharer	Adaptor	Air
July 7th	10:37 AM	Sponge – The Sensitive	Container	Initiator	Water
July 21st	10:42 PM	Rex – The Dignified	Sharer	Sustainer	Fire
Aug 6th	9:52 AM	Details – The Analyst	Container	Adaptor	Earth
Aug 26th	9:11 PM	ProCon – The Diplomat	Sharer	Initiator	Air
Oct 2nd	9:27 AM	Details – The Analyst	Container	Sustainer	Water
Oct 11th	5:57 AM	ProCon – The Diplomat	Sharer	Initiator	Air
Oct 31st	10:44 PM	Sherlock – The Detective	Container	Sustainer	Water
Nov 19th	11:30 AM	Flash – The Pioneer	Sharer	Adaptor	Fire
Dec 8th	8:22 PM	Exec – The Achiever	Container	Initiator	Earth

2003

Date	Time	Style	Reaction	Approach	Uptake
Jan 1st	0:00 AM	Exec – The Achiever	Container	Initiator	Earth
Feb 13th	1:01 AM	Boffin – The Innovator	Sharer	Sustainer	Air
Mar 5th	2:05 AM	Sonar – The Intuitive	Container	Adaptor	Water
Mar 21st	12:17 PM	Scout – The Trailblazer	Sharer	Initiator	Fire
April 5th	2:38 PM	Steady – The Vault	Container	Sustainer	Earth
June 13th	1:35 AM	Buzz – The Curious	Sharer	Adaptor	Air
June 29th	10:18 AM	Sponge – The Sensitive	Container	Initiator	Water
July 13th	12:11 PM	Rex – The Dignified	Sharer	Sustainer	Fire
July 30th	2:06 PM	Details – The Analyst	Container	Adaptor	Earth
Oct 7th	1:29 PM	ProCon – The Diplomat	Sharer	Initiator	Air
Oct 24th	11:21 PM	Sherlock – The Detective	Container	Sustainer	Water
Nov 12th	7:20 AM	Flash – The Pioneer	Sharer	Adaptor	Fire
Dec 2nd	9:35 PM	Exec – The Achiever	Container	Initiator	Earth
Dec 30th	7:54 PM	Flash – The Pioneer	Sharer	Adaptor	Fire

2004

Date	Time	Style	Reaction	Approach	Uptake
Jan 1st	0:00 AM	Flash – The Pioneer	Sharer	Adaptor	Fire
Jan 14th	11:03 AM	Exec – The Achiever	Container	Initiator	Earth
Feb 7th	4:21 AM	Boffin – The Innovator	Sharer	Sustainer	Air
Feb 25th	12:59 PM	Sonar – The Intuitive	Container	Adaptor	Water
Mar 12th	9:45 AM	Scout – The Trailblazer	Sharer	Initiator	Fire
April 1st	2:29 AM	Steady – The Vault	Container	Sustainer	Earth
April 13th	1:24 AM	Scout – The Trailblazer	Sharer	Initiator	Fire
May 16th	6:55 AM	Steady – The Vault	Container	Sustainer	Earth
June 5th	12:49 PM	Buzz – The Curious	Sharer	Adaptor	Air
June 19th	7:51 PM	Sponge – The Sensitive	Container	Initiator	Water
July 4th	2:53 PM	Rex – The Dignified	Sharer	Sustainer	Fire
July 25th	1:59 PM	Details – The Analyst	Container	Adaptor	Earth
Aug 25th	1:34 AM	Rex – The Dignified	Sharer	Initiator	Air
Sept 10th	7:39 AM	Details – The Analyst	Container	Sustainer	Water
Sept 28th	2:14 PM	ProCon – The Diplomat	Sharer	Initiator	Air
Oct 1st	10:58 PM	Sherlock – The Detective	Container	Sustainer	Water
Nov 4th	2:41 PM	Flash – The Pioneer	Sharer	Adaptor	Fire

2005

Date	Time	Style	Reaction	Approach	Uptake
Jan 1st	0:00 AM	Flash – The Pioneer	Sharer	Adaptor	Fire
Jan 10th	4:10 AM	Exec – The Achiever	Container	Initiator	Earth
Jan 30th	5:38 AM	Boffin – The Innovator	Sharer	Sustainer	Air
Feb 16th	5:47 PM	Sonar – The Intuitive	Container	Adaptor	Water
Mar 5th	1:35 AM	Scout – The Trailblazer	Sharer	Initiator	Fire
May 12th	9:15 AM	Steady – The Vault	Container	Sustainer	Earth
May 28th	10:45 AM	Buzz – The Curious	Sharer	Adaptor	Air
June 11th	7:04 AM	Sponge – The Sensitive	Container	Initiator	Water
June 28th	4:02 AM	Rex – The Dignified	Sharer	Sustainer	Fire
Sept 4th	5:54 PM	Details – The Analyst	Container	Adaptor	Earth
Sept 20th	4:41 PM	ProCon – The Diplomat	Sharer	Initiator	Air
Oct 8th	5:16 PM	Sherlock – The Detective	Container	Sustainer	Water
Oct 30th	9:03 AM	Flash – The Pioneer	Sharer	Adaptor	Fire
Nov 26th	11:55 AM	Sherlock – The Detective	Container	Sustainer	Water
Dec 12th	9:20 PM	Flash – The Pioneer	Sharer	Adaptor	Fire

2006

Date	Time	Style	Reaction	Approach	Uptake
Jan 1st	0:00 AM	Flash – The Pioneer	Sharer	Adaptor	Fire
Jan 3rd	9:27 PM	Exec – The Achiever	Container	Initiator	Earth
Jan 22nd	8:43 PM	Boffin – The Innovator	Sharer	Sustainer	Air
Feb 9th	1:23 AM	Sonar – The Intuitive	Container	Adaptor	Water
April 16th	12:21 PM	Scout – The Trailblazer	Sharer	Initiator	Fire
May 5th	8:29 AM	Steady – The Vault	Container	Sustainer	Earth
May 19th	8:53 PM	Buzz – The Curious	Sharer	Adaptor	Air
June 3rd	11:22 AM	Sponge – The Sensitive	Container	Initiator	Water
June 28th	7:58 PM	Rex – The Dignified	Sharer	Sustainer	Fire
July 10th	8:19 PM	Sponge – The Sensitive	Container	Initiator	Water
Aug 11th	4:11 AM	Rex – The Dignified	Sharer	Sustainer	Fire
Aug 27th	7:32 PM	Details – The Analyst	Container	Adaptor	Earth
Sept 12th	9:09 PM	ProCon – The Diplomat	Sharer	Initiator	Air
Oct 2nd	4:39 AM	Sherlock – The Detective	Container	Sustainer	Water
Dec 8th	5:53 AM	Flash – The Pioneer	Sharer	Adaptor	Fire
Dec 27th	8:56 PM	Exec – The Achiever	Container	Initiator	Earth

2007

Date	Time	Style	Reaction	Approach	Uptake
Jan 1st	0:00 AM	Exec – The Achiever	Container	Initiator	Earth
Jan 15th	9:26 AM	Boffin – The Innovator	Sharer	Sustainer	Air
Feb 2nd	9:21 AM	Sonar – The Intuitive	Container	Adaptor	Water
Feb 27th	3:02 AM	Boffin – The Innovator	Sharer	Sustainer	Air
Mar 18th	9:36 AM	Sonar – The Intuitive	Container	Adaptor	Water
April 10th	11:08 PM	Scout – The Trailblazer	Sharer	Initiator	Fire
April 27th	7:17 AM	Steady – The Vault	Container	Sustainer	Earth
May 11th	9:18 AM	Buzz – The Curious	Sharer	Adaptor	Air
May 29th	12:57 AM	Sponge – The Sensitive	Container	Initiator	Water
Aug 4th	5:16 PM	Rex – The Dignified	Sharer	Sustainer	Fire
Aug 19th	1:02 PM	Details – The Analyst	Container	Adaptor	Earth
Sept 5th	12:03 PM	ProCon – The Diplomat	Sharer	Initiator	Air
Sept 27th	5:19 PM	Sherlock – The Detective	Container	Sustainer	Water
Oct 24th	3:38 AM	ProCon – The Diplomat	Sharer	Initiator	Air
Nov 11th	8:42 AM	Sherlock – The Detective	Container	Sustainer	Water
Dec 1st	12:22 PM	Flash – The Pioneer	Sharer	Adaptor	Fire
Dec 20th	2:44 PM	Exec – The Achiever	Container	Initiator	Earth

2008

Date	Time	Style	Reaction	Approach	Uptake
Jan 1st	0:00 AM	Exec – The Achiever	Container	Initiator	Earth
Jan 8th	4:47 AM	Boffin – The Innovator	Sharer	Sustainer	Air
Mar 14th	10:47 PM	Sonar – The Intuitive	Container	Adaptor	Water
April 2nd	5:46 PM	Scout – The Trailblazer	Sharer	Initiator	Fire
April 17th	9:08 PM	Steady – The Vault	Container	Sustainer	Earth
May 2nd	8:01 PM	Buzz – The Curious	Sharer	Adaptor	Air
July 10th	8:18 PM	Sponge – The Sensitive	Container	Initiator	Water
July 26th	11:49 AM	Rex – The Dignified	Sharer	Sustainer	Fire
Aug 10th	10:52 AM	Details – The Analyst	Container	Adaptor	Earth
Aug 29th	2:51 AM	ProCon – The Diplomat	Sharer	Initiator	Air
Nov 4th	4:01 PM	Sherlock – The Detective	Container	Sustainer	Water
Nov 23rd	7:10 AM	Flash – The Pioneer	Sharer	Adaptor	Fire
Dec 12th	10:14 AM	Exec – The Achiever	Container	Initiator	Earth

2009

Date	Time	Style	Reaction	Approach	Uptake
Jan 1st	0:00 AM	Exec – The Achiever	Container	Initiator	Earth
Jan 1st	9:52 AM	Boffin – The Innovator	Sharer	Sustainer	Air
Jan 21st	5:37 AM	Exec – The Achiever	Container	Initiator	Earth
Feb 14th	3:40 PM	Boffin – The Innovator	Sharer	Sustainer	Air
Mar 8th	6:57 PM	Sonar – The Intuitive	Container	Adaptor	Water
Mar 25th	7:56 PM	Scout – The Trailblazer	Sharer	Initiator	Fire
April 9th	2:22 PM	Steady – The Vault	Container	Sustainer	Earth
April 30th	10:30 PM	Buzz – The Curious	Sharer	Adaptor	Air
May 13th	11:54 PM	Steady – The Vault	Container	Sustainer	Earth
June 14th	2:48 AM	Buzz – The Curious	Sharer	Adaptor	Air
July 3rd	7:21 PM	Sponge – The Sensitive	Container	Initiator	Water
July 17th	11:09 PM	Rex – The Dignified	Sharer	Sustainer	Fire
Aug 2nd	11:08 PM	Details – The Analyst	Container	Adaptor	Earth
Aug 25th	8:19 PM	ProCon – The Diplomat	Sharer	Initiator	Air
Sept 18th	3:27 AM	Details – The Analyst	Container	Adaptor	Earth
Oct 10th	3:47 AM	ProCon – The Diplomat	Sharer	Initiator	Air
Oct 28th	10:10 AM	Sherlock – The Detective	Container	Sustainer	Water
Nov 16th	12:29 AM	Flash – The Pioneer	Sharer	Adaptor	Fire
Dec 5th	5:25 PM	Exec – The Achiever	Container	Initiator	Earth

2010

Date	Time	Style	Reaction	Approach	Uptake
Jan 1st	0:00 AM	Exec – The Achiever	Container	Initiator	Earth
Feb 10th	9:07 AM	Boffin – The Innovator	Sharer	Sustainer	Air
Mar 1st	1:29 PM	Sonar – The Intuitive	Container	Adaptor	Water
Mar 17th	4:13 PM	Scout – The Trailblazer	Sharer	Initiator	Fire
April 2nd	1:07 PM	Steady – The Vault	Container	Sustainer	Earth
June 10th	5:42 AM	Buzz – The Curious	Sharer	Adaptor	Air
June 25th	10:33 AM	Sponge – The Sensitive	Container	Initiator	Water
July 9th	4:30 PM	Rex – The Dignified	Sharer	Sustainer	Fire
July 27th	9:44 PM	Details – The Analyst	Container	Adaptor	Earth
Oct 3rd	3:05 PM	ProCon – The Diplomat	Sharer	Initiator	Air
Oct 20th	9:20 PM	Sherlock – The Detective	Container	Sustainer	Water
Nov 8th	11:44 PM	Flash – The Pioneer	Sharer	Adaptor	Fire
Dec 1st	12:12 AM	Exec – The Achiever	Container	Initiator	Earth
Dec 18th	2:54 PM	Flash – The Pioneer	Sharer	Adaptor	Fire

2011

Date	Time	Style	Reaction	Approach	Uptake
Jan 1st	0:00 AM	Flash – The Pioneer	Sharer	Adaptor	Fire
Jan 13th	11:26 AM	Exec – The Achiever	Container	Initiator	Earth
Feb 3rd	10:20 PM	Boffin – The Innovator	Sharer	Sustainer	Air
Feb 21st	8:54 PM	Sonar – The Intuitive	Container	Adaptor	Water
Mar 9th	5:48 PM	Scout – The Trailblazer	Sharer	Initiator	Fire
May 15th	11:19 PM	Steady – The Vault	Container	Sustainer	Earth
June 2nd	8:04 PM	Buzz – The Curious	Sharer	Adaptor	Air
June 16th	7:10 PM	Sponge – The Sensitive	Container	Initiator	Water
July 2nd	5:39 AM	Rex – The Dignified	Sharer	Sustainer	Fire
July 28th	6:00 PM	Details – The Analyst	Container	Adaptor	Earth
Aug 8th	9:47 AM	Rex – The Dignified	Sharer	Sustainer	Fire
Sept 9th	6:00 AM	Details – The Analyst	Container	Adaptor	Earth
Sept 25th	9:10 PM	ProCon – The Diplomat	Sharer	Initiator	Air
Oct 13th	10:53 AM	Sherlock – The Detective	Container	Sustainer	Water
Nov 2nd	4:55 PM	Flash – The Pioneer	Sharer	Adaptor	Fire

2012

Date	Time	Style	Reaction	Approach	Uptake
Jan 1st	0:00 AM	Flash – The Pioneer	Sharer	Adaptor	Fire
Jan 8th	6:35 AM	Exec – The Achiever	Container	Initiator	Earth
Jan 27th	6:13 PM	Boffin – The Innovator	Sharer	Sustainer	Air
Feb 14th	1:39 AM	Sonar – The Intuitive	Container	Adaptor	Water
Mar 2nd	11:42 AM	Scout – The Trailblazer	Sharer	Initiator	Fire
Mar 23rd	1:23 PM	Sonar – The Intuitive	Container	Adaptor	Water
April 16th	10:43 PM	Scout – The Trailblazer	Sharer	Initiator	Fire
May 9th	5:16 AM	Steady – The Vault	Container	Sustainer	Earth
May 24th	11:13 AM	Buzz – The Curious	Sharer	Adaptor	Air
June 7th	11:17 AM	Sponge – The Sensitive	Container	Initiator	Water
June 26th	2:25 AM	Rex – The Dignified	Sharer	Sustainer	Fire
Sept 1st	2:33 AM	Details – The Analyst	Container	Adaptor	Earth
Sept 16th	11:23 PM	ProCon – The Diplomat	Sharer	Initiator	Air
Oct 5th	10:36 AM	Sherlock – The Detective	Container	Sustainer	Water
Oct 29th	6:19 AM	Flash – The Pioneer	Sharer	Adaptor	Fire
Nov 14th	7:43 AM	Sherlock – The Detective	Container	Sustainer	Water
Dec 11th	1:41 AM	Flash – The Pioneer	Sharer	Adaptor	Fire
Dec 31st	2:04 PM	Exec – The Achiever	Container	Initiator	Earth

2013

Date	Time	Style	Reaction	Approach	Uptake
Jan 1st	0:00 AM	Exec – The Achiever	Container	Initiator	Earth
Jan 19th	7:26 AM	Boffin – The Innovator	Sharer	Sustainer	Air
Feb 5th	2:57 PM	Sonar – The Intuitive	Container	Adaptor	Water
April 14th	2:38 AM	Scout – The Trailblazer	Sharer	Initiator	Fire
May 1st	3:38 PM	Steady – The Vault	Container	Sustainer	Earth
May 15th	8:42 PM	Buzz – The Curious	Sharer	Adaptor	Air
May 31st	7:08 AM	Sponge – The Sensitive	Container	Initiator	Water
Aug 8th	12:14 PM	Rex – The Dignified	Sharer	Sustainer	Fire
Aug 23rd	10:39 PM	Details – The Analyst	Container	Adaptor	Earth
Sept 9th	7:08 AM	ProCon – The Diplomat	Sharer	Initiator	Air
Sept 29th	11:39 AM	Sherlock – The Detective	Container	Sustainer	Water
Dec 5th	2:43 AM	Flash – The Pioneer	Sharer	Adaptor	Fire
Dec 24th	10:13 AM	Exec – The Achiever	Container	Initiator	Earth

2014

Date	Time	Style	Reaction	Approach	Uptake
Jan 1st	0:00 AM	Exec – The Achiever	Container	Initiator	Earth
Jan 11th	9:36 PM	Boffin – The Innovator	Sharer	Sustainer	Air
Jan 31st	2:30 PM	Sonar – The Intuitive	Container	Adaptor	Water
Feb 13th	3:31 AM	Boffin – The Innovator	Sharer	Sustainer	Air
Mar 17th	10:25 PM	Sonar – The Intuitive	Container	Adaptor	Water
April 7th	3:36 PM	Scout – The Trailblazer	Sharer	Initiator	Fire
April 23rd	9:17 AM	Steady – The Vault	Container	Sustainer	Earth
May 7th	2:58 PM	Buzz – The Curious	Sharer	Adaptor	Air
May 29th	9:13 AM	Sponge – The Sensitive	Container	Initiator	Water
June 17th	10:06 AM	Buzz – The Curious	Sharer	Adaptor	Air
July 13th	4:46 AM	Sponge – The Sensitive	Container	Initiator	Water
July 31st	10:47 PM	Rex – The Dignified	Sharer	Sustainer	Fire
Aug 15th	4:45 PM	Details – The Analyst	Container	Adaptor	Earth
Sept 2nd	5:39 PM	ProCon – The Diplomat	Sharer	Initiator	Air
Sept 27th	10:40 PM	Sherlock – The Detective	Container	Sustainer	Water
Oct 10th	5:28 PM	ProCon – The Diplomat	Sharer	Initiator	Air
Nov 8th	11:10 PM	Sherlock – The Detective	Container	Sustainer	Water
Nov 28th	2:27 AM	Flash – The Pioneer	Sharer	Adaptor	Fire
Dec 17th	3:54 AM	Exec – The Achiever	Container	Initiator	Earth

The Characters in Colour

One out of four of us is a visual learner, for whom absorption of new information is greatly assisted by pictures, graphics, illustrations of all sorts, and especially by colour. Words alone just don't do it for members of the Water Family – neither does black and white.

For the rest of us, colour pictures are still fun or lively or pretty or simply entertaining.

Here are all twelve characters, the three Divisions and the Big Picture, which represents the Mercury Model graphically, in larger scale than elsewhere in the text and in colour.

Scout – The Trailblazer

Quick on the uptake, this mind is active, direct, energetic, positive, lively and bright. It can be unflaggingly forceful and competitive. And to a parent it can be both stimulating and exhausting.

Steady – The Vault

Have you heard the one about leading a Highland calf to water
only to find the decision to drink it is totally his own?
That statement was first written about a boy with this learning
style. Sometimes you can't even get him within half a mile
of the trough.

Buzz – The Curious

Here is a child who is inquisitive about absolutely everything,
from bison to butterflies. One WHY question will follow another,
and another, and another.

Sponge – The Sensitive

Regardless of this child's outward behaviour, despite how robust she may appear to be, she has a supersensitive mind. By the time she's a teenager she will be sick and tired of hearing people say 'Oh, why do you have to be so sensitive?'
Well, here's the simple truth: she just is.

Rex – The Dignified

Your child might try out new ideas, have a good sniff around them, but she absolutely will not invite them into the kingdom of her mind, unless she knows they will be worthy subjects.

Details – The Analyst

Your child's mind learns by separating large pieces of information into tiny bite-sized bits. It dissects. It analyses. It can tear an idea apart limb from limb in the blink of an eye.

It has to do this in order to learn.

ProCon – The Diplomat

Always ready for an exchange of ideas, your child thoroughly enjoys conversation, dialogue and debate. His mind establishes relationships with all kinds of information – with the spoken or written word, with other people's ideas and with the variety of points of view within himself.

Sherlock – The Detective

The Detective attempts to conceal his extreme sensitivity.
And you will tend to observe the defensiveness more than you
will see what's going on inside him.

Flash – The Pioneer

If you are raising a child with this learning style, you'd better have your mental roller skates on just to keep up. His mind might seem like a little ball of flame rampaging through the house, a pint-sized conflagration on the loose.

Exec – The Achiever

This group thinks along more responsible, more adult lines than much older children. Don't worry, it's natural. They are still being themselves and enjoying childhood.

Boffin – The Innovator

*These children excel at cracking the mould of the Traditional,
the Customary and the Expected in current-day thinking,
allowing an opening for the New, the Unusual and the Innovative.*

Sonar – The Intuitive

Your child's mind links pieces of information together – it unifies, it includes. It naturally sees the big picture in which everything is connected and integrated. He understands a new idea by sensing how it fits into the context of the larger whole.

The Two Families of the Reaction Division

Sharers

Scout, Buzz, Rex, ProCon, Flash, Boffin

Half of us are Sharers and know that information exists to be passed around – right now!

Containers

Steady, Sponge, Details, Sherlock, Exec, Sonar

Half of us are Containers and are sure that information should be held, at least for a while.

The Three Families of the Approach Division

The Initiators

Scout, Sponge, ProCon and Exec

The 'Let's Get On To The Next Topic' Family

The Sustainers

Steady, Rex, Sherlock and Boffin

The 'Once An Idea Is In There, Well, It's In There' Family

The Adaptors

Buzz, Details, Flash and Sonar

The 'What Else Is There To Learn?' Family

The Four Families of the Mode of Uptake Division

The Fire Family
Scout, Rex and Flash

They breathe in information in a flash, without needing to alter it in any way.

The Air Family
Buzz, ProCon and Boffin

They shape information into logical concepts to learn it.

The Water Family
Sponge, Sherlock and Sonar

They absorb information and filter it through their feelings.

The Earth Family
Steady, Details and Exec

They incorporate practical ideas at a physical level.

The Big Picture